Education's End

EDUCATION'S END

WHY OUR COLLEGES AND UNIVERSITIES

HAVE GIVEN UP ON THE MEANING OF LIFE

ANTHONY T. KRONMAN

Yale University Press/New Haven and London

A Caravan book. For more information, visit www.caravanbooks.org

Published with assistance from the Mary Cady Tew Memorial Fund.

Printed in the United States of America.
First Large Print edition 2007
ISBN (Large Print) 978-0-300-13864-1
ISBN (Hardcover) 978-0-300-12288-6

Library of Congress Cataloging-in-Publication Data is available on request.

A catalogue record for this book is available from the British Library.

This Large Print Book carries the Seal of Approval of N.A.V.H.

When I was six and asked her,
"What's beyond the stars?,"
she said, "That's a metaphysical question,"
and made it clear by her tone of voice
that questions of this sort are the most
important kind. This book is for
my mother, Rosella.

The pleasures of the intellect are notoriously less vivid than either the pleasures of sense or the pleasures of the affections; and therefore, especially in the season of youth, the pursuit of knowledge is likely enough to be neglected and lightly esteemed in comparison with other pursuits offering much stronger immediate attractions. But the pleasure of learning and knowing, though not the keenest, is yet the least perishable of pleasures; the least subject to external things, and the play of chance, and the wear of time. And as a prudent man puts money by to serve as a provision for the material wants of his old age, so too he needs to lay up against the end of his days provision for the intellect. As the years go by, comparative values are found to alter: Time, says Sophocles, takes many things which once were pleasures and brings them nearer to pain. In the day when the strong men shall bow themselves, and desire shall fail, it will be a matter of yet more concern than now, whether one can say "my mind to me a kingdom is"; and whether the windows of the soul look out upon a broad and delightful landscape, or face nothing but a brick wall.

—A. E. Housman, 1892

What is education? I should suppose that education was the curriculum one had to run through in order to catch up with oneself, and he who will not pass through this curriculum is helped very little by the fact that he was born in the most enlightened age.

—Søren Kierkegaard, 1843

CONTENTS

ACKNOWLEDGMENTS

I'm grateful to my colleagues Bruce Ackerman and Paul Kahn for their comments on an
earlier draft of this book, to my friend Justin
Zaremby for his helpful comments as well, to
Justin Shubow of the Yale Law School Class of
2008 and Jamie Dycus of the Class of 2006 for
valuable research assistance, and to my assis-
tant, Marge Camera, for her cheerful and competent help. And I'm grateful to the Yale Law
School for providing the supportive environment in which I could discover my own mind
about the matters discussed in these pages.
My friend and agent Wendy Strothman provided much helpful guidance, and Jonathan
Brent, the editorial director of Yale University
Press, has been a wonderful interlocutor and
stimulating critic. As always, my greatest debt
is to my wife, Nancy Greenberg, without whose
encouragement neither this book nor anything
else in my life would be possible.

INTRODUCTION

In the fall of 1965, I was a sophomore at Williams College—for the second time. The year before, I had left Williams to work as an organizer for Students for a Democratic Society (SDS). It was an exciting time to be in college. Black students in the South were at the forefront of the civil rights movement. Their courage had set an example for the world to admire. In the North, the (mostly white) student leaders of SDS had begun a movement of their own for social and economic change. The Port Huron Statement of 1962 was their manifesto. It described with passionate clarity the gap between America's ideals and the realities of racism and poverty and summoned my generation of students— "bred in at least modest comfort, housed now in universities, looking uncomfortably to the world we inherit"—to close it.[1] The war in Vietnam was on the horizon. The campuses of America's colleges and universities were beginning to stir with an energy they had not seen since the 1930s. By the time the decade was over, these stirrings would grow into the most powerful student movement the country has ever known.

Many of us who were students at the time were part of this movement. We felt in touch with history. We believed we were participating in events much larger than our individual lives. It was a thrilling idea that made the rest of life—and school in particular—seem unimportant by comparison. Like others of my generation, I embraced this idea, and like some I acted on it. With my parents' strained support, I left Williams at Thanksgiving in 1964 and a month later was living with four other organizers in a small apartment in a poor white neighborhood on the north side of Chicago, hoping to help start what we called "an interracial movement of the poor."

My parents were Democrats of liberal conviction. They had voted for Henry Wallace in 1948, and twice for Adlai Stevenson. They hated Joseph McCarthy and revered Martin Luther King. I absorbed their beliefs and took them with me to college. But at Williams I met a new idea that put my beliefs to the test. The student leaders of the civil rights movement had shown by their example that it is not enough merely to believe in justice and equality. They had shown that one must struggle and sacrifice to achieve these things as well. They had proved that it is necessary to enter the fray and become a participant in the great contests of life or risk not having a life of any consequence at all. This was a terrifying idea but an exhilarating one too, for it implied that if one just picked up the banner and marched, one's life might be consequential after all. In the fall of 1964, I was nineteen years old. I had been in school all my life. What, I thought, was more important—a few more years of college, all leading to an end I couldn't see, or action in the service of a cause I saw as plain as day? How, exactly, I came to frame the choice in these terms remains obscure to me even today. What other longings fed it I can't say. But when I left Williams, in the middle of my first sophomore year, it was because I had come to believe that the meaning of my life was at stake and that if I stayed in school, and continued on the path I was following, I risked living a life with no meaning at all.

The work in Chicago was hard—long days of ringing doorbells and handing out leaflets, followed by evening meetings to take stock and make plans. Our goal was the creation of a union of neighborhood residents mobilized to press their landlords and the city for reform—for cleaner buildings, safer streets, and, ultimately, a greater voice in their economic and political fates. The neighborhood was called "Uptown," and when I lived there most of the residents were former coal miners from Kentucky and West Virginia who had come to Chicago looking for work when the mines gave out. They understood, from long experience, the value of a union. They were polite, but suspicious of the well-spoken kids who knocked on their doors and tried to persuade them that a union of neighbors is the same as a union of workers and that a rent strike is no different from shutting down a mine.

After seven months, with not much more to show for my efforts than one failed rent strike and a sidewalk protest at the office of our city councilman (where my fellow organizers and I outnumbered the other protesters), I had begun to doubt whether my next thirty years of organizing would produce results to justify a lifetime of labor. My politics were unchanged, and I admired the organizers who had made a permanent home in Uptown. I still felt the same drive to live a life of purpose and value. But I was less confident that the life I wanted was the life that I was leading. I was less sure of *what* I wanted. I had come to Chicago to find the answer to the question of life's meaning and because I believed I would never find the answer in school. After seven months, the question remained, but a life of political activism no longer seemed the clearly right answer. And I was beginning to miss the life I had left.

Williams is a comfortable place and that is part of what I missed. But I also missed reading—for which I now had almost no time—and the aimless conversations of college life that the hard realities of my organizing work discouraged. And there was gentle pressure from my parents, who accepted my decision to leave school even though they had already paid the full year's tuition (a sacrifice that as a parent with children of my own in college, I now recognize for the gift it was). My parents never said, "Go back to school," but when I came home to Los Angeles that summer and told them I wanted to return to Williams, their relief was physical. It was no clearer to me then, than it had been the year before, where school was leading. I was no more confident that school had anything to do with the meaning of life. The demands of the world seemed as large and urgent as they had when I left Williams to meet them. It was the summer of 1965, and as my parents and I discussed my plans to return to Williams that fall, we watched Watts burn on the television screen, twenty miles and another country away. But I was ready to go back to school and the life I had left and to sort things out as best I could.

It was in this mood that I enrolled that fall in a seminar taught by Nathaniel Lawrence, who was then the chair of the philosophy department at Williams. I had taken the introductory course in philosophy my freshman year and wanted to study the subject further. I had some dim sense that I might find in philosophy, and in Professor Lawrence's seminar, answers to the questions that plagued me. The seminar was titled "Existentialism." Most of the other students were juniors and seniors, and I felt a bit over my head. The readings were difficult. We read Kierkegaard's *Either/Or,* Sartre's *Being and Nothingness*, and *The Mystery of Being* by the great Catholic philosopher Gabriel Marcel. We met once a week, in Professor Lawrence's home at the end of Main Street, a few blocks from campus. Each session lasted three hours. We broke in the middle for tea, and there were always fresh cookies (courtesy of Mrs. Lawrence). The fall came on, the days shortened, the air grew chilly. The Berkshires were covered in scarlet and gold. When we arrived at Professor Lawrence's home, late in the afternoon, we found a fire going, and his two golden retrievers asleep like bookends beside the hearth.

The discussions were animated, often passionate. It seemed to all of us that much was at stake—just what one would expect in a seminar on existentialism. At the heart of the seminar was the question of how best to live, of what to care about and why, the question of the meaning of life. It was the question that Kierkegaard, Sartre, and Marcel all addressed in different ways and that we discussed— awkwardly, confusedly, eagerly—around the fire in Professor Lawrence's living room. By the third or fourth week of the term, I had begun to look forward to our meetings with growing excitement. The seminar became the center of everything I did that fall, in class and out. Partly it was because the readings were deep and enlightening, partly because I discovered I could keep up with my more advanced classmates and even make a contribution or two, partly because Professor Lawrence's wisdom and kindness enveloped us all. But mostly it was because I made a discovery in that class that has been a central conviction of mine ever since. I discovered that the meaning of life is a subject that can be studied in school.

There are many things to study in a college or university. The question of what constitutes a life of significance and value is only one of them. And there are other places to search for an answer. There are other institutions—religious ones most notably—that offer instruction in the meaning of life and other settings, including many that have nothing to do with formal education, in which people make discoveries that help them to say, "My life has a value I recognize and cherish." What I discovered in Professor Lawrence's seminar forty years ago was that an institution of higher education is one of the places where the question of what living is for can be pursued in an organized way. I had left Williams looking for a place where the question has more reality than I thought it ever could in school. What I found when I returned was the place for which I had been searching. It has been my professional home ever since.

For the past forty years, I have been by turns a student, a teacher, and a dean. I am now, after ten years as a dean, a teacher once again. For the past twenty-eight years, I have been a member of the faculty of the Yale Law School. At present, I am teaching in a freshman program in Yale College that is devoted to the study of the great works of philosophy, history, literature, and politics that form the foundation of the Western tradition. For all this time, and in the different roles that I have occupied in my career, my deepest belief has remained unchanged: that a college or university is not just a place for the transmission of knowledge but a forum for the exploration of life's mystery and meaning through the careful but critical reading of the great works of literary and philosophical imagination that we have inherited from the past. Over the years, many of my beliefs have changed but not this one. My confidence that the meaning of life is a teachable topic has never faltered since Professor Lawrence first helped me to have it, and my whole professional life has been devoted to vindicating this confidence and to transmitting it to my students.

That is why I have written this book. For as I have watched the question of life's meaning lose its status as a subject of organized academic instruction and seen it pushed to the margins of professional respectability in the humanities, where it once occupied a central and honored place, I have felt what I can only describe as a sense of personal loss on account of my own very substantial investment in the belief that the question is one that can and must be taught in our schools. In my time as a teacher and dean, I have seen this question exiled from the humanities, first as a result of the growing authority of the modern research ideal and then on account of the culture of political correctness that has undermined the legitimacy of the question itself and the authority of humanities teachers to ask it. I have felt puzzlement and anger at the easy sweeping aside of values that seem to me so obvious and important. And watching these developments, I have been moved to wonder about their causes and consequences and the likelihood of a cure.

Why did the question of what living is for disappear from the roster of questions our colleges and universities address in a deliberate and disciplined way? What is the source of the appeal of the research ideal, and why is it so hostile to this question? Why are the ideas of diversity and multiculturalism and the belief that values are merely expressions of power so corrosive of the attempt to explore the question of life's purpose and meaning? What have the consequences of the disappearance of this question from our colleges and universities been for the culture at large, where our churches now monopolize the authority to address it? And what are the prospects for its restoration to a position of respect in the academy?

These are the questions I ask and answer in this book. I ask them as a student who fell in love with the humanities at Williams long ago. I ask them as a teacher of law and philosophy who has tried to keep the question of life's meaning alive in his classroom. And I ask them as a former dean who worried every day that the demands of the research ideal and the spirit of political correctness have together put the humanities on the defensive and their authority to guide us in the exploration of life's meaning under a cloud.

These questions have a personal urgency for me. My attempt to answer them is a defense of what I care about and have done in my life. But there are others for whom they have great importance too. There are the humanities teachers who need to recover the confidence they once possessed in their authority to lead the search for an answer to the question of life's purpose and value—who were originally drawn to their work by this question itself and need to be reconnected to it. There are the students who depend upon their teachers for such guidance—who are excited and confused and perhaps even frightened by the question but for whatever reason find the answers that religion offers incomplete. And there are the parents of students who, despite all their cautionary advice about the realities of life, yearn for their children to have an education that goes beyond the merely vocational and equips them for a challenge larger than that of succeeding in a career. It is for these—teachers, students, and parents—that I have written this book, in puzzlement and anger, yes, but also in the confident hope that the question of what is living for will soon be restored to its proper place in American higher education.

1

What Is Living For?

Our lives are the most precious resource we possess, and the question of how to spend them is the most important question we face. The lives we actually lead are the more-or-less well-thought-out answers we give to this question. Our answers depend, of course, on what we value and where we find fulfillment. How should I spend my life? That question immediately invites another. What do I most care about and why? For the sake of what—or who—am I living? What is my life for?

But what sort of question is this exactly? There are philosophers who have said it is not a real question at all, but only a mirage that looks like one because it has the same form as other, real questions, like the question of what my job is for, or my bank account, or the clock on the wall in my kitchen.[1] And there are comics who, trading on our instinctive sense that there is, at a minimum, something highly peculiar about the question and that it may indeed be an illusion in the end, poke wonderful fun at those who ask it. Woody Allen, in particular, has made a career of puncturing the balloons of intellectuals who go around pontificating about the meaning of life. Monty Python has made a brilliant contribution to the deflation of such pretensions as well.[2] We all laugh at their jokes because there is something ridiculous about the question of the meaning of life. But if it were merely ridiculous, the humor would be shallow. The jokes are funny in a deep way because they touch a nerve and remind us that however absurd the question seems, we cannot get away from or do without it. The question of what living is for is like no other. It is at once fundamental and illusory, urgent and absurd, solitary and shared. At certain moments, it presses on us with a crushing weight. At others, it tickles like a feather. Most of the time, it isn't a question for us at all.

Perhaps the most obvious thing to be said about the question is that it has an unavoidably personal quality. How I answer it depends upon my interests, tastes, and talents, as well as my upbringing and social and economic circumstances—in short, upon a thousand factors that distinguish me from you and everyone else. These differences all have a bearing on what I care about, and hence on how I choose to spend my life. The variety of lives that people lead reflects the variety of endowments—temperamental, cultural, and other—with which they start. These differences of endowment fix the perspective or point of view from which we approach the question of what living is for. In a real and important sense, they "personalize" it. The question looks different to me because I see it from the angle of my own distinctive constitution. And of course the same is true for you and everyone else.

But there is a second, deeper sense in which the question of what my life is for is personal to me. For it is a question that only I can answer. No one else in the world is competent to answer it for me, even if they know as much about my makeup as I do. I may of course learn from others and take instruction from their example. But however enlightening or inspiring I find what they say and do, the answer I give to the question of life's meaning has validity for me only because it is my answer. My answer may be the same as yours. We may care about the same things and lead lives of a similar kind. We may agree on the standards for judging whether the lives of others have purpose and value. I may take comfort in our agreement and be encouraged by it. But what matters most to me—what is of overriding importance—is not that the question of what living is for have a right answer, which someone else perhaps has already found, but that my answer be the right one, even if others discovered it long ago.

This is not true of all questions. There are many, in fact, of which it is not true. Consider, for example, questions in mathematics. After the seventeenth-century French mathematician Pierre de Fermat died, a book was discovered in his library with a note, written in the margin, that he had discovered a "marvelous proof" for the proposition that there are no non-zero integers x, y, and z such that $x^n + y^n = z^n$ where n is an integer greater than two. Fermat noted that the margins of his book were too narrow to contain the proof he had found. This became known as Fermat's "last" theorem, last because it was the last to be proved. It was not in fact proved until 1995, when the Princeton mathematician Andrew Wiles published his proof. When he did, the world celebrated and his discovery was the subject of much discussion in the popular press. The cause for celebration was obvious. For though only a handful of specialists could follow Wiles's reasoning, it appeared that a troubling question in mathematics had now been decisively answered, and others could scratch it off their list. Other questions remained, but this one, at least, had been settled. There was no longer any reason for other mathematicians to ask themselves whether Fermat's Last Theorem can be proven.[3]

Some of Wiles's fellow mathematicians were no doubt jealous of his discovery. They wished they had been the one to make it. That is only human. But to the extent they were faithful to their discipline, to the extent they were, as we might say, "true" mathematicians, they had to acknowledge that the important thing was not who made the discovery but that it was made.

There is a distinction between the personal and impersonal views we take of such discoveries. From an impersonal point of view—from the point of view of the world, which we sometimes call the objective point of view—all that matters is the discovery itself, not the fact that it happens to have been made by one person rather than another. By contrast, from a personal point of view, what matters is that I be that person, that I be the one to have answered the question correctly. Thus while it doesn't matter from an impersonal perspective who first discovered the calculus, Leibniz or Newton, it mattered personally to both Leibniz and Newton, and the quarrel between them on this score eventually became quite bitter.[4] But their quarrel illustrates an important point about the relative priority of these two points of view, the personal and the impersonal, so far as the discovery of the calculus is concerned. For their quarrel seems quite petty and unworthy of the two great geniuses involved. That they quarreled is understandable and forgivable. Like the rest of us, Leibniz and Newton felt the pull of vanity and self-interest. But as mathematicians, they ought to have suppressed these all-too-human instincts in favor of a more "objective" attitude from whose perspective the identity of the discoverer of the calculus is a matter of indifference. And if we feel they "ought" to have done this, that is because, where discoveries of this sort are concerned, the latter, impersonal point of view takes precedence over the personal one which, though it cannot be extinguished, is subordinate in relevance and importance.

The distinction between these two points of view, and the priority of the impersonal over the personal, is especially clear in disciplines like mathematics where there is an unequivocally right answer to most (if not all) questions one might ask. But the same distinction exists in other fields, where there is more room for debate about the correctness of particular answers. So in history, for example, the question of what caused the Civil War is one that historians have answered in different ways, and that can never have a final and conclusive answer like the answer to the question of whether Fermat's Last Theorem has a proof. There will always be room for disagreement as to whether the answer that any particular historian gives is the right one. Yet still we can distinguish between a historian's conviction that his answer is correct, that he has discovered the truth of the matter, and his satisfaction in being the one to discover it. And here, too, as in the field of mathematics, we believe that what ought to matter most to a historian is the soundness of his answer, which should— in principle—matter just as much if someone else has found it (though that is an attitude requiring a suppression of vanity that borders on the heroic). If a historian is asked whether she would prefer to be the author of a famous and well-regarded book containing an account of the Civil War that she alone knows to be wrong, or be proven wrong by another historian whose reputation consequently eclipses her own, and chooses the former, we say that this shows she is not really a historian at heart because her decision, however understandable in human terms, reverses the order of importance that real historians should attach to their personal and impersonal interests in getting the answer right. And the fact that "right" is here harder (and perhaps impossible) to determine, and that all sorts of subjective elements enter into the answers that historians give to questions of this sort, makes not a whit of difference so far as the priority of the impersonal point of view is concerned.

In my search for an answer to the question of how I should spend my life, of what commitments and pursuits will give it meaning and value, the priority is the reverse. Here what matters most is not that the right answer be found, by someone or other, but that it be me who finds it. This is, indeed, the only thing that matters. To other questions, like those that mathematicians and historians ask, I naturally want to give the right answer, and it is a disappointment to me if I don't—perhaps even a big disappointment if I'm asked the question on a test. But it is always some consolation that another person has found the right answer even if I haven't. By contrast, my interest in the question of what living is for is overwhelmingly personal. It is no consolation at all that others answer it correctly (whatever that means) if I don't. All I care about, all I should care about, is the quality of the answer I give, not that the "truth of the matter" be grasped and brought to light by someone or other, regardless of who that might be. If my answer is a poor one (whatever that means), that is not merely a disappointment, like failing a math exam. It is a disaster unmitigated by the existence of the right answer I happen to miss. With respect to this question, and perhaps only with respect to it, the personal point of view completely trumps the impersonal one in its importance to the person asking the question. Nor do we think there is anything wrong about according it this priority. Indeed, we would consider it perverse—faithless to the spirit and nature of the question—to do otherwise.

This is what, in a deeper sense, gives the question its personal character. The question of whether Fermat's Last Theorem has a proof is settled for me because Andrew Wiles settled it. But the question of what living is for can never be settled for me just because it is settled for you or anyone else. I may have much to learn from your words and actions. I may benefit from the study of other people's lives, as recorded in books or presented to me in experience. But I can never defer to their judgment in this

matter, as I do in so many others. For nothing
that anyone else says or does can ever by itself
justify my thinking that the question of the
meaning of my life has been answered. Deference and delegation, which are appropriate
where an impersonal concern for the truth has
priority, are out of place here. The question of
how to spend my life, of what my life is for, is a
question posed only to me, and I can no more
delegate the responsibility for answering it than I
can delegate the task of dying.

The essentially personal nature of this question
is one reason why the meaning of life is such a
rich vein of comic fun. For the idea that one can
learn the meaning of life in the same way that
one learns the names of the kings of England or
the periodic table or masters the elements of economic theory is not just mistaken. It is absurd. I
can study all these things in an impersonal way.
I can go to school to learn the truth about them
without taking the slightest interest in the subject. I can happily acknowledge that the truths
of history and chemistry and economics have a
value apart from and superior to the value of my
own personal knowledge of them. But none of
this makes sense if the question is how to spend
my life—how to live a life that has purpose and
value. It is perverse not to take an interest in the

question or to think that the truth of the matter, whatever it might be, has any value at all apart from my recognition of it. The question of what living is for is personal to me in a way the others I study in school are not, and I can't answer it simply by following someone's instructions or reading the right books. This is one source of the humor in Woody Allen's remark that he cheated on his metaphysics exam by looking into the soul of the boy sitting next to him.

A second reason why the question of life's meaning often seems so funny is the rarity with which we ask it. It is not a question that arises with any regularity in the course of everyday life. It is an "eccentric" question and whole periods in our lives can pass without our asking it. And on those rare occasions when we do, we find it a hard question to confront. We find it difficult to get and keep in focus. La Rochefoucauld compared death to the sun.[5] Just as we cannot stare at the sun for more than a moment, he said, we cannot bear to look death in the eye. The question of the meaning of life is like this too. It seems absurdly disconnected from the questions of everyday living which preoccupy us most of the time, and when we do put it to ourselves in a deliberate way it has a blinding immensity that threatens to blot out all the more familiar landmarks by which we steer our course from day to day. Woody Allen joked that he couldn't understand why some people want to know the secrets of the universe when it's hard enough to find your way around China-town. He was reminding us how funny the question of the value and purpose of life looks from the standpoint of everyday living.

To be sure, history does record the careers of a few rare individuals, like Socrates and Jesus, who were able to keep this question before themselves with a steadiness the rest of us can never attain. We are drawn to them for this reason, quite apart from the substance of their teachings. We are fascinated by their ability to pursue the question of life's meaning with such unflagging seriousness, and divided between our admiration for them and our wonder at their inhuman remoteness (a source both of pathos and humor). Unlike Socrates and Jesus, we confront this question only at long intervals and obliquely at best. For the most part, we spend our days addressing questions of a humbler kind. Should I take an umbrella to work? Call a friend and make a date? Sometimes we face questions of a larger sort. Should I change jobs? Invite an aging parent to live in my home? And sometimes, though rarely, these questions spiral up to an even higher level of concern. How important is my job, relative to the other things in my life? Am I loved by my children? Am I worthy of their love? And once in a very long while, we ask ourselves the question to which all these others seem to lead and in which they are gathered as a final conundrum, the question of what living is for, of whether and why our lives have a meaning that makes them worth living at all. But this last question emerges only rarely and under exceptional circumstances, and when it does, we glimpse it just for a moment, like a distant peak, before it disappears again behind the fog of everyday life, which only a few extraordinary people seem ever to escape for very long.

Because we confront it so rarely and have such difficulty holding it in view when we do, the question of the value and purpose of life might therefore seem to be one we need not spend much time preparing to meet. Our time and energy are limited, and the demands of everyday life immense. Each day presents a thousand questions that must be answered just to get to the next. Common sense encourages us to devote ourselves to these. It advises us not to be distracted by a question we face so infrequently and that is so difficult to grasp. Prudence counsels us to economize our mental and spiritual resources by concentrating on the issues at hand, for these are challenging enough, and to let the meaning of life look after itself—or risk pointless distraction and the danger of appearing a fool.

But a nagging thought puts this counsel in doubt. For however eccentric the question of life's meaning may be, however remote from the immediate concerns of everyday life, however sprawling and indefinite, however intimidating, it is always there, hovering in the background, threatening to break through into conscious attention and, when it does, to challenge or upset my established routines and cause a crisis that compels me to consider what I most care about and why.

My life is a pyramid of decisions and commitments. At the wide bottom of the pyramid are the many decisions I make every day about matters of little consequence and the modest commitments these imply. Further up in the pyramid are decisions and commitments of greater importance. These provide the foundation—the framework and supporting justification—for those nearer the base. And above these, closer to the apex of the pyramid, are decisions and commitments of still greater importance, which in turn provide the foundation for those below them. And so on up to the very top, where my life comes to a point in the deepest and most important commitments I have.

In the pyramid of my commitments, unlike the pyramid paperweight sitting on my desk, it is the apex that supports the base, not the other way around. The base is broad because it includes so many small commitments. The apex is pointed because it includes so few. But it is these few—my deepest and least changeable attachments—that support and justify all the many, modest ones below them, that hold them in place and secure their purpose and value.

And yet because all my commitments are connected in an ascending hierarchy, each tranche or level depending on those above it, a disturbance at a lower level can always create a disturbance at a higher one, rippling upward in the pyramid of my life. This need not happen and typically doesn't. But the possibility that it might is always there, and it is just this possibility that keeps the question of life's meaning right offstage, waiting to be called into the spotlight at any moment, forcing me to attend to the hierarchy of commitments on which my life depends, or better, of which it consists: a crisis of living whose potential is as permanent as its manifestation is rare.[6]

I have a cold. Shall I take the day off from work and stay home? It's probably best that I go. Why? Because a meeting has been scheduled and I'm expected. So? Others are counting on me being there. Why do I care? Because I want our project to succeed. For what reason? To increase my chances of promotion. And if I don't get it? I may need to look for another job. And what's so bad about that? I like my job. I like the money and prestige it affords. But wouldn't I be better off if I cared less about these things? Shouldn't I look for a job that would allow me to spend more time with my family and books?

Aren't there more important things for me to care about than money and prestige, before I'm dead and can't care about anything at all? Maybe I should take the day off after all.

From the wide bottom of the pyramid of my life, a question spirals up to the apex of my deepest commitments. It becomes a question about them. A head cold turns into a question about the meaning of life. This almost never happens. But it always can. And if it is imprudent to waste too much of my everyday life thinking about this question, it seems imprudent in another way to ignore the possibility of the escalating crisis of meaning with which my life is permanently pregnant.

For the most part, the question of the purpose and value of life lies in the unnoticed background of the many, smaller questions I face and decide each day. But I know it is there. I know that even my smallest decisions are hinged on a set of ascending commitments to increasingly important values, each dependent on commitments and values of still greater importance. I know that the smallest units of meaning in my life are held in place by larger and larger units, reaching up, at their apex, to some conception of what living itself is for—unexpressed, perhaps inexpressible, but foundational. I know that my most ordinary and inconsequential decisions are saved from meaninglessness only because they rest upon this hierarchy of commitments. And I know that however rarely I confront this

hierarchy directly, the least significant question—"Shall I part my hair behind? Do I dare to
eat a peach?"[7]—has the power to trigger a crisis
that will force the confrontation on me. I know
that the question of life's meaning is with me at
every moment, out of view but exerting a pull,
and this knowledge is the source of that anxiety,
familiar to us all, that enlivens and sustains my
belief in the importance of the question, however
strange or humorous it seems from the standpoint of common sense.

This anxiety is always with us, from the
moment we become reflectively aware of our
engagement in the mortal enterprise of living
until the enterprise is done. At different points
in our lives, the anxiety assumes different forms.
When we are young, the question of what living
is for is largely prospective. It draws our attention
to the choices before us and reminds us that our
lives are significantly subject to our own direction
and design, though never perfectly so. We ask the
question in order to make the right choices and
for the sake of the lives we want to lead. When
we are old, the question becomes more retrospec-
tive. It draws our attention to the choices we have
made, which are now embodied in the increasingly finished story of our lives. Near the end of
life, we ask the question in order to make sense
of the lives we have lived and to know what has
made them worth living. This shift in orientation
does not happen all at once, of course, nor is it
ever complete. For the living, life is never either

perfectly open or entirely done. The shift is gradual and follows the natural trajectory that sets the common frame of our lives. As we move forward on this path, which nature prescribes, the question of life's meaning changes direction and form. But its urgency never diminishes. It is no less important at one stage of life than another. It can produce a crisis in youth or old age, for Goethe's Werther or Mann's Aschenbach.[8] And our anxious sense that everything else depends on the answer we give to it remains with us as long as we live, however rarely we acknowledge our anxieties or permit them to intrude on the serious business of everyday life.

I care about many things. I care about my health. I care about my wife and children. I care about my garden. I care about my retirement portfolio. I care about my appearance. I care about finishing this book. But not all my cares are of the same caliber. Not all are as important in my life. Some of my cares are more important than others. If I had to, I could arrange them in a rough order of priority by asking which I would retain and which I would let go if forced to choose among them. The idea of a hierarchy of cares is familiar and intuitive.[9]

Perhaps the hierarchy does not come to a head in a single care—one thing (or person) I care more about than any other and for whose sake I am prepared to sacrifice all the rest. Perhaps there is more than one thing (or person) I care about in this way. Perhaps my highest-level cares are connected in some fashion and form a sort of family; perhaps they are disjointed or even conflicting. But whether my highest-level cares are one or many, coordinated or conflicting, the notion that I have such cares, that there are certain things (or persons) that matter more to me than any others, seems obvious, and if I do in fact have certain highest-order cares, it seems especially important that I be confident these are the cares I want to occupy this position in my life.

If the things (or persons) that matter most to me are not the ones that, on reflection, I want to matter most, no adjustment or correction is more important. And if I am uncertain or confused as to what it is that matters most, no clarification is more urgent. For error or ignorance regarding my highest-order cares gives my life as a whole the wrong kind of meaning or none. The question of the meaning of my life can therefore be reframed as the question of what I should ultimately care about and why. A person who says that he cares about many things—the cut of his hair, the size of his bank account, his reputation as a scholar—but, ultimately, about nothing at all, is pathological. And a person who says he has no interest in discovering what he most cares about, or in deciding whether he ought to care about these things, displays a shocking carelessness about his life itself—about the expenditure of the most precious resource he possesses. If the question, "What is the meaning of life?," strikes us as odd and more than a little funny, its equivalent, "What, in the end, should I care about?," is more familiar and its urgency easier to see.

This formulation presupposes that I have some choice in the matter, that it is open to me to care about one thing rather than another. It may be doubted whether this is so. In any case, it seems plain that I am not free, at the highest or any other level, to care about whatever I wish. What I care about, both trivially and fundamentally, is a function of my history and makeup. These circumscribe the range of what I am able to care about, realistically and effectively. Still, they do not eliminate all my deliberative freedom to consider some set of options. This is clear at lower levels of caring. Should I care as much as I do about the neatness of my office? Perhaps it is a neurotic habit that I would be better off without. No matter how deeply entrenched the habit, nothing prevents me from coming to this judgment about it, and I may even be able to make some progress in its practical reform. Even at higher levels of caring—even, indeed, at the highest—I retain the reflective independence that permits me to ask whether my cares are the right ones, the best ones for me, and to conclude that they are not. However high I go in the hierarchy of my cares, it always makes sense to ask this question, and it is always possible for me to answer it in the negative. Of course, if I do, it may be hard or impossible to bring my cares into alignment with my assessment of them—to reform them along the lines my negative judgment requires. My success in this regard depends on a host of factors that have been a subject of philosophical inquiry from Aristotle's discussion of weakness of the will to Freud's account of resistance.[10] But even if I fail, or only partially succeed, this does not mean that the inquiry that led to my frustrated effort at reform was itself pointless. For it has at least led to a deepened self-awareness about my highest-order cares and that is not only good in itself but also the most potent source of self-reform I have, the best basis for continuing to hope that the life I want to live will one day approximate more closely the life I am actually living.

When I ask myself what I should do, the question most often has a moral meaning. What should I do? That is, what are my moral responsibilities? But the question of what I should care about is not a moral question in this sense. For even after I have met all my moral responsibilities, the question of how I should spend my life remains. I may decide to spend it in pursuit of some moral objective— for example, eliminating famines or promoting human rights. But that decision is not dictated by the requirements of morality itself, which always leave me some discretionary space to decide what I should care about. For some, the decision leads to a life organized around moral values at the highest level of care. For others, it leads to a life respectful of morality but devoted, at the highest level, to values of a different kind, to the study of philosophy, for example, or the pursuit of athletic prowess. And for a few, it leads to a life whose highest values conflict with those of morality, like the life of Paul Gauguin, who cared so much about art that he abandoned his family for its sake.[11] But whatever answer a person gives, the question of what he ought ultimately to care about is a question that cannot be answered within the boundaries of moral reflection. It is not a moral question. It is a question that in fact arises only at the point at which morality leaves off. And for me to think that I can answer it by identifying my moral and legal responsibilities is to conflate—reassuringly, perhaps, but falsely—a larger issue with a narrower one that can never capture or exhaust the full challenge of deciding what to care about and why.

This way of formulating the question of life's meaning has the further advantage of highlighting a curious but familiar feature that any answer to the question must have. To "care" about something is, in ordinary parlance, to take an interest in its protection or preservation or perfection. It is to be interested in the welfare of who or what one cares about, for that person's or thing's own sake. Thus to care about one's family, or the study of Renaissance art, or the game of baseball is to wish to see these things succeed and flourish, to be protected against what threatens them and to be made happier or more perfect, if possible. The kind of interest involved in caring is thus not a self-interest, as we ordinarily use the term. It is directed away from the caring person at someone or something else—not as a means for promoting, in a circuitous and indirect way, the welfare of the person who cares but that of the person or thing that is the object of her caring. A person who cares about her parents or children only because it increases her stature in the community or who cares about baseball only because she is betting on the game is someone, we would say, who cares only about herself, and this familiar criticism underscores that real caring is always directed at the welfare of another—that its other-directedness is what gives it the quality of care in the first place.

If the meaning of my life is a function of what I care about at the very highest level, it therefore seems to follow that my life has the meaning it does only on account of something outside of or beyond it that I have an interest in protecting or preserving. For if caring is other-directed, then my ultimate cares, which give my life as a whole its meaning, must be directed at something other than my life itself. That is true regardless of what my ultimate cares are. They must have as their object something other than my own well-being or even my existence, for if they do not, if I have myself as my own object of greatest care, then, though I may be supremely interested in myself, I do not really care about anything at all, and if I don't, and the meaning of my life consists of what I care about, my careless life has no meaning. This sounds like an extravagant conclusion. But it is only a generalization of the very common and very human belief that the willingness of most parents to die for their children gives the parents' lives purpose and value. Others are prepared to die for other things. Their highest-order cares are different. But one cannot live a meaningful life unless there is something one is prepared to give it up for. People's lives are therefore meaningful in proportion to their acknowledgment that there is something more important than the lives that they are leading: something worth caring about in an ultimate way. The question, of course, is what that something is or ought to be. It is a supremely difficult question. But the difficulty of the question should not be mistaken for its absurdity or irrelevance. It is the question that Socrates (who died for philosophy) and Jesus (who died for humanity) installed at the center of our civilization and that we each face in our individual lives.

✦

The question of what living is for—of what we should care most about and why—seems so urgent because all our lesser attachments appear at times to depend upon it. At certain moments and in certain moods, all these other attachments can seem vulnerable and on the verge of collapse unless they are secured by an answer to the question that frames them and holds them in place. Such moments are rare but never completely out of mind. They hover at the edge of our more mundane concerns, and we are always aware, vaguely at least, of their power to disrupt our otherwise well-organized lives.

And yet it is precisely at these moments, when the question of life's meaning seems most pressing, that it is also likely to appear most strange. For the more pointedly we ask ourselves about the meaning of our lives as a whole, the more we may be inclined to conclude that this is not a real question at all. The more we may see it as a phantom question that has the same form as the ordinary questions we ask every day and whose legitimacy common sense accepts but which, unlike them, lacks all content and purpose. The more we may judge it a mirage and our anxious preoccupation with it the consequence of an illusion or mistake, of the confused belief that the familiar words we use when we ask what living is for—words that make sense and have an obvious utility in other settings—make similar sense and have the same utility here. In the end, we may conclude that this question is an example of what happens when, in Wittgenstein's famous phrase, "language goes on holiday."[12] And if we do, we are likely to dismiss it as a nonsense question—one that cannot be answered because it has no meaning itself.

The conviction that this is so arises in the following way.

When we are asked what something in our lives is for—an activity, a relationship, or a project of some sort—we generally answer by pointing out its connection to something else. The connection is meant to establish its purpose or value and in this way to explain its significance. The connection can be of different sorts. Sometimes it is instrumental. If, for example, I am asked what my job is for, I may answer that it is for the money I make from it. I may say that I value my job on account of the material benefits it affords. My job is for these other things. It is a means to an end, an instrument for the achievement of some other goal. That of course does not deprive my job of value. It merely identifies the kind of value it has. My job has the value of an instrument, something I explain by pointing out its connection to the end it serves.

Of course, there are many things in my life whose value is, in whole or part, of a non-instrumental kind. Though I value my job for the money it brings, I may also value it because it gives me an opportunity to use skills whose exercise is, for me, a source of pleasure in its own right. And I am likely to value my relationships with my friends mostly or entirely because of the intrinsic satisfactions they afford (though some degree of instrumentalism may be present here as well).

But even the value of these aspects of my life, the ones I find intrinsically rewarding, can only be explained by pointing out their connection to something else. Suppose I am asked what my friendships are for. What purpose do they serve? What value do they have for me? The question is not absurd. I understand it, and can frame an answer. I might say, for example, that my friendships create the occasion for me to love and be loved. They embody, for me, the experience of love. They give love a place in my life. It would be a mistake to say that my friendships are instruments for the attainment of love. They do not exist separately from the love they embody, in the way that an instrument exists apart from the end it serves. And yet the love I feel for my friends, and they for me, is something larger than my friendships themselves. No one of my friendships exhausts it, nor even all of them together. In this sense, my friendships and the love that gives them their vitality and value are not the same, and that makes it possible for me to speak of a relation between the two—between my friendships and the love they embody.[13]

If a word were wanted, we might call this relation one of revelation. My friendships create a place for me to experience—to feel and know—what love is like. They reveal its meaning. Explaining this helps me answer the question of what my friendships are for, and though the answer in this case is non-instrumental, it too depends on my pointing out the connection between one thing (my friendships) and another (the love they allow and display).

There are other possibilities. If I am asked, for example, why I read or exercise or travel—what any of these things are for—I may give an instrumental answer by pointing out their usefulness as means to something else (being well-informed or physically fit or skilled in another language). But I may also give an answer of a different kind by observing that these activities contribute to a well-balanced life, not in the way an instrument contributes to its goal but in the different way that an ingredient contributes to a dish or the background of a portrait to its subject—in the way that one part of some larger composite contributes to the whole of which it is an element. I may value reading and exercise and travel not because they contribute to some discrete good other than themselves, but because my life would be less interesting or pleasurable without them. They are, for me, intrinsic goods—I find them satisfying in their own right—but they are also parts of a complex whole that would be diminished by their elimination, just as they would be diminished if they were somehow separated from it or expanded to absorb my life completely.

The value of these activities is therefore also explained by their relation to something else— in this case, to a balanced life that includes many different things. This relation is not an instrumental one, nor can it reasonably be described as one of revelation. Again, if a word is needed, we might say that the relation is one of composition, the relation in which a needed part stands to the larger whole that requires it in order to be completed in the best or most fulfilling way. Pointing out that some aspect of my life stands in this relation of composition to my life as a whole is another way of answering the question of what it is for.

There may be still other ways of answering this question than the three I have considered. But it is difficult—in the end, I think it is impossible—to conceive of any answer that does not adopt the general approach these three all do. When we try to explain what something in our lives is for, we always do so by pointing out its relation to something else, recognizing that these relations may be of different sorts (instrumental, revelatory, compositional, or whatever).

But suppose we now ask what living itself is for—what gives our lives as a whole their value and meaning. Can this question be answered in the way we answer questions about the value and meaning of the different parts of our lives?

To do so would seem to require that we place our lives as a whole in relation to something else—which of course is just what is implied by the idea that our lives have meaning only in case we care less about our lives than we do about something outside of or beyond them.

The vast majority of men and women, today as in the past, do in fact hold this belief in one form or another. Patriots committed to their country, believers devoted to their God, parents dedicated to their children, all think of their lives as related to something else of greater value and draw the meaning of their lives from this relation. They place their lives in a wider frame of reference—in the extended, if still mortal, career of their family or country, or in the cosmic pageant of an eternal God. They anchor their lives in this wider frame and derive from it an understanding of the point and purpose of their lives as a whole.

Different people view the relation between their lives and this larger frame of meaning in different ways. Some see themselves in instrumental terms, as tools for the attainment of a greater good; others compositionally, as actors whose participation is needed to make a drama complete; still others, as revelatory presences in whose lives something larger and more lasting comes to light.[14] But however this relation is conceived, it provides an answer to the question of life's meaning that follows the pattern of the answers we give when it is the meaning of some part of our lives that we are trying to explain. It seems natural to extend the pattern in this way, and to address the question of life's meaning by placing our lives as a whole in some larger context, just as we do when it is the meaning of a particular activity or relationship that is in question.

But natural as the extension seems, it represents in one crucial respect a departure from the pattern. For the judgment that our lives have meaning only in relation to something outside of or beyond them is a judgment that can be rendered only within the limits of life itself. Every claim about the meaning of life is made by the living, hence within the boundaries of the very enterprise whose meaning is in question. Nor can we even conceive of any other possibility, for we have no standpoint outside of life from which to make or assess such a claim.

In this respect, judgments about the meaning of life as a whole differ from judgments about the purpose and value of its various parts. For it is not inevitable that these latter judgments be rendered from within the boundaries of the activity, relationship, or experience they seek to explain—from within what might be called its experiential horizon. In most cases, if not all, I construct an explanation of what this or that part of my life is for from some standpoint outside it. I explain what my job is for from a vantage point outside the job itself. I consider my job from the outside and bring it into a relation with something else that explains its meaning—my hobbies, my talents, my family. If I am asked what my friendships are for, or why I read or travel, I do the same. I take up a position outside these relations and activities and answer the question by describing their connection to something else I value.

I do this in my imagination, but I am also able to do it in fact. None of the parts of my life occupies it completely. For every part of my life, there is always some other part from which I can survey it, from which I can see the part in question from a point of view beyond its own horizon, and assess its relation to the other things that give it meaning or value, whatever form this relation takes. But I cannot do this when it is the meaning of my life as a whole that is in question. Here, the only point of view I can attain is in imagination. There is no real outside vantage point that corresponds to those from which I can assess and judge the parts of my life, and answer the question of what they are for.

Thus if the question of what the whole of life is for can be answered only by placing it in a context larger than life itself, it can also never be answered from a point of view that we are really (as opposed to imaginatively) able to adopt. In the first respect, the question of life's meaning looks like the question of the meaning of its parts. It follows the same pattern. But in the second, it differs fundamentally, and this difference is one that gives the question its peculiar aura of unreality.

We feel the special importance of the question of life's meaning, however rarely it breaks through the crust of everyday living. Yet at the same time we recognize the unreality that sets this question apart from all the lesser ones that precede and invite it. We express this unreality by saying that claims about the meaning of life can never be proven, that they lie beyond the province of demonstration, that they must be taken on faith and are therefore essentially religious in nature. In saying these things, we acknowledge the discontinuity between questions about the meaning of life, on the one hand, and the meaning of its parts, on the other. For there is no actually attainable point of view from which the relation of our lives to whatever lies outside them can ever be observed with the same objectivity and detachment to which we at least aspire in reviewing the parts of our lives. There is no real vantage point that we can ever occupy from which our lives can be seen as a whole. And knowing this, we can never escape the disquieting sense that the question of life's meaning is more unreal than all the other questions that point to it as their foundation—yet, just because it is their foundation, more urgent as well.

Unlike questions about the meaning of the various parts of my life, the question of what value and purpose my life as a whole possesses—of what my life is for—cannot be raised except from a point of view that I am able to adopt only in imagination. It is an imaginary question in a way these others are not, and because of this I may be tempted to conclude that despite appearances it is not a real question at all. Some philosophers have drawn this conclusion. But the philosophical judgment that the question of the meaning of life is not a real question can never permanently still the feelings of hope and fear that attend it. Among other things, the persistence of religious belief in the face of such judgments testifies to their impotence to quiet these feelings except, perhaps, for a few rare souls like Spinoza.[15] Despite our philosophical doubts, and the jokes that express in a humorous way our sense of the air of unreality that hovers about the question, few of us can suppress, entirely or for long, our nagging worry that it is both real and supremely important.

But even if it is a real question, and the most important one we ever face, it is a question we face alone, and the answers we give to it can only be our own. No one else can answer for me the question of what I should ultimately care about and why. It is an exquisitely personal question. And if that is true, one might reasonably wonder whether the meaning of life is a subject that can usefully be studied in school, like myriad others that are listed in the catalogues of our colleges and universities.

In what sense, and in what way, can the question of what living is for be made an appropriate and useful subject of academic instruction? Today, in most of our colleges and universities, it is not, in fact, a subject of organized study, and one might infer from what I have said that this is because the question by its very nature precludes it—that it is too personal to be studied in this way. But the question of life's meaning has not always been neglected as it now is. Once upon a time, and not all that long ago, many college and university teachers, especially in the humanities, believed they had a responsibility to lead their students in an organized examination of this question and felt confident in their authority to do so. They recognized that each student's answer must be his or her own but believed that a disciplined survey of the answers the great writers and artists of the past have given to it can be a helpful aid to students in their own personal encounter with the question of what living is for—indeed, an indispensable aid, without which they must face the question not only alone but in disarray.

The loss of this belief and the collapse of the confidence that attended it is not a consequence of the logic of the question itself. There is nothing in the nature of the question that requires its exclusion from the roster of subjects our colleges and universities teach. The inattention that is paid to it today in most corners of higher education is a consequence of historical developments instead. It is to these that I now turn.

2

SECULAR HUMANISM

There are more than six thousand institutions of higher education in America.[1] "Institution" is a colorless word, and I use it for that reason. For the variety of colleges and universities in America today is so vast that only a word with almost no content could possibly encompass them all.

There are the great research universities, with their graduate programs, professional schools, and specialized facilities for advanced research; the residential liberal arts colleges, devoted to undergraduate education; the two-year state and community colleges, serving for the most part a local population and providing career training as well as a preparation for further study elsewhere; and today, the "electronic" universities that offer education at a distance for those who find it easier to work at home. All these schools meet real needs. But the differences among them—of function, character, and aim— are so large that "college" and "university" are only words they share in common.[2]

Of the many functions our colleges and universities serve, most need little explanation or defense. The advancement of research, which our largest universities are set up to promote, is a self-evident good. The new knowledge that research produces is of value in its own right and has immense practical benefits. To a degree that few Americans perhaps fully appreciate, their material well-being is today a consequence of discoveries first made in the libraries and laboratories of the country's research universities.

Vocational training, at all levels, is another unquestioned good. Whether one wants to be an architect or electrician, a doctor or dental hygienist, a lawyer or court reporter, technical training is today a prerequisite. All but the most unskilled forms of labor are increasingly based on knowledge of a kind that can be acquired only in school, and in supplying that knowledge America's colleges and universities provide a tremendous service to the individuals who come to them to learn a trade or profession and make an enormous (if not fully visible) contribution to the country's economy.[3]

There are other, non-economic contributions that our colleges and universities make to the welfare of their communities and of the country as a whole. In broad terms, these might be called political. I have in mind the cultivation of the habits of respectfulness and tolerance on which responsible citizenship in a diverse democracy depends. Colleges and universities do this not so much by preaching the virtues of these habits (though they do that too), as by creating an environment in which students are required to interact with others quite unlike themselves—often for the first time in their lives—and to develop the attitudes of open-mindedness and toleration that this demands. Colleges and universities are not, of course, the only such environment—the contemporary workplace is another—but they are an important one, and the contribution they make to strengthening the spirit of democratic citizenship is one of their most valuable functions.[4]

This is an impressive list of goods. But there is another that must be added to it. It is harder to define but just as real. It is the good of helping students come to grips with the question of what living is for—the good, as Alexander Meiklejohn, the president of Amherst College, described it a century ago, of helping young people fashion "a life worth living" from their given endowments of desire, opportunity, and talent.[5]

College is for many a time to prepare for their careers. It is, in fact, the first stage of their careers, a period of preliminary academic training to be followed by other forms of training or by work itself. For those who approach it with this goal in mind, their college education has a clear and measurable value. It contributes in a direct way to the achievement of an already-fixed objective. But its value depends upon the determinacy of the goal toward which it is directed. For others, who are less sure what they want to do or be, for whom the question of how they should spend their lives is a more open one, a college education can be of value for a different reason. It can help them meet the challenge of gaining a deeper insight into their own commitments, of refining for themselves the picture of a life that has purpose and value, of a life that is worth living and not just successful in the narrower sense of achievement in a career.

For undergraduates who approach their studies in a state of curiosity or confusion about these things, a college education can help them find their bearings. It can help them confront the question, which comes before all vocational training and goes beyond any answer that such training can supply, of what living itself is for. And if it succeeds in doing this, even modestly and incompletely, their education has for them a value very different from the value it has for those who come to college with their expectations fixed. Indeed, it has a value of an opposite sort, for it is the very absence of those settled goals that give all vocational education its utility that makes the question of what living is for so important.

To have the freedom to pursue this question for a period of time in early adulthood is a great luxury. Many cannot afford it. The demands of life press too insistently for them to give the question its due. And some of those who have the time choose not to use it for this purpose. They are distracted or incurious. But for more than a few, who have both the freedom and the inclination, college is a time to explore the meaning of life with an openness that becomes harder to preserve the further one enters into the responsibilities of adulthood, with their many entanglements. College is a time for other things too, but it is also a time to survey, with as open a mind as one can manage, the horizons of the stirring and mysterious venture in which, by the age of eighteen or twenty, an attentive young person will have begun to grasp that he or she, like every human being, is fatefully engaged. For those who see the value of this survey, and have the time to make it, a college education affords an opportunity that may not come again. And however few they are in number or in proportion to the student population as a whole, it seems natural to regard this opportunity as a very great good that we would wish others to share and regret if they can't for lack of money or time.

It is the goal of every undergraduate liberal arts program to provide its students with an opportunity of this kind. Every college and university that has such a program describes it in essentially similar terms—as a means to acquaint its students with a wide range of human pursuits and to equip them with a general knowledge of themselves and of the world that will prepare them to meet the personal, ethical, and social challenges of life, regardless of the career they eventually choose. All liberal arts education is defined in consciously non-vocational terms. It is not a preparation for this job or that, for one career rather than another. It is a preparation for the "job" of living, which of course is not a job at all. Different schools undertake to do this in different ways. The variety of liberal arts programs is enormous. But all rest on the assumption that one important aim of undergraduate education is to afford the young men and women who are its beneficiaries an opportunity to reflect on the curious and inspiring adventure of life before they have gone too far in it and lost the time and perhaps the nerve for such reflections.[6]

Yet curiously, while emphasizing the importance of questions of meaning and purpose that transcend the narrowly vocational, few liberal arts programs today provide a place for their sustained and structured exploration. Few offer organized programs of the kind once associated with (now politically charged) phrases like "the great books curriculum," or "the Western tradition," or "the tradition of arts and letters," in which students and teachers pursued the perennial puzzles of human existence through the disciplined study of an interrelated series of works in which the question of how a person ought to spend his or her life provided a connecting theme and organizing focus of inquiry. Some programs of this sort still exist, of course, including some very famous ones like the Contemporary Civilization Course at Columbia, introduced at the time of the First World War. And individual courses that address these issues in a deliberate way can be found in every liberal arts program. But the attempt to provide the students in these programs with a broad, structured, and shared introduction to the alternative views of life's purpose and value that ought to be weighed as they struggle to define life's meaning for themselves is today an increasing rarity in American higher education. Fewer and fewer schools attempt to do this and the idea that it is even worth trying to do so—that it is a valuable and constructive goal to pursue—is one that many teachers and students now reject.

Today, many of those teaching in liberal arts programs, even teachers of the humanities, feel uncomfortable asserting the competence or authority to lead their students in an organized inquiry of this sort. They claim not to possess any special wisdom about the meaning of life that might be communicated to their students in a disciplined way. They insist that they are not professionally qualified to lead their students in the search for an answer to the question of what living is for. The subject may of course come up outside of class, where teacher and student feel free to speak in more intimate terms. But few college or university teachers today believe they have either the right or duty to offer their students organized instruction in the value and purpose of living. And this belief is by and large shared by their students, who for the most part do not hope or expect to receive such instruction in class.

That of course is not to say that students are uninterested in these questions, or think their academic studies irrelevant to them. Most students, especially those enrolled in liberal arts programs, have a passionate (if intermittent) interest in the question of what makes a life valuable and fulfilling. And most regard their academic work—all of it potentially—as a useful source of information and inspiration in reflecting on this question. But like their teachers, they regard the question as a personal one that cannot usefully be studied in a public and organized way.

What is the physical world made of and why does matter behave as it does? How do living organisms function and evolve? When are markets competitive? Is democracy the best form of government? Does the number pi have a pattern? How do we know what we know? These and countless other questions are appropriate subjects of classroom instruction. They can all be studied in a structured and rigorous fashion. In most colleges and universities, there are courses and departments devoted to their examination and teachers trained to guide students in their study. But the question of what living is for, of what ultimately matters in our lives and why, is only rarely a subject of explicit instruction in the way these others are. There are departments of geology and sociology and Spanish, but no departments in the meaning of life. Indeed, the very idea seems laughable. Who can imagine an Associate Professor of the Meaning of Life? Unlike the countless subjects best studied in a classroom with an organized curriculum under the supervisory eye of a professionally qualified teacher, the question of what living is for is one that today even those students gripped by the question are likely to regard as a personal matter most usefully explored outside of school, in the company of family and friends. And their teachers are for the most part likely to agree.

A student who holds this view might express it as follows. "Only I," he might say, "can decide what ultimately matters in my life. That is something I must do on my own. It is true that everything I learn in school, or outside it for that matter, bears on my search for an answer. All of my experience, academic and otherwise, deserves to be taken into account. But there is no academic discipline to guide me in my search for an answer to the question of life's meaning. There is no method or technique, no organized body of knowledge, no disciplined course of study, on which I can rely. There are no teachers whose special responsibility it is to frame this question or lead me in the investigation of it. No teacher has either the competence or right to do this. Perhaps no one does, but at least my family and friends know me personally, and love me. If I take the question up with anyone at all, I ought to take it up with them. The question of what living is for cannot be studied in school."

This describes the attitude of many students in our colleges and universities today, even those in liberal arts programs devoted to preparing them for the non-vocational task of fashioning what Meiklejohn called a "life worth living." And it describes the attitude of many of their teachers, who join in the judgment that the question of life's meaning is not a fit topic for study in school. Their agreement on this point is an important premise of American higher education at the start of the twenty-first century.

But this has not always been so. Even a half-century ago, the question of life's meaning had a more central and respected place in higher education than it does today.[7] It was not always given this name. But the question of how to spend one's life, of what to care about and why, the question of which commitments, relations, projects, and pleasures are capable of giving a life purpose and value: regardless of the name it was given, and even if, as was often the case, it was given no name at all, this question was taken more seriously by more of our colleges and universities in the middle years of the twentieth century than it is today. It was a question that institutions of higher learning felt they had the right and duty to address in an explicit and disciplined way. The responsibility for doing this fell in particular to the humanities. A half-century ago, many teachers in these fields still believed in the possibility and value of an organized study of the mysteries of life. But under pressure, first, from the modern research ideal whose authority today dominates the humanities as it does all branches of learning, and, second, from the culture of political correctness that has been so particularly influential in these disciplines for the past forty years, the question of the value and purpose of living, of the sources of fulfillment available to us as mortal creatures with ambitions of the most varied kinds, has been pushed to the margins of respectability even in the humanities. It has been stripped of its legitimacy as a question that teachers of the humanities feel they may properly and competently address with their students in a formal program of instruction. It has been exiled from the classroom and kicked out of school, so that today it survives only in private, in *pianissimo*, in the extracurricular lives of teachers and students, even in those liberal arts programs whose distinctive purpose presupposes the vital importance of this question itself: the depressing conclusion of an historical development that has privatized a subject the humanities once undertook to investigate in a public and organized way, before the modern research ideal and the culture of political correctness made it an embarrassment to do so.

✦

If one asks whether the purpose and value of life is a subject that can usefully be studied in school, and surveys the history of American higher education with this question in mind, that history can be divided into three phases. The first, and longest, begins with the founding of Harvard College in the early seventeenth century and lasts until the Civil War. It might be called the "age of piety." College education (and there were of course as yet no universities) rested on the premise that the ends of human living are not merely a fit subject of instruction but the one subject, before all others, that young men must study and learn. Instruction in the meaning of life proceeded on the basis of dogmatic assumptions that were simply taken for granted.

The second phase begins with the establishment of the first universities in the decades following the Civil War and ends in the middle years of the twentieth century. It might be called the "age of secular humanism," a term I shall define with more precision later on. The meaning of life continues to be an organized subject of undergraduate teaching. But it is now the special responsibility of the humanities to provide such instruction, which can no longer proceed on the old dogmatic assumptions that had once been accepted without question. A more pluralistic approach to the subject, based on a critical study of the great works of Western literature, philosophy, and art, emerges as a successor to the dogmatic program of the antebellum college.

The third phase, in which we find ourselves today, begins in the late 1960s. How long it will last is uncertain. In this third phase, the question of life's meaning has ceased to be a recognized and valued subject of instruction even in the humanities. It has been expelled from our colleges and universities, under pressure from the research ideal and the demands of political correctness.

At the start, America's colleges were all religious institutions. What they taught their students about the purpose and value of life was itself a branch of religious instruction. Later, in the age of secular humanism, church and school drew apart. America's colleges and universities distanced themselves from religion and claimed the authority to provide instruction in the meaning of life in a different way, and on different terms, from the instruction that America's churches continued to offer. In this second phase of American higher education, the authority to address the question of what living is for was divided between church and school. In the third phase—our phase—the abandonment by our colleges and universities of any claim to such authority has left it entirely in the hands of the churches, who now enjoy a near monopoly in the institutionally organized provision of instruction in the meaning of life. But at the start, America's colleges offered such instruction with a confidence that today only our churches possess.

The history of American higher education begins with the establishment of Harvard College in 1636. The first students at Harvard lived in a world unimaginably remote from our own. Their entire material universe consisted of a handful of crude structures, huddled on the edge of an immense and unyielding wilderness, which a few devout souls had crossed the Atlantic to build so that they might live a life of exemplary Christian piety and be a model for those they left behind, "a City on the Hill."[8] Those who came to build this city had to make a world from the ground up, and it can never cease to be a source of wonder that one of their first acts was the establishment of a college for the education of the young men in their midst. "After God had carried us safe to *New England,* and wee had builded our houses, provided necessaries for our liveli-hood, rear'd convenient places for Gods worship, and setled the Civil

Government: One of the next things we longed for, and looked after, was to advance *Learning* and to perpetuate it to Posterity."[9] But if the Puritan divines who founded Harvard College were pioneers, creating the first institution of its kind in North America, they were also heirs to a long tradition of learning, from which they took the design for their new college. Nearly all of Harvard's founders had been educated at Cambridge or Oxford, and their own education naturally served as a model for the college they built.

The educational program at Cambridge and Oxford in the early seventeenth century had been shaped in part by the traditions of medieval scholasticism and in part by the humanist revival of the century before. In broad terms, it combined a training in Latin and Greek and the close reading of works written in these languages with a rigorous study of theology that was meant to put the great works of pagan antiquity in their proper Christian perspective.[10] Students at Oxford and Cambridge in the early seventeenth century heard lectures on Homer, Herodotus, Sophocles, and Cicero. They read Aristotle's writings on ethics and studied ancient history and law. They read the Bible in Greek and listened as their teachers discussed fine points of religious doctrine. They engaged in highly structured debates of their own on classical and theological subjects. They learned the basic elements of natural science, in the Aristotlean terms in which these were still conceived. And in every branch of study, they worked mainly by copying, memorizing, and reciting passages from the texts they had been assigned. The Puritans who founded Harvard College were products of this program and brought it with them as a model.[11]

They brought something else as well. They brought the idea, so deeply embedded in their thinking that it would not even have occurred to them to formulate it as a principle, that the purpose of a college is to shape its students' souls. In their minds, a college was above all a place for the training of character, for the nurturing of those intellectual and moral habits that together form the basis for living the best life that one can—a life of discernment and piety, shaped by the example of the great men of the past and enlivened by a deep and unassailable love of God. Such a life might be described as the life of a Christian gentleman, and if the founders of Harvard College had been asked whether it was their aim to promote this way of life, the answer would have seemed to them self-evident. They did not think that Harvard's task was merely to impart certain useful knowledge, which its students were then free to exploit as they chose. Harvard's job was to make its students into men of a certain kind, with distinctive attitudes and dispositions, specific cares and concerns. It would never have occurred to the founders of the College that its students should be left to answer the question of life's meaning on their own.

At most, they would have recognized that a Christian gentleman might pursue one of several different careers—that he might become a minister, lawyer, teacher, or something else of the kind. But they would have rejected the idea that their college had been set up as a vocational school to prepare its students for their various post-graduate employments. They would have said that it had been created for a more elementary purpose—to provide the common base of character on which success and honor in all these endeavors depend. They would have insisted that Harvard had been established, first and most importantly, for the good of its students' souls.

They also believed they had chosen the best means to achieve this goal. This was the method of memorization and recitation. Memorization has always been a useful method for acquiring knowledge. But to the founders of Harvard, it seemed a natural technique for achieving the higher purpose of character building as well. To acquire a text by memory is to fix in one's mind the image and example of the author and his subject. Memory is the storehouse of the soul. We draw encouragement and guidance from it. To have a well-stocked memory is to be equipped for the challenges of life—to have a repertoire of stories, speeches, and the like from which to draw, as we face our choices and evaluate the alternatives before us. Memory (and recitation, which is its public display) are in this sense not distinct from character. They are its nursery bed, a sustaining source of enlightenment and inspiration for the soul. We might even go so far as to say that memory is character itself; a man is what he remembers, and reveals himself to be the person he is in his public speech.

That, in any case, was the ideal that lay behind the practice of memorization and recitation on which the earliest experiment in American higher education was based. It is an ideal that can be traced back to ancient beginnings, to the Roman discipline of rhetoric, and even earlier sources.[12] Today, we no longer see these methods in the attractive light of this tradition. Influenced by the writings of Rousseau and Dewey, among others, we view them not as aids to the growth and equipment of the soul but as a damper on spontaneity instead.[13] But for the Cambridge- and Oxford-educated Puritans who founded our first college, these techniques seemed the perfect means to achieve the goal of making Christian gentlemen—their main, indeed their only, object.

It is unlikely that the founders of Harvard College would have described its program as an education in the meaning of life. That is a modern formulation they would not have chosen, or perhaps even understood. But that they were concerned with life's ultimate values, thought they possessed a stable and authoritative wisdom about them, and understood the principal responsibility of their college to be the transmission of these values by means of methods designed to implant them in its students' souls: of all this there can be no doubt.

Harvard struggled to survive in material circumstances as challenging as any ever faced by an institution of higher learning. Intellectual developments in Europe put increasing pressure on the ideal of education with which the college had begun its "errand into the wilderness."[14] But at its heart, the enterprise was enlivened by a confident belief that the purpose of a college education is to answer the question of what living is for—to transmit the knowledge of what matters most in life and why, and to convey, in a psychologically compelling fashion, an understanding of the cosmic structures of meaning in which our human lives are anchored and that guarantee their own meaning in turn. Higher education in America begins with the belief that a college's first duty is to provide instruction in the meaning of life and for a long time afterward, and under pressure from many directions, this idea remained essentially unchallenged.

In the two centuries that followed Harvard's founding, hundreds of other colleges were established to serve the educational needs of their communities. By 1840, the American landscape was dotted with institutions of higher learning. Most drew their students from the local region, though a small number had already achieved national prominence and were attracting students from farther afield. Nearly all were affiliated with a particular church but varied in the degree to which that affiliation influenced the life of the college. And of course some were more financially secure than others, though by 1840 few had achieved a reliably comfortable distance from the threat of insolvency, which eventually forced many to close their doors.

The American collegiate scene, two hundred years after the founding of Harvard College, was one of vitality and variety. During this long formative period, the American people poured their wealth and ambitions into the creation of institutions of higher learning to an extent unprecedented in the history of any other nation. In Europe, higher education had always been the privileged preserve of a social and intellectual elite. In America, it became uniquely democratic—not perfectly so, of course, but to a greater degree than at any other time or place in human history.[15] The colleges that sprang up everywhere in America in the eighteenth and early nineteenth centuries were and remain one of the enduring expressions of the peculiarly American belief that everyone is educable, even up to the highest levels of intellectual ambition. Colleges, it was said, "break up and diffuse among the people that monopoly and mental power which despotic governments accumulate for purposes of arbitrary rule, and bring to the children of the humblest families of the nation a full and fair opportunity" for higher learning— a conviction that combined democratic and aristocratic ideas in a distinctively American way.[16] The antebellum college was a landmark of American civilization.

The colleges with which America was beginning to fill up in the early years of the nineteenth century differed in many respects. But nearly all shared certain features and continued to follow, in modified form, an educational tradition that could be traced back to the founding of Harvard. Two features were especially characteristic of their organization and intellectual culture. The first was the absence of a sharp distinction among different branches of study, each the province of a separate group of teachers and students. The second was the absence of any meaningful distinction between the faculty of the college and its administration.

In colleges of the early nineteenth century, the entire curriculum was fixed. Students were required to take specific courses in a set sequence, and the reading for each course was generally prescribed for the whole student body. At Yale, which played a leading role in setting and defending curricular standards in the first half of the nineteenth century, freshmen read Livy, Horace, Homer, and Herodotus; sophomores, Cicero and Xenophon; and juniors, Aeschylus, Euripides, Plato, Thucydides, and Demosthenes. In their senior year, Yale students read texts in logic and representative writings of the philosophers of the Scottish Enlightenment, such as Dugald Stewart and Thomas Reid. Freshmen began their study of mathematics with Euclid's *Elements* and continued the following year with Dutton's treatise on conic sections. Astronomy, geology, and chemistry were all taught using prescribed textbooks, as were geography and political economy, where the French economist Jean-Baptiste Say's book on the subject and later Francis Wayland's served as the primary texts. In every branch of study, the Yale curriculum before the Civil War was fixed in lockstep fashion, so that each student in a graduating class would have studied a nearly identical list of books that changed only gradually from year to year.[17] The course of study at other schools varied in certain details, but in broad outline resembled that of Yale, which served as a model for many.[18]

If students studied the same things in the same order and were expected to master a common curriculum, each of their teachers was expected to be able to teach the whole of it to them. The faculty of the antebellum college were jacks-of-all-trades, competent to teach whatever needed teaching, from Latin to natural science, at all levels of instruction.[19] Even at Yale, where there was a greater division of labor than at most schools, instructors were expected to teach their students "in all subjects throughout the first three years of their college course."[20] The college thus demanded a commonality of effort on the part of students and faculty alike. If students did the same work, their teachers had a common assignment as well. Students did not choose which course of study to pursue. They followed a prescribed curriculum. And their teachers did not specialize in a subject and limit their teaching to it. They taught the entire curriculum from beginning to end. There were no disciplinary distinctions of the kind we now take for granted, no "divisions" or "departments" or "majors." Everyone was a generalist, and did more or less the same thing.

This included the administrators of the college, who were members of the teaching faculty too. The distinction between faculty and administration, which we now take for granted, did not yet exist. Before the Civil War, most colleges in fact had only a single full-time administrator—a president—who not only taught but was often the most influential teacher on the faculty, entrusted with the senior course that served as the capstone of the students' college experience.[21] Even late in the nineteenth century, this continued to be the practice at many schools, including large ones like Princeton and Brown. During Timothy Dwight's presidency at Yale (1866–99), the senior class met with him for recitation once a day.[22] The president of an antebellum college was not a mere functionary or fundraiser as many college and university presidents are today. He was the leading voice in his community, and others on the faculty looked to him to articulate the aims of the common enterprise in which they were engaged—the moral education of their students.

It was an enterprise based on two assumptions. The first was that teachers possess an unassailable authority on account of their superior understanding of the moral and spiritual aims of the educational process in which they and their students are involved. A teacher might be unpopular—hated, even— but still retain his moral authority. Faculty typically lived in the college buildings, along with their students, and supervised their every movement, meting out harsh punishments even for minor infractions of the rules that regulated the students' "entire existence."[23] This inevitably produced tensions between faculty and students, and occasionally even a violent reaction. At the University of Georgia, angry students stoned the president of the school and one of its professors.[24] But for the most part, the authoritarian premises of collegiate life remained unchallenged. Students simply assumed that their teachers knew best which habits and beliefs one must acquire in order to become a morally mature person, and which books, read in what order, are most likely to produce this result. The suggestion that moral maturity is an ambiguous idea, subject to conflicting interpretations; that teachers are in no better position to define it than their students; and that students should be free to select a course of study, in accordance with their own varying conceptions of the purpose and value of a college education, would have struck both students and faculty as absurd.

The second assumption was that every branch of study has its place in a single, integrated program of instruction and contributes to its common goal. In 1840, most American colleges still placed special weight on the study of the classics, which continued to occupy a central place in the curriculum. It is true that by the beginning of the nineteenth century, more and more attention was being given to the natural sciences, which had been revolutionized by the work of Galileo, Kepler, and Newton. The Newtonian revolution put immense pressure on the world view that for centuries had successfully accommodated Aristotle's physics and cosmology to the revealed truths of Christianity.[25] There were some, of course, who concluded that science and religion must henceforth go their separate ways. But in America's antebellum colleges, most of which had strong denominational affiliations, confidence remained high that science and religion could be reconciled, and much effort was expended to harmonize their claims. Courses in the new science of nature were typically followed by a course in theology, where it was demonstrated that Newton's laws of motion can be adjusted to, indeed can only be explained by, the idea of an all-knowing and beneficent God whose works, which run with clockwork precision, constitute a moral as well as mechanical order, in which man's spiritual needs and responsibilities also have their place. At Williams College, an observatory was built to better study the stars, but also so that students could elevate their thoughts "toward that fathomless fountain and author of being, who has constituted matter and all its accidents as lively emblems of the immaterial kingdom."[26] In this way, the seamlessness of the world was preserved. It continued to be a moral world of purposes and values.

Even the increasingly influential discipline of political economy—a fluid blend of subjects that would later be distributed among the separate fields of economics, political science, and sociology—continued to be shaped by moral assumptions, while claiming to provide a more methodical approach to the study of human society. The curriculum of the antebellum college yielded to this claim of greater rigor. The new science of society acquired a growing authority in American colleges, along with the new science of nature.[27] But it too remained anchored in a set of moral beliefs, and these in turn in a set of theological assumptions that guaranteed the spiritual integrity of the world as students were taught to understand it. At Brown, Francis Wayland, the president of the college and one of the most influential educators of the period, taught courses in political economy and moral science, which he treated as different facets of a single subject.[28] In this regard, he was a representative of his age. For teachers everywhere continued to believe that every branch of study—classics, mathematics, natural science, political economy, and theology—has its place within a unified program of instruction whose purpose is to shape the souls of students by demonstrating to them the common moral order of the natural and social worlds, and by nurturing the habits required to meet the duties entailed by their position within it.

The founders of Harvard would hardly have recognized the landscape of American higher education two centuries later. The sheer number of colleges, their denominational variety, the growing diversity of their student bodies—all of this would have amazed them. And they would have been shocked to learn how the study of nature and of human society had changed, and what a large influence these changes had had on the curriculum of America's colleges.

But despite all this, they would also have recognized something deeply familiar. They would have understood that the educational program of most colleges in 1840 was still directed toward a goal not all that different from their own. For two centuries on, American college life remained based on the belief that the first responsibility of a college is to provide its students with methodical assistance in their search for an answer to the question of what living is for. It still rested on the assumption that the faculty and administrators of a college are joined in a common and carefully planned campaign to provide this assistance.

The question of life's meaning was becoming more complex. The challenge to religious belief was deepening. The new sciences of nature and society were on the verge of forcing a separation of science and morality.[29] The intensifying national debate over slavery was having an unsettling effect on America's colleges, as on everything else.[30] But in 1840, the old order was still largely intact. College teachers were still confident that they possessed an authoritative wisdom about the meaning of life. They still felt it was their collective duty to convey this wisdom to their students. All this would change in the next half century. But for the moment, the spiritual confidence with which Harvard had been founded two centuries before remained alive in America's colleges.

In the decades following the Civil War, the world of American higher education was transformed. The changes that took place between 1860 and 1910 eventually brought about a near-total rupture with the old order in education, which had prevailed from the Puritan migration of the 1630s to the Civil War, and set American higher education on a different path, one we are still following today.

At the center of these changes and of the new regime they brought about was an entirely new institution: the American university.[31] Institutions called universities had existed in Europe for centuries. America's early colleges were modeled on them. But in the early nineteenth century, a new kind of university emerged in Europe, one that shared the name but had an importantly different purpose. This happened first and most influentially in Germany.

The new German university was organized on a novel assumption that had no precedent in the history of higher education. This was the idea that universities exist primarily to sponsor research, that their first responsibility is to provide the space, books, and other resources that scholars need to engage in the work of producing new knowledge. There had always been a few private scholars, in Germany and elsewhere, who made this their goal. But never before had the work of original scholarship been viewed as an activity of such overriding importance or made the object of such deliberate and disciplined support. Never before had the sponsorship of research been so organized, centralized, and continuous. The German university of the early nineteenth century institutionalized the idea of research and gave it, for the first time, the authority and prestige it has had ever since.

At the start, only a few teachers in a few fields embraced this idea. But its influence grew steadily, and by the second half of the nineteenth century there were many German university professors who viewed themselves primarily as scholars working to make an incremental contribution to the endlessly expanding knowledge in their fields.[32] This new ideal of scholarship contrasted sharply with the older notion that a college teacher's first duty is to give his students moral and spiritual guidance by introducing them to the more-or-less fixed system of knowledge and norms that constitutes their intellectual inheritance. This older conception, which had shaped European higher education since the Middle Ages and been transported to America in the seventeenth century, encouraged a more stable and holistic view of knowledge, one that stressed the continuity of human knowledge from each generation to the next and the capacity of a well-educated mind to grasp it as a whole. It underscored the role that teachers play as keepers of a tradition. By contrast, the new ideal of scholarship emphasized the progressive character of human knowledge, which changes and increases over time; the immensity of such knowledge, which makes it impossible for anyone to understand the whole of it and therefore requires specialization; and the importance, as scholarly virtues, of invention and originality, of the ability to upset traditions rather than sustain them.

In all these respects, the scholarly ideal represented a profound intellectual break with the past, and its acceptance brought with it equally profound changes in the organization of the institutions that embraced it. The research seminar, the graduate course, the scientific laboratory with its state-of-the-art equipment: these and other innovations were among the lasting consequences of the revolution in higher education that began in Germany's universities in the late eighteenth century and eventually spread to every corner of the world.

In the first half of the nineteenth century, several thousand Americans traveled to Germany to study in its universities. There they encountered the new ideal of scholarship, and some attempted, though with little initial success, to transplant this ideal to American soil.[33] It was only after the Civil War, in the 1860s and 1870s, that the research ideal began to take root in America, when a few older colleges embraced it and several prominent new universities were established for the purpose of promoting scholarly work. Harvard, under the leadership of Charles Eliot; Cornell and Johns Hopkins (which opened in 1869 and 1876, respectively); the Universities of Michigan and California: these and a handful of other schools were among the first to recognize, and institutionalize, the German ideal of research scholarship in American higher education.

An emphasis on research was not, of course, the only thing that set these new American universities apart. Many also broke from tradition by offering instruction in practical and vocational subjects—ranging from veterinary medicine to business management—that had no place in the classical curriculum of the antebellum college. In Texas, professors taught advanced techniques of cotton farming and in Washington studied the best ways of raising salmon.[34] The idea that a university exists to serve the people in concretely helpful ways, that it is devoted not only to the education of an elite and to the advancement of theoretical knowledge but to the material improvement of the lives of the citizens of its state (or of the country as a whole), was an idea that had tremendous influence on American higher education during this period, under the provocative stimulus, in particular, of the Morrill Land Grant Act of 1862, which transferred federal land to the states for the purpose of establishing colleges on the condition that they teach "agriculture and the mechanic arts" along with more traditional subjects.[35]

Not every university responded to the call for more practical studies with the same enthusiasm, however, and some actively opposed it (Harvard and other elite private universities, in particular). But every institution that aspired to be a university, or to be called one, felt compelled to embrace the ethic of scholarly research. In the fifty years that followed the end of the Civil War, the acceptance of the research ideal became the one common characteristic of all American universities, large and small, public and private, Eastern and Western, however much they differed in other respects.

The acceptance of the research ideal had many institutional consequences of lasting importance. In addition to the ones I have mentioned, these included the provision of sabbatical leaves for the pursuit of research; the establishment of professional journals for the publication of research; and the adoption of hiring and promotion standards based upon scholarly achievement. These developments came more quickly at some schools than at others and were embraced with varying degrees of enthusiasm and completeness at different institutions. But the embrace of the research ideal had two broad consequences that affected the whole of American higher education in especially significant ways. The first was the demise of the so-called "prescriptive" curriculum and the second the rise of academic specialization.

Students in the antebellum college had taken the same courses in the same order. Their curriculum was entirely prescribed. It was assumed that a student who followed this program for four years would, by the end, know everything a well-educated gentleman needs to know to be prepared for life's intellectual and moral challenges. The idea that knowledge is accretive, that it is constantly expanding and becoming more refined, and that the more refined a branch of knowledge becomes the more expertise one needs to grasp it, put tremendous pressure on this older ideal. It made it increasingly implausible to think that any student—even the brightest and most disciplined—could master the barest outlines of human knowledge in four years.

If not, then a choice of some kind had to be made. Something had to be selected for study and made a subject of special attention. Other things had to be ignored. And if it was unavoidable that a selection be made, who better to make it than the student himself?[36] For who knows better than the student which fields of study are well-suited to his interests and talents, and likely to reward the effort their mastery requires? President Eliot of Harvard was the great champion of this view.[37] The late-nineteenth-century romantic belief in the virtue of expressing one's personality against the forces of convention and the very practical idea that a college education should be fitted to a student's vocational plans lent additional support to the notion that students be allowed to elect (at least some of) their own courses.[38] This has remained an axiom in American higher education ever since. The tide has gone back and forth, with the principle of prescription at times regaining at least some of the ground it lost to that of election. The perennial debate over the wisdom of a "core curriculum" is one expression of the continuing contest between these two great principles.[39] But the idea of a single, comprehensive program of instruction that every student must accept on identical terms has never regained the legitimacy it enjoyed before the explosive expansion of knowledge driven by the research ideal.

The widening acceptance of the research ideal had a second consequence. In addition to promoting the principle of student election, it hastened the emergence of distinct academic disciplines with separate subjects and discrete bodies of knowledge, out of the undifferentiated faculty of the old-time college. As the research ideal took hold, faculties divided into departments and then into ever more specialized units of teaching and scholarship. In the 1880s, philosophy emerged as "an important and well-defined department at leading American universities."[40] Departments of English soon followed. At most schools, the teaching of modern European languages other than English became a distinct discipline too, which further divided into departments of French and German. In 1893, the department of biology at the University of Chicago was reorganized into five separate departments of zoology, botany, anatomy, neurology, and physiology.[41]

Those who embraced the research ideal sought above all to make an original contribution to some expanding body of scholarly knowledge. This became for them the new benchmark of professional success. To succeed on these terms one had to specialize, to become an expert in some particular branch of study. Teachers who held onto the older ideal and continued to aspire to a comprehensive grasp of human knowledge were doomed to remain dilettantes in the new world of specialized research. Their lack of expertise disabled them from making an original contribution in any area of work. Only those who concentrated on a single discipline while ignoring all others could hope to add in a meaningful way to the expanding storehouse of learning in their fields.

By the last decades of the nineteenth century, the world of the antebellum college, with its prescriptive curriculum and unitary faculty, seemed more and more remote. Increasingly, college and university teachers (even those not directly engaged in research) were expected to have some special knowledge of a particular discipline, an expectation that over time was equated with graduate training, and eventually with the possession of a Ph.D.[42] Students were expected to specialize too—to "major" or "concentrate" in a particular field—so that they might acquire an understanding of at least one subject that went beyond the shallow dilettantism of the gentleman-amateur. The curriculum was rearranged along subject matter lines, with introductory courses in each discipline leading to more advanced ones. And faculties were divided into separate departments, each responsible for instruction in a single subject and exercising a growing autonomy over the hiring and promotion of its members. In 1840, with the rarest of exceptions, America's colleges exhibited none of these features. Sixty years later, its leading universities and a growing number of liberal arts colleges displayed them all, at least in nascent form.

The faculty of the antebellum college had been concerned mainly with the moral and spiritual education of its students. The expectations and ambitions engendered by the research ideal encouraged a shift away from this concern toward a preoccupation with the advancement of knowledge in a particular field of scholarly work. Increasingly, the old idea that a program of higher education should be—or even could be—organized around the question of the ends of human life, of how and for the sake of what one ought to live, lost its appeal in favor of the new idea that a college or university is, first and foremost, a gathering of academic special- ists inspired by their shared commitment to scholarship as a vocation.

No discipline that hoped to secure a place in the new university system could escape the imperatives of the research ideal. Still, there were some in which the older concern with the purpose and value of human life continued to be felt more strongly and to retain greater credibility than in other areas of study. These were the disciplines we call the humanities— literature, philosophy, history, classics, and the fine arts—the fields that make up one of the three great families of academic subjects into which university and college faculties came to be divided in the latter part of the nineteenth century. Only in the humanities did the question of life's meaning retain its salience in an educational regime now dominated by the specialized interests and needs of the scholar. In the natural and social sciences, it quickly ceased to be a recognizable question at all.

In the old order, even the natural sciences had been closely tied to human concerns. Under the heading of "natural philosophy," physics and ethics were joined in a continuum along which a student might move without interruption, studying first the mechanics of God's creation and then the attributes of God Himself, including His moral relation to mankind. By the end of the nineteenth century, the study of nature had been thoroughly disenchanted, in part because of the intensifying demands of research itself, which could be met only if the investigation of the physical world were purged of all moral and theological presumptions. Their elimination left a material universe whose structure could now be described with astounding precision but which was itself devoid of meaning and purpose. As a result, the physical sciences ceased to be concerned with, or to have much to contribute to, the search for an answer to the question of the meaning of life. To the extent that human beings now figured in these disciplines at all, they did so only as physical or biological units subject to the same laws of spiritless motion that govern the behavior of nonhuman bodies as well.[43]

The new social sciences, which emerged as distinct disciplines in the second half of the nineteenth century, were similarly disconnected from the question of life's meaning. In one important respect, of course, the social sciences bore a close relation to

the humanities, for the subjects they studied—
the nature and workings of government and
of human society generally—had been topics
of observation and analysis in the humanistic
tradition for centuries. But practitioners of
the social sciences claimed to have something
their humanist predecessors lacked: a set of
methods that made it possible, for the first
time, to study these age-old topics in a rigorous
and systematic fashion. The great humanists
who had written about the nature of human
society had done so on the basis of their own,
unsystematic experience of the world and their
personal judgments of it. Their findings had
necessarily been incomplete and anecdotal. The
new social sciences began with the ambition
to study the various aspects of society—its
political, cultural, and economic dimensions—in
a more impersonal and organized way, with the
aid of novel quantitative methods that enabled
them to achieve a previously unattainable
degree of precision and objectivity both in the
empirical description of human society and in
the analysis of its governing laws.[44]

It was this drive toward greater rigor and
objectivity, more than anything else, that
set the new disciplines of political science,
economics, and sociology apart from the older
humanistic disciplines of philosophy, history,
and rhetoric. Like their humanist counterparts,
the social scientists who first self-consciously
identified themselves as such hoped to

understand the social life of mankind. But in contrast to the humanists, who had only their own experience, taste, and judgment on which to rely, the social scientists who took up the humanists' questions were equipped with a panoply of methods that enabled them to search for answers of a more impersonal and ethically neutral kind. This new approach produced remarkable results. But at the same time it severed the social sciences' connection to the personal and value-laden question of what living is for. For the new methods of the social sciences necessarily directed attention away from the struggles of the individual soul toward the general structures of society— toward man in the aggregate. Those who embraced these methods postponed, or eliminated entirely, the questions of ultimate value around which these struggles revolve and put a passion for objective knowledge in the place of spiritual concerns.[45]

This displacement was not an accident, but a deliberate adjustment of outlook essential to the social sciences' success. For only by eliminating all personal questions of value from their scholarly work could the practitioners of the new social sciences associate themselves, however loosely, with their colleagues in the natural sciences, whose achievements set then, as they do today, the standard by which the objectivity of all knowledge is measured. Only in this way were the social sciences able to accumulate the tremendous authority and prestige they now enjoy under the aegis of the research ideal. But this very adjustment of outlook and method, which brought the social sciences closer to the natural sciences and dramatically increased their intellectual authority, depersonalized and despiritualized these disciplines in a way that disabled them from providing organized help in the search for an answer to the question of the meaning of life.

Once the college dissolved into separate departments, each dedicated to the advancement of knowledge in a particular field, it was no longer clear where help of this kind might be found. Neither the natural nor the social sciences were able to supply it. Neither even claimed or aspired to do so. The responsibility for providing such help thus fell, by default, to the humanities. The humanities seemed, moreover, well-suited to the task. For in contrast to the natural and social sciences, which demand that teacher and student put personal values aside for the sake of objectivity, the humanities impose no such requirement. They do not aspire to value-free knowledge. To the contrary, they address questions of value directly. They study human values as these have been expressed in one setting or another and invite—indeed, compel—students to engage these values themselves by asking whether they are sound and attractive. It is not enough for a student of philosophy to know that Plato held one view of justice and John Stuart Mill another. He must consider which, if either, to endorse himself. He must enter the conversation, join the debate, and take sides in it. He cannot put brackets around questions of value in order to preserve his objective detachment. The natural and social sciences require such detachment. Philosophy, literature, art, and the other humanities forbid it. They study the world of human values, but not from without. They study it from within and compel those who follow their path to decide where they stand in this world and why. As a result, the study of the humanities has an unavoidably personal dimension. It forces an engagement with intimate questions of meaning and touches on matters of identity and ultimate concern. Unlike the natural and social sciences, which lead away from the question of what living is for, the humanities lead irresistibly to it.

The humanities were themselves profoundly reshaped by the research ideal. By the end of the nineteenth century, a growing number of humanities teachers in America's colleges and universities viewed themselves mainly as scholars, and the fruits of their research were impressive.[46] But there were others who continued to think of the humanities as a forum for exploring the meaning of life, not just as a body of knowledge to be transferred from one generation of specialists to the next, and it

was to them that the responsibility for guiding
this exploration now fell, after their colleagues
in the natural and social sciences had given
it up. They were the residual legatees of the
older tradition to which all college teachers in
America once belonged.

But even those humanities teachers who still
believed in the importance of this tradition
could not carry it forward unaltered. Too much
had changed for that to be possible. The classics had lost their central place in the curriculum. Theology no longer provided a shared
moral and spiritual perspective. The comforting
assumption that science and faith are congru-
ent had been exploded. And the conviction that
there is a single right way of living for which
a college education prepares its students was
giving way to a more pluralist conception that
acknowledges a diversity of fulfilling and honorable lives, distinct in their motivations and
concerns.[47]

All of these developments contributed to
the culture of experimentation and doubt, of
skepticism and adventure, that flourished in
the last decades of the nineteenth century.[48] Its
growth and increasing influence coincided with
the emergence of the modern university which

was in many ways its institutional expression. By 1880, the world of the antebellum college had disappeared. For those teachers of the humanities who felt some loyalty to the traditions of the old regime and still believed they had a duty to guide their students in the search for an answer to the question of what ultimately matters in life and why, a new way of providing such guidance had to be found amidst the ruins of the old order, in a culture of skeptical pluralism that had no antecedent in American higher education.

Those who took up the challenge agreed on two basic points. The first was that the tendency toward specialization must be resisted. The purpose of a college education is not, they said, merely or even mainly to prepare students for their careers by conveying to them the specialized knowledge they need for their work. More fundamentally, a college must equip its students for the comprehensive challenges of life by giving them what Alexander Meiklejohn called a training in the general "art of living."[49] A college's first duty, he said, is to help its students acquire this art—not to equip them for the more limited responsibilities associated with a particular job.

Second, there was broad agreement that the humanities are the disciplines best suited to do this. Literary studies were thought particularly important in this regard. The study of literature, as we now understand it, was still something of a novelty in 1900. Before 1850, modern, vernacular literature had no place in the college curriculum. Only the classics were read, and they less as literature than as grammar texts and ethical guidebooks. By 1900, English literature had become a recognized field of study. Students were reading Wordsworth and Tennyson along with Homer and Virgil, and they were reading the classics themselves in a more literary spirit—as works whose primary value lies in their "power to stimulate thought about life," "to stir the emotions," to "kindle the imagination."[50] The study of literature, classical and modern, had become an important vehicle for training students in Meiklejohn's art of living.

The same was true of philosophy. In the antebellum college, philosophy had been an adjunct to theology. Its main function was to indoctrinate—to provide argumentative support for religious belief. By the end of the nineteenth century, philosophy had declared its independence from religion and, partly in response to the characteristically American demand that speculative thought have practical value, become a less dogmatic discipline in which the various ways of playing what William James called "the total game of life" could be compared and assessed.[51] It had become a testing ground for the examination of competing philosophies of life and the arguments that support them. Those who agreed with

Meiklejohn's definition of education as a "preparation for the art of living"[52] saw in this new and more free-ranging style of philosophy another valuable means to provide it. The study of history, which supplies an organizing framework for the examination of man's cultural achievements and helps bring these to bear in an orderly way on the central problems of life, seemed relevant to Meiklejohn's goal as well.[53] Among the many specialized fields of study that now had a place in the university system, it was the humanities—literature, philosophy, history, and art—that still seemed most alive to the old, unspecialized question of how best to live.

Agreement on these two basic points, however, was accompanied by disagreement on many others. Some who accepted the general idea that a college education should be a preparation for life understood this goal in aesthetic terms, as the cultivation of a sensibility that reacts with pleasure to beautiful things.[54] Others understood the goal more intellectually, as the mastery of a set of ideas. Some thought these ideas fit together in a harmonious way. Paul Elmer More insisted that the entire tradition of thought "from Plato to St. Chrystostom and beyond that to the Council of Chalcedon in 451 A.D., is essentially a unit and follows at the center a straight line."[55] Others, like William James, believed that there is an eternal conflict between certain fundamental ideas, like those summarized under the headings of "idealism" and "materialism," and that our endorsement of one or the other depends ultimately on considerations of "personal temperament."[56] Some stressed the importance of character and well-roundedness as the goal of a humanistic preparation for life.[57] Others were more skeptical of these claims, in which they detected an inappropriately narrow, class-based conception, both of the goal and the best means to reach it.[58]

The search for a way to sustain the older tradition of providing instruction in the meaning of life did not, therefore, result in a unified movement with common slogans and a single agenda. Woodrow Wilson expressed the goal one way when he said that what our colleges should seek to impart is "not so much learning as the spirit of learning."[59] Irving Babbitt, the brilliant and belligerent Harvard professor of literature, put it differently when he declared that the most important thing "is humane selection, in other words a choice of studies that will reflect in some measure the total experience of the race as to the things that have been found to be permanently important to its essential nature."[60] These were expressions not of a movement but a tendency, and even where the tendency prevailed the outcome was always shaped by the views of its local champions and the history and traditions of the school in question. The Contemporary Civilization Course at Columbia (1919), the Humanities Course at Reed College (1924), Harvard's General Education Program (1946), the Directed Studies Program at Yale (1947): these and dozens of other curricular reforms were the product of a shared desire to see the question of how one should live kept at the center of undergraduate education and pursued in an organized way. But no two programs used the same words to describe their ambitions or prescribed the same course of study. Each was distinctive and followed a path of its own.

Yet despite their variety, most of these programs rested on several important (and today controversial) assumptions that went beyond the general idea that a student's education should be a preparation for life and that the humanities are the disciplines best equipped to provide it. Together these assumptions defined a philosophy of humanistic education. They defined its goal and the best means to reach it. This philosophy was never expressed in just the way I shall describe it here. I have gathered its elements from different sources and arranged them in an idealized fashion. But the ideal helps to explain how it was possible for many teachers of the humanities to continue to believe in their authority to guide their students in a search for the purpose and value of life, after the traditions of the antebellum college had fallen away.

I shall call this ideal "secular humanism." Others have used the name and given it different meanings.[61] Some of these have implications I do not wish to endorse. But it is a good name nonetheless. For it underscores the single most important feature of the outlook I have in mind. This was the conviction that it is possible to explore the meaning of life in a deliberate and organized way even after its religious foundations have been called into doubt. In a culture of deepening skepticism, secular humanism offered modest but real grounds for hope to teachers of the humanities who wanted to believe they still had the competence to lead their students in a disciplined study of the human condition and to help them locate their own personal search for meaning within it. For the better part of a century, secular humanism remained a source of inspiration—sometimes noticed, often not—for teachers who wanted to do this and who recognized that their efforts had to be based on something other than man's well-understood relation to God.

Secular humanism was a response to two questions that teachers in the antebellum college never had to confront. The first arose as a result of the shift that took place in the decades following the Civil War (and partly on account of it) from a single, fixed conception of human fulfillment toward a more pluralistic view.[62] Once we abandon the idea that there is a single right way of living and accept the notion that human beings can find different yet fulfilling answers to the question of what living is for, a new challenge arises. For now we must decide how wide the range of such answers can be and which ways of life it includes. More important, we must decide where to draw the line between the universal interests and concerns that all men and women share and those that are peculiar to a way of life organized around a particular set of values in which only some human beings find fulfillment.

The second question arose as a result of growing doubts about the role that God plays in the search for such fulfillment. To many generations of American college teachers, it had seemed self-evident that a person's life can have meaning only if it is anchored in faith, in the loving and devoted acceptance of God's commands. In the increasingly skeptical culture of the late nineteenth century, this theocentric premise no longer seemed so obvious, to put it mildly. Doubts about the teachings of religion—about religion itself—multiplied and acquired a credibility that would have been hard to imagine a half-century before. These doubts spawned new and disturbing questions. Can a life without God have meaning? Can we supply, for ourselves, the meaning we want our lives to have? Or do we have spiritual needs, along with our material and social ones, that can only be met by a source of meaning outside ourselves, one we can never supply on our own? And if God is no longer available to play this role, who or what else is? What other sources of meaning might there be?

Humanities teachers who wanted to continue the tradition of offering instruction in the meaning of life in the age of the research university had to face and answer these questions. The philosophy of education they offered in response—the philosophy of secular humanism—rested on three assumptions.

The first was that pluralism is compatible with, indeed presupposes, the existence of a common human nature. There are facts of life we all confront and have no choice but to accept. There are needs we share and must satisfy in one way or another. We all die, and know we will, and must adjust ourselves to the shadow which the foreknowledge of death casts over the whole of our lives. We all hunger for love and recognition and a satisfying connection with others. These and certain other basic and immutable facts—that we are physical beings with recurrent bodily needs; that we possess the capacity to form and use abstractions; that we are limited and yet relatively equal in our powers, so that cooperation among us is both possible and required; that we create laws and live in political communities; that we take pleasure in knowledge for its own sake—together fix the parameters of human living. They define the human condition. They limit our opportunities and choices—everywhere and always. Together, they provide a common foundation for the different ways of life in which human beings have at one time or another found a satisfying answer to the question of what living is for. There is no human life outside the boundaries they establish. In combination, they make us the kind of creature we are.

Other living things die, but only we are tormented or inspired by the knowledge that we will. Other creatures mate, and show affection, but only we hope for love. Some animals communicate, but none with language and laws. Some seem capable of learning, and of using what they learn to practical advantage, but only human beings delight in learning for its own sake. We inhabit a condition uniquely our own. It is something that all—and only—human beings share. The question of life's meaning arises for each of us only within the boundaries of this condition and in response to the distinctive combination of limit and transcendence it defines.

Secular humanism affirmed the existence of this shared condition. This was the first of its three core assumptions. If the humanities are to help us address the question of the meaning of life in a disciplined way, their first task must therefore be to identify the elements of our common human nature and to help us understand the consequences that flow from them. Their first task must be to acquaint us with our shared and fateful destiny as human beings.

A second assumption, and a second task, followed from the acknowledgment of pluralism itself. For if human nature fixes our most elementary needs and establishes the limiting conditions under which these must be met, it also leaves room to fulfill them in a variety of ways, and even permits these needs themselves to assume different forms. The openness and plasticity of human nature are as impressive as its limits. Indeed, each of us can make, and wants to make, a life uniquely our own—a life that has no precise precedent in all the lives that have gone before and that will never be repeated exactly. Lives only look alike. If we knew more about them we would know that no two have ever been the same. Every birth is a new beginning of the world.[63] When we ask what living is for, we challenge ourselves to imagine the perfectly unique trajectory our lives might follow, unprecedented and unrepeatable in all of time.

But though the variations of human living are endless, they are not without pattern or form. There are certain patterns of life that have had a perennial attraction for human beings, living in the most diverse historical conditions. Each of these might be thought of as a template for living, subject to individual variation but offering a distinctive core of values, interests, and attitudes around which a fulfilling life can be arranged.[64] There is the life of the warrior, for example, and of the thinker, the artist, the lover, the scientist, the politician, the priest. Each has had its followers in every period and place. Their individual lives have of course been shaped in distinctive ways by contemporary habits and beliefs. Alcibiades is not Napoleon, and Plato is not Spinoza. Yet their lives are also recognizably linked, over immense periods of time and vast cultural divides, to the lives of others following the same pattern or path. When everything peculiar to the expression of a particular way of life at a given time and place has been removed, an enduring core remains. Thinkers in all ages share certain values in common, as do warriors and politicians and priests. They share a set of beliefs and concerns that define a way of life with a unity that connects its diverse historical manifestations.

It is not clear how many such ways of life there are, nor is it clear whether they are merely different or antagonistic. The record of human experience suggests that their number is not large—certainly not infinite—and that their organizing values are, in certain cases at least, mutually exclusive and perhaps even hostile, for the basic commitments of some (the life of the warrior) appear to require the repudiation of those of others (the lives of the poet and lover).

In broad terms, secular humanism accepts the pluralistic belief in a variety of paths to fulfillment; assumes their number to be modest but remains agnostic as to how many there are; and acknowledges that some ways of life are likely to be incompatible with others.

Thus if the first task of the humanities is to help us understand the common condition of mankind—the circumstances in which all human ambition unfolds—their second task is to identify and vivify the main lines into which the infinitely various individual expressions of this ambition have most often been channeled, to organize the tableau of our diversity. The humanities acquaint us with the core commitments of the different patterns of life that represent the most durable forms of human striving and explore the tensions among them, drawing from the storehouse of the past diverse examples that display each in its most compelling form. There is the life of Achilles, the brilliant brief life of battlefield honor and comradeship in arms; of Socrates, who put fidelity to philosophy before all else; the life of the prudent and measured man of practical virtue whose portrait Aristotle paints in the *Nicomachean Ethics*; of Augustine and Paul, the convert who hears the word of God amidst the busy noise of the world; of Michelangelo, for whom the making of beautiful things was a kind of salvation; of Galileo, the scientist prepared to follow the logic of discovery wherever it leads; of Jane Austen's Emma, searching for happiness in the tangles of domestic life.

Each of these lives is oriented toward a distinctive set of ultimate cares. Each illustrates a pattern or model to which we may look in an effort to gain clarity about our own deepest commitments. Each represents a permanent possibility of living, in response to whose demands men and women in all ages have found fulfillment. Understanding these patterns can never eliminate the demand we make on ourselves to live a life that recognizes, honors, and expresses our own uniqueness. Nor can it ever by itself answer the question of what living is for. Nothing can ever convert this personal question into an intellectual one. But the humanities can give us the guidance we need to organize a response. They can provide us with landmarks on the landscape of life and help us frame our search, one by one as individuals, for an answer to the question. They cannot supply the answer itself but they can make the search for it more tractable, and that is a help of no small value.

This was the second key premise of secular humanism. Its third addressed the challenge posed by the weakening of religious belief as a starting point in higher education.

Teachers in the antebellum college had an answer to the question of life's meaning. Their confidence in the answer was anchored

in a shared religious faith. By 1880, that
faith could no longer be taken for granted.
There were, of course, many who still believed
in God, just as there were many who now
doubted His existence and viewed religion with
suspicion or contempt. But between these two
camps, of believers and skeptics, little common
ground remained. A gulf had opened and was
widening.[65] The only thing the two camps
now shared was the question of whether it
is possible for human beings to live lives of
meaning in a godless world. Is it possible for
men to establish, on their own, the meaning
that their lives were once thought to possess on
account of their location in a divinely ordered
universe? The faithful said no, and insisted
this can never be done. Skeptics said yes, and
argued that human beings are able to provide
for themselves what superstitious and ignorant
men once believed only God can supply.

Secular humanism neither reaffirmed the
religious dogmas of the old order nor embraced
the most radical doubts of the new one. It
refused to endorse the idea that human life
has meaning only in a world created by God
and directed toward His ends. But it also
rejected the notion that we are able to create for
ourselves, as individuals, whatever structures
of meaning our lives require in order to have
purpose and value. Instead, it emphasized our
dependence on structures of value larger and
more lasting than those that any individual

can create. It stressed the need for individuals to locate themselves within these structures as a condition of their leading purposeful lives. This much secular humanism shared with the religious outlook of the old-time college. But it did not insist that these structures be eternal, like the ideas in God's mind. It accepted their mortality, and liability to decay, requiring only that they have a longer life than the lives of the individuals who are born into them and die out of them, one by one.

Nor did secular humanism imagine these more durable structures of meaning to be beyond the power of human beings to change or even, for that matter, to create and destroy. Indeed, it regarded them as products of human creativity, subject to deliberate change by human beings and requiring their constant, caring attention to survive at all—unlike God's plan for the world, which He creates and sustains without our help. But it also stressed that the creativity and care in question are the work of many hands, over long periods of time, the achievement of many human beings working together to establish and sustain something greater than anything any one of them can ever make on his or her own.[66]

These structures do not transcend the realm of human things in the way that God transcends the world. They are products of human invention, made by men, changed by men, preserved only through human attention and toil. But they do transcend the life of the individual, and it is only within their wider frame of meaning that individuals can ever hope to lead lives of a meaningful kind. God may no longer be there to sustain us in our search for an answer to the question of what living is for. But in that search we cannot make do without enframing structures of value and significance that, as individuals, we lack the power to create on our own. To think we can is to arrogate God's power to ourselves, to assume His self-sufficiency. Secular humanism did not require a God to give the world meaning. But it did insist that even if our faith in God has lost its force, we remain dependent for the meaning of our lives on structures of meaning that transcend our individual powers of creation and for whose existence the most appropriate attitude is therefore one of thanks.

There is, of course, more than one structure that satisfies this general requirement. For many people, their families and countries fulfill it. The structures of political and family life are of human origin and subject to decay. But they have a longer life than the lives of their individual members. For countless human beings, in every age, their families and countries have provided the more durable framework of meaning that must be present, in some form, if the lives of those within it are to have any meaning at all.

Secular humanism did not discount the importance of any of these frameworks. But it did insist on the importance of one in particular, and the distinctiveness of secular humanism as a philosophy of education was a function, in large part, of the emphasis it placed upon this particular framework of meaning. I have in mind the long tradition of writing and reflection, and of artistic creation, that is still sometimes referred to as the tradition of European arts and letters. It was here, more than anywhere else, that secular humanism located the enduring yet temporal structures of value and purpose that are a condition of value and purpose at the individual level.

The tradition of arts and letters grew out of the earlier program of classical studies that had dominated American college education before the Civil War, but differed from it in content and purpose. The study of the classics is limited to Greek and Roman authors. The classical period is a bounded historical epoch and no new classical works will ever be composed (though a new one may occasionally be discovered). The tradition of arts and letters included the study of classical texts. But it also included the study of great medieval and modern works of European philosophy and literature as well—the writings of Dante, Chaucer, Petrarch, Cervantes, Descartes, Montaigne, Shakespeare, Milton, Kant, Hegel, and Goethe, among others. Most of these were composed in the still-living languages of Europe and belong to a tradition of writing that remains open today. New works continue to be written in these languages and from time to time achieve a status comparable to theirs. Joyce's *Ulysses* and Wittgenstein's *Philosophical Investigations* are twentieth-century examples. The tradition of arts and letters thus has an openness that classical studies lacks and raises questions of a kind the classics alone cannot—most importantly, the question of how to understand the relation between the world of Greco-Roman antiquity, as reflected in its surviving works, and the very different world of modern European civilization. The expansion of arts and letters to include vernacular works of the modern period necessarily gave their study a living historical significance the classics alone can never possess.

The study of the classics in the antebellum college was essentially "conformist." The purpose of studying the classics was to acquaint oneself with certain lasting models of thought and behavior and to develop the habits needed to apply these models in life: to conform oneself to them. Because of this, memorization and recitation seemed appropriate methods of teaching. When the field of arts and letters was widened to include modern materials as well, neither these methods nor the conformist goal that justified them could be sustained. For the student of arts and letters was presented not with a single model but two. On the one hand, there was the ancient model of virtue and order; on the other, modern ideas of individuality and creative freedom.[67] These ideals cannot easily be reconciled, and a student encountering them is bound to be impressed with the plurality of human values and experience. He is less likely to believe in the existence of a single, fixed model of life, to which he has only to conform his own habits and actions, and more likely to see himself as having some choice in the matter. He is more likely to see his own situation in historical terms—as the position of a person in a long and evolving story, with twists and turns and new developments, and no end yet in sight. He is less likely to view himself as the acquiescent mimic of some finished form of life and more likely to see himself as a participant in an active, ongoing, unfinished process to which he may someday contribute something himself.

The tradition of arts and letters invited each student to see himself as a participant in what Michael Oakeshott memorably called a "great conversation."[68] The student was encouraged to think of previous participants—poets, philosophers, novelists, historians, and artists—as addressing each other in a long, unbroken conversation about the most important matters in life, a conversation that has both the continuity and variability all real conversations possess. And he was taught to think of himself as a respectful but not subservient latecomer to this conversation, who has much to learn but also something to add. He was taught that he must study the great works of the past with attention and care, but not memorize them with a slavishness (as a defender of the tradition of arts and letters might have put it) inconsistent with the openness of this tradition itself and with the need for even the latest arrival to carry it forward and make it his own.

But open though it was, the tradition of arts and letters was most emphatically a tradition. It had central texts and abiding themes. It had a history and an internal life of its own. It could be taught in an organized way. It offered students a common set of references, a shared lexicon of works, and a fund of developed ideas with which to formulate their individual judgments and express them to others. It provoked, in the way that any living tradition does, a feeling of reverence for its previous contributors, a sense of responsibility for protecting their achievements, and the experience of freedom in being able to build something distinctively one's own from these inherited materials.

For those who felt an allegiance to it, the tradition of arts and letters thus provided a more durable frame of reference within which to engage the question of life's meaning, without assuming this frame to be immortal or divine. It framed the question by locating the confrontation with it in a conversation longer and more lasting than anything any individual can ever produce on his own. In this respect, the tradition of arts and letters served the same function for its followers that the structures of political and family life serve for so many others. It provided them with the backdrop of meaning that must be present, in one form or another, if the individual's search for the meaning of his or her own life is to be sustainable at all, without relying on theological beliefs whose truth could no longer be assumed.

In the new university system that arose in the later years of the nineteenth century, teachers of the humanities were increasingly alone in their belief that they had the responsibility and competence to guide their students in an exploration of the value and purpose of life. They alone still felt a connection to the older tradition of college teaching in which this subject had had a central place. But the religious foundations of that tradition had been shattered beyond repair, and the classics no longer enjoyed the unquestioned primacy they once did. Accepting the need for some larger framework of meaning as a condition of the individual's search for fulfillment, while denying that only an eternal God can provide it, teachers of the humanities joined the study of the classics to more modern works of literature, philosophy, and art in a complex and evolving tradition that forms a conversation of sufficient richness and strength to frame the student's search for an answer to

the question of what living is for. This was the
tradition of arts and letters whose spiritual
vitality secular humanism affirmed. Shaped
by a belief in the validity of the idea of human
nature and by a confidence in the perennial
significance of a limited number of exemplary
types of human fulfillment, its study formed, for
many years, the core of an educational program
that enabled teachers of the humanities to meet
their duties as residual legatees of the older
tradition of offering instruction in the meaning
of life, in colleges and universities now defined
by specialization and in a culture marked by
pluralism and doubt.

✦

For roughly a century, from Charles Eliot's
appointment as president of Harvard in 1869—
a date as fitting as any to mark the birth of
the new university system in America—to the
watershed year of 1968, secular humanism
continued to give credence to the idea that
the question of life's meaning is one that can
be taught. In the modified form that secular
humanism gave it, the older tradition of offering such instruction survived for a hundred
years, flickering and occasionally flaring, until
it finally went out.

Today, increasingly few teachers of the humanities believe they have either the competence or

duty to offer their students an education in the meaning of life. Even those who express this view in private are generally reluctant to do so in public. What they are likely to say instead is that the humanities are no better equipped than other disciplines to provide organized help in the search for life's meaning; that it is not their special responsibility as teachers of the humanities to do so; and that college and university students, like the rest of us, must wrestle with this question on their own, outside of school, and without the illusion that any academic discipline can teach them how or what to think about it. A subject that was once, at the dawn of American higher education, a universal topic of instruction and later the special responsibility of the humanities, is thus today no longer taught even in these fields.

Beginning in the 1960s, and at an accelerating pace in the decades that followed, the principal tenets of secular humanism came under attack.[69] The idea that there is such a thing as human nature seemed increasingly implausible to many. In place of the older notion that there are enduring features of human existence that form the permanent framework of human experience and ambition, a new idea gained support—that any claim about human nature is an expression of power in disguise, an attempt by some to impose their will on others, not much different from a punch in the face. For the older belief that the principal patterns of human living are modest in number and steady over time, a new conviction took hold—that these patterns are innumerable and local to their place and period, making the appearance of historical continuity an illusion. And in sharp contrast to the tradition of arts and letters, a new attitude flourished—one that was hostile to the idea of a great conversation; that challenged its canonical selection of works; that emphasized the voices it excluded; and that insisted that the intellectual and artistic achievements of the West, to which the humanities have always paid special attention, are themselves the product of only one culture among many, no better or more interesting than the others that human beings have created, a single thread in the multicultural skein of human experience and expression.

Together, these new ideas caused many humanities teachers to denounce what they saw as the pieties of secular humanism. By the end of the twentieth century, secular humanism had little more authority than the Christian classicism it replaced. Like its predecessor, it had come to seem just an article of faith.

Some attribute these developments to the turmoil of the 1960s and the resulting politicization of American academic life.[70] In these years, teachers, courses, and school policies all came under political scrutiny to an unprecedented degree. Existing practices were attacked as biased and unfair, and the traditional justifications for them denounced as "ideological." Ideas came to be seen as camouflaged expressions of power, promoting a skepticism about truth and a relativism about values. The 1960s—so the story goes— converted truth to power and legitimated a relativism that compromised the authority of secular humanism in ways that have sapped the confidence of the humanities ever since.

There is some truth in this story. But there is a deeper truth that it fails to convey. For if the humanities had still been strong and self-confident disciplines in the 1960s, they would never have yielded as quickly and completely as they did to these destructive ideas. The politicization of the academy in the 1960s did not destroy the humanities. The humanities destroyed themselves by abandoning secular humanism in favor of the research ideal, which for a century and a half now has been gaining ground as the principal arbiter of authority and prestige in American higher education.

The humanities' embrace of the research ideal compromised their sense of purpose and self-esteem by cutting them off from their connection to the question of what living is for. It undermined the tradition of secular humanism that had given the question credibility in an age of skeptical pluralism. It left the humanities adrift and without direction and in their search for a new purpose and a new direction, many in the humanities welcomed the politically inspired ideas of the 1960s and the culture of political correctness that has plagued these disciplines ever since. They embraced these ideas in an effort to restore the special standing of the humanities and to repair the loss of authority brought about by the collapse of secular humanism. But in the process, they caused the humanities great harm, for the culture of political correctness that has dominated the humanities since the 1960s has not restored their authority but further compromised it instead.

This damage was not the result of an attack from without. It was not caused by barbarians crashing the gates. It was a self-destructive response to the crisis of authority that teachers of the humanities brought down on their own heads when they embraced the research ideal and the values associated with it. These values are the real enemy of secular humanism and the cause of its demise. They are the real source of the humanities' crisis of authority. For the modern research ideal, whatever its merits and however great its achievements, devalues the question of what living is for—the question to which the authority of secular humanism, and of the humanities generally, is uniquely and permanently tied.

3

THE RESEARCH IDEAL

In 1918, the great social historian Max Weber delivered a lecture at Munich University titled "Scholarship as a Vocation."[1] It was one of his last and most passionate statements. In his lecture, Weber sought to describe the inner meaning of a scholarly career—its spiritual significance for the scholar himself. Toward the end, Weber's words rise to a near-religious crescendo as he struggles, with great feeling, to explain how a life of academic research can still be experienced as a calling, in the original sense of that word, in "our godless and prophetless time." But Weber begins on a more mundane note by surveying what he terms the "external" conditions of scholarly life in the German universities of his day. "What are the prospects," he asks, "of a graduate student who is resolved to dedicate himself professionally to scholarship in university life?" What are the conditions of his advancement and eventual success in the career that he has chosen?

The scholarly ideal that Weber describes is no longer a peculiarly German obsession. The production and dissemination of scholarship is today a central, organizing purpose of higher education throughout the world. In the United States in particular, the research ideal has acquired a tremendous prestige. This is clearest in our large universities, which are consciously directed toward the production of research and whose teachers are appointed and promoted primarily on the basis of their scholarly achievements. But the pull of the ideal can be felt in our liberal arts colleges too and even in the country's community and other two-year colleges. Appointment to the faculty of any of these schools now generally requires the possession of a Ph.D. or other advanced degree that can be attained only in a research university with a graduate program.[2]

Graduate school is thus the common portal through which nearly all of America's college and university teachers now pass on their way to an academic career. It is the first stage of their professional lives, not just for a few devoted scholars but for all who choose a career in college or university teaching, at whatever level and whether or not they later engage in research themselves. It is in graduate school, therefore, that all but a few of America's college and university teachers are now introduced to the norms of the academic profession and where they first acquire an understanding of who possesses authority within the profession and why. As a result, our graduate schools, and the research universities that house them, exert an enormous influence on the values and expectations of young teachers. They are the nursery beds in which the professional habits of most of our college and university teachers are formed, and the attitudes they acquire there are carried with them to every corner, and level, of American higher education.

All graduate students learn certain lessons in common. They learn to think of their disciplines as distinct "fields" of study, each occupying a limited place within a larger division of intellectual labor. They learn to view their fields as "specialities" that address different questions and employ distinctive methods to answer them. They are taught that each speciality has its own separate "literature" in which the knowledge of that field is contained; that the literature in each field is constantly being augmented and improved as new discoveries are made and fresh interpretations offered; that its "cutting edge" represents the latest and best thinking in the field; and that to become a professionally competent teacher of any subject one must "master" its literature and be able to appreciate the work done on its cutting edge.

Graduate students learn to restrict their attention to a single segment of human knowledge and to accept their incompetence to assess, or even understand, the work of specialists in other areas. But they also learn to accept the idea that this same narrowing of attention, which cuts them off from those in other disciplines, alone qualifies them to join the company of fellow specialists in their own field, spread over many generations and united in a common commitment to the subject they share. They are taught to understand that only by accepting the limits of specialization can they ever hope to make an "original contribution" to the ever-growing body of scholarship in which the fruits of research are contained. And finally, they are encouraged to regard the making of such a contribution as the greatest satisfaction an academic career has to offer, so that if they never publish an article or book but limit themselves to teaching instead, they are likely to feel that their professional lives, however fulfilling in other ways, have been of a lesser sort than those of scholars who have contributed something new to their fields. In short, whatever their discipline, graduate students are taught to accept the limits of specialization and to see these as the price that must be paid for the powers and opportunities it affords.

In this regard, academic work is of course no different from any other. Specialization is today the ruling principle in nearly every productive activity. A young person considering a career of almost any sort faces the same need to find his or her place in a system of specialized labor. The division of intellectual labor within the academy is merely one expression

of a much larger phenomenon that characterizes the modern world of work in its entirety.
One might conclude that the principal motive
for specialization in scholarly work is the same
as it is everywhere else.

In *The Wealth of Nations*, Adam Smith uses
the example of a pin factory to explain the
advantages of specialization. These are, in his
view, advantages of efficiency. Many more pins
can be made at much less cost if those making them divide the labor amongst themselves,
each concentrating on one aspect of the process
only, instead of working in parallel fashion to
produce whole pins from start to finish. "Each
person," Smith says, "making a tenth part of
forty-eight thousand pins, might be considered
as making four thousand eight hundred pins in
a day. But if they had all wrought separately
and independently, and without any of them
having been educated to this peculiar business,
they certainly could not each of them have
made twenty, perhaps not one pin in a day."[3]

Smith's argument applies with equal force
to the intellectual work of research and teaching. If each member of a college or university studied and taught every subject
instead of concentrating on a single field, the
result would be the same as in the pin factory—a wasteful duplication of effort, a dramatic decline in output, and a degradation in
the quality of the work produced. Within the
academy as outside it, more and better work

can be done through specialization. This necessarily implies a narrowing of attention to some single aspect of a much larger whole, and if the loss of wholeness that results is thought to be dehumanizing (as Marx and others have suggested)[4] it is no greater for the academic worker than for the factory worker on an assembly line. And in both cases the loss is more than offset by a tremendous increase in efficiency that benefits not only the consumers (of knowledge or pins) but their producers as well, who are, after all, consumers of these and countless other things too.

This is a powerful argument, and it goes a long way toward explaining the division of labor that now exists in academic work—the "fate" of specialization, as Weber calls it, that graduate students must accept as the inescapable condition of their professional lives. But the modern system of specialized research is a result not merely of the drive for greater efficiency in the production of ideas. It is also the descendant of a spiritual ideal that was first self-consciously embraced by German scholars of the nineteenth century who understood their work to be a calling in the sense that Weber used that religiously charged term.

For them, the concept of an academic specialty and of the scholar's commitment to make an original contribution to his field were ideals deeply shaped by spiritual values. Today, the origins of these ideals are largely forgotten. Few young college and university teachers know anything of their history. Yet most still feel the vocational impulse that lay behind them. Most still experience their work as a calling. Most believe that the requirements of academic specialization are not merely a response to the demand for efficiency but a way of answering the call that gives their work its personal meaning. Though compelled to bend to the logic of specialization, most graduate students do not think of themselves as assembly line workers like those in Adam Smith's pin factory. They believe they are responding to something deeper than the imperative to be efficient. And this belief, too, is a part of their devotion to the research ideal, and an important source of its commanding authority.

The modern research ideal is a creature of the nineteenth century. But scholarship, in the broad sense, is of course much older than that.

The humanist revival of letters in the fifteenth century and the Reformation in the sixteenth spurred a vast outpouring of new scholarly work.[5] Throughout Europe, learned scholars devoted themselves with increasing energy to the translation and interpretation of ancient texts, both secular and religious, and to the exploration of the historical, philosophical, and theological questions these raised. Erasmus is the outstanding example of the type.[6] In 1516, he published a nine-volume edition of the writings of St. Jerome and (that same year!) a critical edition of the New Testament in Greek and Latin. Others worked in a similar spirit, corresponding by letter and contributing to various fields of study.[7] Some organized groups to promote their efforts. In London, a "Society of Dilettanti" was established to support the classical scholarship of its members, men like Robert Wood, a widely traveled gentleman-scholar who served in William Pitt's government and wrote one of the eighteenth century's most important books on Homer.[8] Nor was scholarship confined to humanistic and theological subjects. By the end of the eighteenth century, scientists were conducting experiments and reporting their results to an audience on both sides of the Atlantic. Franklin's experiments with electricity were closely followed in London and Paris.[9]

But before the nineteenth century, most scholars and scientists worked on their own, outside of any organized institutional setting. They typically owned their own books and laboratory equipment and supported themselves with income from a source unrelated to their scholarly endeavors. Ficino in the fifteenth century, Bacon in the sixteenth, Leibniz and Spinoza in the seventeenth are all examples of the type. The work of these scholars was, in the strict sense, "avocational"—something they pursued as a private passion, not a means of making a living, though it sometimes attracted the support of a wealthy patron (as in Ficino's and Leibniz's case).[10] And though a scholar might choose to concentrate on some particular area of research—on one text or author or scientific puzzle—most were generalists who remained interested in and competent to judge the work of those in related areas. Descartes made special contributions to the science of optics and invented analytic geometry, but he was involved in most of the important philosophical debates of his time.[11] Scholars of this older type were typically generalists who worked on their own. Their efforts were not coordinated through an agreed-upon division of labor managed by a centralized institution that paid their salaries and provided them with the means for conducting research—the situation of every college and university teacher today.[12]

The modern research system, in the form we know it now, had its beginnings in the German universities of the early nineteenth century. There were, of course, related developments elsewhere. In 1795, the French established a National Institute to promote the production of knowledge aimed at advancing the goals of happiness and progress identified by the authors of the *Encyclopedia*.[13] It was the first institutionalized program of social scientific research.

But it was in Germany that the new research ideal was articulated with the greatest clarity and where its adoption led to the establishment of the first modern research universities. And curiously, when this happened the impetus for it came not from the emergent social sciences or even, as one might have expected, from the natural sciences, but from the humanities, and from the field of classical studies in particular, where a new ideal of scholarship had taken hold in response to the changed conception of the field brought about by the romantic revolt against enlightenment rationalism.

Romanticism is a term of many meanings, but as applied to the earliest phase of German romanticism and to the writings of its two most influential figures, Gottfried Herder and his predecessor J. G. Hamann, it suggests above all else a determined opposition to the leveling tendencies of enlightenment thought, exemplified by the work of Voltaire and the French *philosophes*.[14] Voltaire had insisted on the uniformity of human nature and experience. He maintained that all men and societies, regardless of their location in historical time, are essentially alike. The differences among them, he said, are insignificant by comparison with the attributes they share. These constitute our common humanity, which reason by itself is competent to grasp. For Voltaire and those who shared his views, the homogeneity and rational intelligibility of human affairs were articles of faith, the two related principles on which their enlightened rationalism was based.

Herder and Hamann attacked these claims with ferocity. They argued that Voltaire's rationalism underestimates the differences that distinguish one culture from another. They insisted that Voltaire and his followers had exaggerated the power of reason to comprehend and appreciate these differences. In opposition to those who deny their importance, Herder and Hamann attached supreme significance precisely to these differences themselves. What is most interesting and valuable in a culture or period, they said, is its distinctive personality—the practices, beliefs, and works that give it a unique identity—and not the general traits it shares with every other. Voltaire had equated our humanity with mankind's common nature. The Romantics turned this equation upside down and made the individuality of a people or age the mark of its humanity.

The distinctive personality of a period or culture is of course always shaped by fateful circumstances of geography, weather, and the like. Following Montesquieu, Herder gathered these under the general heading of "climate."[15] But the true significance of a culture, he said, is less a function of the climatic conditions that shape its way of life than of a people's inventive response to them. And that response, Herder insisted, is always something unique—the soul of a culture's character and the source of its meaning and value.

The same is true of individual human beings. Each of us is born to particular parents in a particular social setting and endowed with gifts and disabilities not of our own choosing. Then, through imagination and effort, we make of these conditions—the climate of our lives— personalities whose value lies, from a romantic point of view, in their freely formed uniqueness. This idea has sometimes been expressed by the thought that a person's life is a work of art.[16] Just as an artist begins his creative work with materials he has not invented but finds already at hand, so we begin our lives with opportunities and limitations we have no choice but to accept. And just as an artist strives to make something singularly expressive of his materials, we work to fashion distinctive lives out of the conditions that determine our natal fate. The product is in each case something unique—a work of art, a life—whose value lies in its distinctiveness and whose distinctiveness is the result of a free and creative imagination working on materials that are neither distinctive nor free.[17]

Herder and Hamann endorsed this idea. They agreed that the value of a person's life lies in the distinctive shape he gives it through his creative adaptation to the given circumstances of his existence. And (like Vico before and Dilthey after)[18] they thought this principle applies not just to individuals but to whole ages and civilizations. Each age, they said, ought to be considered a work of art too—the product of a long, imaginative campaign to infuse its given, "climatic" conditions with an expressive personality whose relative value, like that of any artistic creation, must be judged by the singularity and beauty of the result.

For centuries, classical studies had enjoyed a special prestige in Germany and Europe generally. The classics were thought to provide timelessly valid standards of conduct and taste and were assumed to define a permanent pattern of right living, as accessible and authoritative today as in the past. The late-eighteenth- and early-nineteenth-century classicists who were influenced by the romanticism of Herder and Hamann no longer looked at their subject in this way. For them, the classics were not a set of permanently valid norms, to be learned and copied by their modern readers—the once-and-for-all best statement of how men ought to live—but were the products of a unique civilization, now irretrievably gone, that could be studied but not reproduced. The task of the scholar, as they saw it, is to grasp the unique identity of the civilization these characteristics reflect. For the greatest classical scholars of the period—like F. A. Wolf,[19] whose philological research laid the foundation for all modern studies of Homer—the romantic belief in the value of the individual was fundamental. It was the premise on which their new conception of scholarship was based. It reoriented their work and redefined the special prestige of their field, which henceforth was to be explained not by the timeless validity of the norms of the classical world but by the outstanding beauty and utter singularity of their expression.

This new, romantically inspired view had a revolutionary effect on the field of classical studies. It encouraged a more historical approach to the subject, placed greater weight on the knowledge of facts, and put the possibility of ever knowing the classical world as a whole forever beyond reach.

If we want to understand what makes the life of a human being unique, we need to study his biography—his distinct and unrepeatable career in time. It is not enough to know the general ways in which his life resembles that of others. In addition, we must know and understand the course of events that sets his life apart—the accidents and experiences that distinguish it from other lives. The same is true of cultures. If they are individuals with their own distinctive personalities, they too must be studied biographically. We can understand the uniqueness of a period or culture only by studying the trajectory of its movement in time, for the same reason that we can grasp the uniqueness of an individual's life only in this way. The more one stresses the significance of a (person's or age's) individuality, the more one is bound to feel the need for a dynamic (biographical or historical) view of it.

The classicist view of antiquity was essentially static. It paid little or no attention to its historical development. By attaching the importance it did to individuality, romanticism encouraged a more dynamic view of the ancient world. The meaning and value of that world were now seen to reside not in a set of timeless forms, transparent to the intellect and permanently available as standards of judgment, but in its movement along the arc of a unique career in time. Nowhere was this shift of orientation clearer than in the field of philology, where Wolf and others labored to reconstruct the linguistic genealogy of Homer's poems and other classical texts.[20]

The shift from a static to a historical conception of the ancient world in turn demanded an increased attention to facts. To write the biography of a person, one must be acquainted with the facts of that person's life. Ideas alone are insufficient. The uniqueness of a person's life cannot be grasped apart from the facts that make it distinctive. A biographer of course needs ideas too. An assemblage of facts without organizing ideas has no significance at all. But for a biographer, facts have a relevance and value they can never have so long as one believes that the worth and interest of a life is measured by its conformity to some abstract, timeless pattern of conduct. The same is true if one is writing the biography of a culture or period. Here, too, facts have a relevance they lack on a classicist view. Classicism assumes that the timeless values of the past can be expressed in the form of general ideas that we are able to grasp by reason alone. If instead one wants to understand what is distinctive about a culture or period, one needs to know the facts of its biography. A romantic emphasis on the value of the individual demands a historical approach to the subject, which in turn requires a heightened attention to facts, reversing the order of importance that classicism had assigned to facts and ideas.

This insistence on the importance of facts had the further consequence of making a complete knowledge of the classics unattainable. For if the works of the classical authors are conceived as facts, as one set of data among others (archeological, numismatic, etc.), all of which must be weighed and interpreted in an attempt to understand the unique career of the classical world, then no perfect mastery of them, or of the relevant facts generally, can ever be achieved. One can never get to the bottom of a single fact, let alone a limit-lessly expanding set of facts. Facts are inexhaustible. It is always possible to see something new in them that has not been seen before. That is true even where the facts are fixed. But if fresh facts are constantly coming to light, and show every sign of continuing to do so without limit, the first infinity (of each fact taken by itself) is augmented by a second (of the endless series of facts awaiting discovery). Only ideas are fully comprehensible.

Hence only so long as the classics are conceived as a collection of generalized norms is the goal of acquiring an exhaustive knowledge of them a goal that can be reached in a finite period of disciplined study.

Romantic individualism exploded the closed world of classicism with its limited number of comprehensible ideals and replaced it with an infinite universe of facts that can never be exhausted or perfectly explained.[21] In doing so it put the goal of a complete understanding of antiquity forever beyond reach, beyond the furthest horizon of the greatest knowledge any person can ever acquire. This became the premise on which all classical scholarship was henceforth to be based. To those in the field, this presented a novel challenge. How was their work to proceed on these new assumptions? The modern research ideal evolved in response.

Given the infinity of facts now potentially relevant to an understanding of the classical world, formulating a method to guide their exploration now became imperative. Only a set of rules for determining the relative importance of different facts, of interpreting their meaning, and of assembling these interpretations into a coherent scheme could provide the direction needed to find one's way about in an infinitely large universe of possibilities. Without a method, one was condemned to wander aimlessly. The increasing insistence in classical studies on the importance of agreed-upon methods of research; the long campaign to formulate these methods and to police their application by insisting that they alone can generate "meaningful" results; the increasing attention paid to methodological issues of all sorts: these were a predictable, indeed inevitable, response to the challenge of making the now infinite material of classical studies accessible to the finite minds of its students and of transforming what would otherwise be a trackless forest into a manageable plot.

Furthermore, since every scholar now confronted a limited number of possible lines of inquiry to which he might devote his time and energy, a selection obviously had to be made among them. Nothing could be gained by flitting aimlessly from one topic to the next, and all the possible topics could never be exhausted. The explosion of the boundaries of classical studies thus compelled a process of specialization. By devaluing the knowledge of the generalist, who was concerned only with abstract ideals, the romantic insistence on the value of the individual forced scholars to become specialists whose deep but limited understanding of some selected portion of the vast range of materials one might usefully investigate was now deemed the only true, authentic, and worthwhile knowledge a person could possess about the subject.

Finally, classical studies (and, by implication, every branch of specialized research) now had to be viewed as an accretive enterprise extending over many generations of time. For even if he narrows his focus to a single topic, no scholar can hope to grasp it fully in his lifetime. His subject matter is endlessly rich and can never be exhausted. This would be true even if his material consisted of a few well-defined facts, since even a single fact can be made to yield additional knowledge when inspected from a fresh point of view. And of course the narrowest research agenda consists of numberless facts and countless interpretive possibilities. Every field of research, however specialized, is therefore infinitely deep, and hence incapable of being fully explored in the finite span of a single human lifetime.

The acknowledgment that this is so forced those who accepted the new scholarly ideal of specialized work to recognize that their goal can only be achieved by many generations of scholars. It compelled them to acknowledge that their work can, in truth, *never* be completed and that the notion of its completion is what Kant called a "regulative ideal"—a goal which, though unattainable, gives purpose and direction to the effort to reach it.[22] Those who embraced the idea of specialization were thus required to view themselves as participants in a timeless endeavor, governed by a regulative ideal toward whose achievement they might contribute but which they could not reach themselves within the limits of their own mortal careers.

This made it necessary for scholars working in accordance with the new research ideal to find a stable institutional home for their endeavors. The more specialized their research became, the greater was the need for a coordinating mechanism of some sort to bring their work into alignment and to gather their separate discoveries into an organized whole. And the more the work of scholarship came to be viewed as a multi-generational enterprise reaching over a limitless span of time, the more urgent was the need for an enduring institutional setting to provide a link between the generations, preserving the work of each as a capital asset for those that follow. As the research ideal gained authority, and more of those working in classical studies and other fields came to accept its demands, it became increasingly clear that their work could be pursued only in universities—in institutions set up, or redesigned, for the very purpose of providing these links.

Scholars of earlier generations had sometimes enjoyed the support of a patron. More often, they supported themselves with their own resources. Many were wealthy men for whom scholarship was a hobby. Like Robert Wood, they were "dilettantes" who pursued their studies in large part for the sake of the pleasure these afforded. The nineteenth-century German research scholars who worked in the universities that had been created to coordinate their efforts and to provide a stable home for their disciplines approached their task in a different spirit. Their goal was not the cultivation and enjoyment of a refined connoisseurship, as it had been for many scholars of the older type. They did not work for the sake of pleasure, however refined. They worked to advance the state of knowledge in their fields, for whose sake many were prepared to *sacrifice* their happiness—their health, hobbies, family relations, and the like.[23] They approached their work in professional terms, distinguishing (with a sharpness earlier scholars had not) between the objective interests of their disciplines and their own private needs, viewing the latter as a resource to be spent in pursuit of their discipline's goals.

In this respect, their attitude resembled that of two other groups whose historical emergence coincided roughly with their own. One was the class of professional bureaucrats who in the nineteenth century took over many of the administrative responsibilities of the modern nation state, performing their tasks in a similar spirit of self-denying devotion to office.[24] The other was the class of capitalist entrepreneurs whose defining ambition was not to increase their private wealth but the profitability of their businesses instead.[25] Like the bureaucrat and the capitalist, the professional research scholar who emerged as a recognizable type in the German universities of the early nineteenth century worked not for his own sake but for the benefit of the discipline to which he belonged, distinguishing its interests from his own with a clarity foreign to the tradition of learned scholarship that for centuries had been the main carrier of most forms of knowledge in the West.

It may seem surprising that romanticism produced these results. For the spirit of romanticism, with its passion and extravagant self expression, seems far removed from the cool and self-sacrificing spirit of the new scholarly ideal. But it was the romantic affirmation of individual uniqueness—the heart of its revolt against enlightenment rationalism—that created the conditions that gave birth to this ideal with its requirements of specialization and professional restraint. However distant in affect or tone, the modern research ideal is the professionally disciplined child of its hot-blooded parent.

From the field of classical studies, this ideal spread to other areas of historical research, to medicine and the natural sciences, and to the nascent social sciences which began to assume their present form in the middle years of the nineteenth century. Slowly but steadily, its dominion expanded over the whole of academic life. In the process, the new research ideal acquired an increasingly "vocational" cast. The career of the research specialist came to be seen as a calling in the original sense of that term. It came to be viewed not merely as a means to the more efficient production of knowledge but as a path to a spiritual end, a path (to put it most extravagantly) to salvation. This happened first and most emphatically in the German universities of the nineteenth century. It was here that the new ideal of specialized research, born in the field of classical studies, first acquired the moral and spiritual significance it still possesses today, through its interaction with a larger complex of ideas centered around the uniquely German concept of *Bildung*.

The word itself implies a process of self-cultivation, of inward development, that Thomas Mann in 1923 called "the finest characteristic of the typical German."[26] Mann assigned this characteristic a high spiritual value and believed that a form of personal salvation may be found in its achievement. In this regard, he echoed the views of other German writers—of Goethe in the eighteenth century, Schleiermacher, Schopenhauer, and Nietzsche in the nineteenth, Freud and Weber in the twentieth. The value of Bildung was a central organizing premise of the literary and philosophical tradition to which all these writers belonged and of which Mann himself was one of the last great representatives.[27]

Different writers in this tradition interpreted the concept differently. But during the century and a half that the ideal of spiritual self-cultivation associated with the notion of Bildung remained a premise of German culture and thought, specialized academic research continued to be viewed as one of its most characteristic expressions. The professor working in his study on some arcane and specialized problem of research, devoting himself at great personal cost to the advancement of knowledge in his field: here the defenders of Bildung saw a striking example of the values and attitudes they most respected. For them, the work of scholarship was more than a form of productive labor. It was a calling with salvific goals that embodied the highest spiritual values of the civilization to which this distinctively German idea gave expression.

Two features of the Bildung ideal meshed in an especially close and supportive way with the requirements of specialized academic research and help to explain why it acquired the vocational meaning it did. The first was an insistence on the one-sidedness of all responsible self-cultivation. Every human being is born with powers he or she shares with other members of the species. But no one person can develop these to full expression. Life is too short for that. And though we each possess certain universal aptitudes and inclinations, we do not possess them all to the same degree. Every human being is a unique bundle of capacities, interests, and traits. The distinctiveness of a person's talents and inclinations is fixed in part by nature and in part by early experience. But whatever relative weight we assign these two great determining influences in a person's life, by the time he reaches the stage at which the question of what he shall make of himself can be meaningfully framed, the specific gifts (of nature and nurture) on which his efforts of self-cultivation must be trained will already for the most part be fixed, and it is on these that the ethic of Bildung requires him to concentrate his attention.[28]

To aim at a universal humanity that encompasses the whole of mankind's powers is not only fruitless, and hence imprudent, but self-indulgent as well. What one must do instead is develop to their fullest the distinctive talents one possesses, leaving it to others to develop theirs in turn. One should think of oneself as having been assigned a part in a larger drama and as having a duty to play that part with the greatest possible refinement and skill. One should not seek to master the play as a whole. The ancient Aristotlean ideal of well-roundedness must be rejected as both impractical and immoral.[29]

In contrast to the pagan ideal of a well-rounded life, the notion of Bildung assigned supreme moral value to the uniqueness of the individual and to the development of his or her distinctive gifts for the sake of a greater good. It encouraged those who embraced it to see the cultivation of their individuality as a moral responsibility. In this respect, it drew upon the Christian belief in the sanctity of the individual, of which the concept of Bildung was in many ways a secularized expression.[30] It preserved the spiritual power of this Christian idea in a secular form, as an innerworldly ideal of living, without the theological assumptions on which it had originally been based—much like the concept of life as a work of art, which defenders of the Bildung ideal often treated as its equivalent.

It is easy to see how this ideal fit with the new conception of scholarly research and lent spiritual dignity to it. Scholarship demands specialization, a narrowing of effort and attention. This makes all serious scholarship one-sided. That we have each been given our assignment in life and must work to make the most of it is what the notion of Bildung counsels as a general ideal of living. For the research scholar, this means that the development of his expertise is not merely efficient but morally praiseworthy too. The concept of Bildung encourages the equation of scholarly specialization with duty and honor. It makes the development of one's place in the division of intellectual labor a spiritually meaningful goal and not just an economic or organizational necessity. It condemns all efforts to achieve a complete, well-rounded knowledge of the world as pointless and irresponsible. It promotes the idea that in collaboration with others, the specialist can contribute to the development of human knowledge and to the cultivation of humanity in general. The concept of Bildung connects the work of the academic specialist to this larger ideal of living, invests it with redemptive significance, and gives him a framework within which to see his work as part of a larger program that embodies humanity's deepest aspirations.

The Bildung ideal helped secure the spiritual dignity of the research ideal in a second way, by emphasizing the disinterestedness of the process of self-cultivation. A cultivated person may, of course, enjoy the capacities he or she has worked to develop. But this is not the end toward which the person's energies are bent, as the Bildung ideal conceives it. The talents we possess have not been given to us for our private enjoyment. We have been given them to develop for the benefit of humanity as a whole. We have been entrusted with a small but distinctive portion of humanity's resources and charged with the responsibility of cultivating them on humanity's behalf. The attitude we take toward our own talents and capacities must therefore not be one of selfish pleasure. It should be the attitude of a trustee who is responsible for making the most of the corpus he or she has been instructed to manage for the benefit of those others whose enjoyment is the trustee's only legitimate object.

This aspect of the Bildung ideal was also deeply colored by Christian belief—by the belief that as unique components of God's diverse creation we have an obligation to help complete His work by developing the gifts that He has given us, not so that we may enjoy them ourselves but in order to glorify God and fulfill His plan for the world.[31] Christianity teaches that we are not the owners but merely the possessors of our gifts, which belong to someone else for whose sake we must manage their development. Here too the concept of Bildung functioned as the secular equivalent of a religious idea, preserving a Christian ethic of trusteeship without its theological trappings and bringing its vocational spirit of other-directed service into the worldly labor of self-cultivation.

In this way, the Bildung ideal helped to give spiritual legitimacy to the culture of academic professionalism that was associated with the new university-based system of specialized research. Unlike the scholars of an earlier day, who often worked for the sake of their own gratification, the research specialist subordinates his personal well-being to the advancement of knowledge in his field. He accepts the demands of specialization not merely for the sake of efficiency, but out of a sense of duty, believing that he must eschew the pleasures of dilettantism in order to meet his responsibilities as a steward of the one small plot of knowledge that has been entrusted to his care. From this morally demanding point of view, the scholar who pursues his studies for the sake of the pleasure they afford him is acting in a selfish and irresponsible way. He is putting himself before others. Only the scholar who accepts the requirements of specialization and the personal sacrifice these entail, who distinguishes the needs of his discipline from his own private welfare and subordinates the second to the first, is acting in a morally praiseworthy fashion. Only he is acting in accordance with the self-denying ethic of trusteeship that the Bildung ideal embodies.

The Bildung ideal made specialization a virtue. It made the dutiful renunciation of pleasure for the sake of responsible work a spiritually compelling demand. Drawing inspiration from an older tradition of Christian belief while recasting that tradition in a secular form, it conferred a moral and spiritual legitimacy on the work of the academic researcher whose selfless and specialized labors the Bildung ideal dignified as a calling not a job—an innerworldly path to salvation. The result was a spiritualization of the research ideal that persists to this day. Even today, most American graduate students believe they have chosen a path that offers more than external rewards. They believe they are embarking on a career that promises a measure of spiritual fulfillment as well. Max Weber was the last to express this idea with the moral grandeur in which it had originally been conceived by the German scholars of the early nineteenth century who grafted onto the new regime of specialized research spurred by the romantic reaction against enlightenment rationalism an ideal of self-cultivation derived from Christian beliefs but trimmed of religious assumptions. Today, few graduate students read Weber's 1918 lecture. Fewer still have any knowledge of the intellectual developments that produced the modern research ideal, with its demand for specialization and insistence on the spiritual dignity of a life devoted to it. But the implicit acceptance of these ideas remains an important if hidden source of the vast authority of the research ideal in American higher education—an authority that flows not only from its efficiency in the production of ideas but its moral potency as well.

The several thousand Americans who went to Germany to study in the middle years of the nineteenth century brought back with them a German passion for scholarship and the vocational ideal of a life devoted to specialized research.[32] When this ideal began to take root in America's universities, however, it was not in the humanities that it gained its first foothold— in contrast to the situation in Germany—but in the natural sciences instead. Several reasons help to explain this. One was the absence in the United States of a strong secondary school system of the sort that existed in Germany and that guaranteed a steady supply of college students already well-trained in the classics.[33] Another was the continuing influence of an older approach to these texts, which treated them as manuals of moral instruction rather than as objects of research. And a third was the characteristically American emphasis on the importance of "useful" knowledge, to which research in the natural sciences makes a more visible contribution.

The humanities, and classical studies in particular, thus proved to be a relatively less congenial medium for the initial transplantation of the German research ideal to American soil.[34] It was in the natural sciences that this ideal established its first American beachhead. But from here it quickly spread to other fields and by the end of the nineteenth century had penetrated every branch of study. The humanities were no exception. In philology, history, and other fields the new ideal of scholarly research attracted American followers who were eager to reorganize their disciplines in accordance with its requirements.[35] But in the humanities—and there alone—the research ideal met a counter-ideal whose deepest values were in many ways antithetical to its own. This was the ideal of secular humanism, which remained a powerful force in the humanities until the middle years of the twentieth century, when it finally lost its authority as a serious competitor to the research ideal.

Secular humanism was the heir of the classicist tradition that had dominated every aspect of American college life before the Civil War. It modified that tradition in important ways but shared certain core values with it. The research ideal attacked these values directly. It made them seem unworthy of respect. And in doing so, it displaced from a central and respected place in higher education the question to which both the classical program of the antebellum college and secular humanism were addressed—the question of what living is for.

Students in an antebellum college were expected to internalize a fixed and finite set of norms inherited from the ancient world and from Christian tradition and to conform their actions and speech to them. The students who acquired these values assumed the place that generations of students before them had occupied. They repeated their experience. They neither expected to make progress beyond what their predecessors knew and believed nor were encouraged to do so. They did not seek to be original. The whole point of their education was to become *un*original by learning the pattern of living that men whose hearts and minds are properly ordered have always followed. Their attitude was not one of active invention but of submission to the authority of values that they were not to embellish, change, or stamp with their own distinctive personality but merely absorb and embrace.

This attitude was shared by their teachers. Teachers in the antebellum college saw themselves as the conservators of a valued tradition of learning. Their principal duty was to preserve this tradition by initiating the next generation of students into its pantheon of norms and ideas. A teacher in the classicist mold had no ambition to make a contribution of his own to this tradition. He had no desire to impress his personality upon it. His aim was the essentially passive one of transmission, and the gratification that his work provided derived from the experience of serving as a link in an unbroken chain, as a custodian helping to preserve a great human achievement. This attitude is today nearly incomprehensible. But the knowledge that he will die out of a world recognizably the same as the one he entered (a source of immense psychic comfort); the experience of having done his part to keep this world intact; the joy of being immediately in touch with those earlier generations of teachers who had labored before him in the same project of preservation—all the satisfactions of trusteeship, in short—were for teachers of the old order benefits more real and vivid than the pleasures of originality, which they hardly recognized at all.[36]

The modern research ideal turned this older system of values upside down.

The goal of a teacher oriented to scholarship is not to transmit unchanged an existing body of knowledge he has inherited from the past. The scholar's goal is to add something new to the storehouse of knowledge he finds in place when he begins his own research. The novelty he adds need not be grand. Every scholar hopes for this, of course, but the failure to have a transforming effect on his field does not mean that the scholar's research has been in vain. The crucial achievement—without which his efforts really would be in vain—is the contribution of some incremental discovery or invention of his own, however small the contribution may be in comparison to what others have done.

The research scholar who succeeds in contributing to her field experiences something that teachers in the classicist tradition neither experienced nor sought. She experiences the excitement of her own creativity, the thrill of originality. But the conditions on which she does so necessarily deprive her of the satisfaction of knowing everything one needs to know—perhaps even everything that can be known—about her subject. So long as classicism retained its vitality, this remained an attainable goal. But by attaching such importance to originality, and by making specialization the inescapable condition of original scholarship, the research ideal puts this goal beyond reach. It makes it seem laughably naive. The scholar who would be original must concentrate her efforts on a single, specialized point of research and abandon the childish pretense of ever attaining that entire knowledge of the world and of humanity to which all learning in the classicist tradition aspired.

The research scholar is also deprived of the satisfaction of being directly in touch with his predecessors, intellectually and morally, and of sharing with them a vantage point that never changes. The point of instruction in the antebellum college was to equip each student to join his ancestors as a contemporary, standing alongside them in the possession of a common knowledge that is always the same. The pleasure of such contemporaneity was one of its chief goals. The modern ideal of scholarly research substitutes for this what might be called an "ethic of supersession."[37] A scholar does not aim to stand where his ancestors did. His goal is not to join but supersede them and his success is measured not by the proximity of his thoughts to theirs but by the distance between them—by how far he has progressed beyond his ancestors' inferior state of knowledge.

By the same token, the ethic of supersession demands that the research scholar acknowledge, even relish, the prospect that his own original contribution will be superseded in turn. Psychologically, perhaps, this is more difficult to accept than the exciting prospect of advancing beyond those who have gone before. But no one who is truly called to scholarship as a vocation can justify the (understandably human) desire to utter the final word on a subject. For a true scholar, this desire must seem a bit of foolish pride. The true scholar wants to be superseded by his successors, just as he wants to supersede those who have preceded him. He seeks originality, but accepts the transience of his own original achievements.

Teachers in the old order saw themselves as participants in an unchanging venture. They stood with their ancestors in what Max Weber called the "eternal yesterday" of tradition.[38] In doing so, they achieved a position immune to the corrupting powers of time. They experienced a kind of immortality, directly in their own lives and within the limits of their own experience. One might say that they enacted the idea of eternity in their lives. For the research scholar, this experience is no longer available. A scholar of course thinks of himself as a participant in a timeless venture too—in his discipline's unending pursuit of perfect knowledge—and identifies with the immortal life of the discipline as a whole. But this life consists in a perpetual series of supersessions, of which his own career is one, and though a scholar can conceive the idea of a timeless project formed of such a series, he cannot experience it directly. He can imagine himself to be part of an eternal enterprise, but cannot realize its timelessness within the bounds of his finite existence. For the research scholar, eternity is just an abstraction and though he may be consoled by the thought of his participation in a venture whose goal of perfect knowledge lies beyond time's power to change, he can never know the greater consolation of reaching this goal in his lifetime, of experiencing eternity directly as opposed to merely contemplating it as an ideal.

Teachers in the old order faced death knowing what eternity is like. They confronted death from the standpoint of an experience that was already beyond it. The research scholar faces death without the consolation of this experience. For him, death casts a more disturbing shadow. Death makes the meaning of his work more insecure, easier to question and doubt. It makes the scholar's life lonelier—which is why some, like Weber, have seen the scholarly vocation as a heroic ideal demanding a form of courage that classicism never required.

It is indeed heroic for a scholar to forge on, for the sake of truths he will never reach and without the consolation of that living experience of immortality that teachers of the old order knew and which for them made death a less significant event. But it is the scholar's own ethic of supersession that shuts him out from this experience and deprives him of its consolation. It is the scholar's own insistence on the importance of originality that compels him to acknowledge the transience of his work, that deprives him of the experience of eternity in the deathless company of his ancestors, and leaves him facing death alone and unconsoled. If specialization is a price that must be paid for originality, then loneliness is too.

The student who approaches his subject in this spirit, and pursues it beyond its first introductory phase, will see the main purpose of his study as being to acquire the resources he needs to make a creative contribution of his own. His goal will be to supersede the achievements of his teachers by adding something new to their discoveries. He will regard the advance of his own work beyond that of his teachers as a fulfillment of their relationship, as the highest form of fidelity he can show to those who have introduced him to the field—which is how his teachers will view it too, so long as they remain faithful to their scholarly vocation and are not distracted by egoistic concerns.

The further a student moves in this direction, the more reconciled she will become to the necessity for specialization as a condition of original research, and to the transience of her own work as an unavoidable consequence of it. Like her teachers, she will come to accept the impossibility of ever possessing all the knowledge in her field or of joining her ancestors in the eternal now of a deathless wisdom that each generation inherits complete from the ones before. She will accept all this, and the loneliness it entails, so long as she makes originality her guiding star. She will know that these ambitions were once pursued by teachers and students in an educational milieu far removed from her own. But she will recognize that their satisfactions must all be foregone for the sake of that ever-expanding storehouse of knowledge, built over many generations through the specialized labor of countless creative researchers, each adding his or her own original but short-lived bit to the growing pile, to which she hopes herself to make a contribution: the heart of the research ideal.

Secular humanism was more pluralistic than the classicism of the antebellum college. It was more skeptical of the theological certitudes on which the latter was based. It recognized, as classicism did not, that the question of what living is for is one we must each answer for ourselves. Yet it also shared certain important values with the tradition to which it succeeded. These shared values formed a link between them and enabled secular humanism to carry that tradition forward. But the values they shared, which made this continuity possible, were the very ones the research ideal attacked.

Like the classicist tradition, secular humanism also assigned a positive value to recurrence and repetition. While emphasizing the plurality of the answers that can be given to the question of what one should ultimately care about and why, it stressed the stability of these answers over time. It presented them as a relatively permanent set of possibilities, the more-or-less fixed framework within which each individual confronts the question of what living is for. A choice must be made among these possibilities. They do not dictate the answer by themselves. But because the framework they establish is unchanging, teachers in the secular humanist tradition could see themselves as the guardians of an educational program that remains unoriginal in each generation, much as their classicist forebears had done.

They could also experience a communion with the great creative spirits of the past and seek to bring their students into this communion themselves. The life of philosophy has never had a greater champion than Socrates or the life of faith a more impassioned and articulate defender than Augustine. For the secular humanist, Socrates and Augustine are contemporaries. They and all the other great thinkers and artists of the past occupy the same changeless if quarrelsome space, endlessly debating the meaning of life in a single unbroken conversation, where new points may be scored but no answer is ever refuted—a conversation that is always alive, where every participant who has ever joined it is still actively engaged, and to which each new generation of students is introduced, meeting their ancestors face-to-face in a direct encounter regarding matters of timeless importance. Even with its more pluralistic and skeptical assumptions, secular humanism continued to emphasize and to value the bonds that join the generations in a real unity, accessible to experience and immune to time, just as the classicist program of the antebellum college had done.

Finally, because secular humanism assumed that the ultimate values toward which a human life may be directed are manageably few in number, its proponents could still think that a student might acquire, in four years of college study, the basic knowledge one needs to be prepared for the question of life's meaning. Secular humanism of course accepted that a choice must be made among different ways of life and left this choice to the person whose life it is—the only person who can make it. But by affirming that a student can acquire, in the span of a college education, a sympathetic acquaintance with the main forms of human living, secular humanism preserved, in a more pluralistic form, the old classicist belief in the possibility of conveying to each generation the (timeless) knowledge one needs to meet even this most "existential" of questions.

The modern research ideal exploded this set of beliefs. It drained them of their plausibility and appeal. It did this not by proving them to be false. It deprived them of their power by championing a new set of values that contradict the values of recurrence, connection, and closure on which secular humanism was founded.

Because the research ideal elevates originality to a position of supreme importance, it makes the notion of a limited set of ways of life, even incommensurably different ones, seem a barrier to individual invention. The unoriginality that secular humanism celebrates—its belief in a stable repertoire of values that form a recurrent framework of choice in each generation—seems, from the vantage point of the research ideal, not a virtue but a vice, a constraint on the passion for original achievement. What from the standpoint of secular humanism was a source of comfort and consolation thus becomes in the system of values promoted by the research ideal something to be resisted, even despised—a narrow menu of stereotypes that cramp the individual's drive to be original.

The research ideal also sharply devalues the communion with past writers and artists to which secular humanism attached such importance. The immediacy of one's engagement with the great works of the past; the sense of being in the present company of their creators; the experience of contemporaneity that is implied by the idea of the great conversation which the tradition of arts and letters sustains: all of these ideas become suspect, or worse, from the standpoint of the ethic of supersession. The notion of a timeless conversation in which the great voices of the past still speak with undiminished authority, that never concludes and never changes, where all the generations are present at once, is to those who judge things from the standpoint of this ethic not an impractical ideal but a bad one that denies the possibility of that very progress in understanding that is the scholar's deepest reward.

And of course the idea that one can acquire in any finite period of time (let alone in four short years of college) a more-or-less complete knowledge of any subject (let alone a subject as large and consequential as the array of alternatives that frame a person's answer to the question of what living is for) is bound to seem to those who embrace the research ideal ridiculously naive and even offensive. For the closure and completeness it assumes, were it achievable, would bring to an end the accretive movement toward an asymptote of perfect knowledge that gives each field its life and dignity from the standpoint of this ideal. Without the prospect of further progress, which completeness rules out, a discipline is dead so far as research is concerned. There is nothing more of value to be accomplished in it. It must be abandoned for more fruitful—which is to say, less finished—branches of inquiry. A belief in the possibility of conveying to one's students a knowledge of all the main forms of human living must therefore be judged, from the perspective of the research ideal, not merely unsound but pernicious—a belief that, if taken seriously, denies the very thing to which the scholar is most devoted.

The research ideal thus promoted a set of counter-values that were the antithesis of those that secular humanism supported. But it undermined the authority of secular humanism in a still more basic way. For it made the question of the meaning of life appear unprofessional—a question that no responsible teacher of the humanities could henceforth take seriously. It demoted the question as a subject of legitimate academic concern by devaluing the point of view from which the question of life's meaning arises most insistently—the only point of view from which it can in fact arise at all.

This is the point of view we take when we consider the purpose and value of our lives as a whole. We cannot, of course, step outside our lives and contemplate them from without. In that sense, the view we take of our lives as a whole is always taken from a vantage point within them, which inevitably has its own special character and varies with our age, mood, and relations to others. "Life as a whole" is something we never experience directly. It is always an idea.

If one were inclined to denigrate this idea, to deny its value and importance, one might say that it is "nothing more" than an idea. This is true, but the denigration is unwarranted. For the idea of life as a whole is one that has tremendous urgency and great practical importance in our lives. We never stop taking the idea seriously and often make important adjustments in our lives on account of our reflections about it. Though we never experience it directly, our life as a whole is rarely far from our attention. When we ask ourselves about the meaning of our lives, about the cares and commitments that give our lives their purpose and direction, it is from the vantage point of this idea that we frame the question.

The idea of life as a whole has two characteristics. The first is its inclusiveness. There is nothing in our lives—no aspect or component of them, no feeling, thought, relation, project, or ambition—which the idea leaves out. The second is its finitude. My life as a whole includes everything within it and nothing beyond it. However much it contains, however many and varied its parts, my life has a limit. One day I shall cease to exist, and in contemplating my life as a whole I have in mind not only the entirety of all it contains but its mortal limits as well.

I may, of course, answer the question of what living is for by imaginatively inserting my life into the framework of something that will survive it—into God's plan for the world, or the history of my country, or the lives of my children and grandchildren. It may even be that the question of life's meaning can only be answered in this way, that our lives as a whole can be meaningful to us only in relation to something larger and more lasting than our selves. But regardless of how we *answer* the question, the vantage point from which we *ask* it is that of life as a whole, and from this perspective the mortality of our lives is as inescapable a premise as the inclusion of all they contain. When I think of my life as a whole I think of it as a bounded totality, as the sum of everything my life contains within the limits fixed by death. If I leave one of its parts out of account, I am not thinking of my life as a *whole*. If I imagine myself living forever, I am not thinking of my *life* as a whole. The thought of my life as a whole joins inclusiveness and finitude in a distinctive way. Their combination produces the idea from whose vantage point the question of life's meaning arises, even if the answer I give emphasizes exclusively one part of my life or places it in a context unbounded by the limits of my own mortality. The logic of the question, as distinct from the answers we give to it, presupposes this peculiar union of totality and mortality, and the more we are in the habit of thinking about both—about the inclusiveness of our lives and their mortal limits—the more familiar the idea of life as a whole is likely to seem and the more urgent the question of its meaning.

The modern research ideal discourages us from thinking about either. It draws our attention away from the whole of our lives and requires that we focus on some small aspect of them instead. It discourages inclusiveness and promotes a narrowing of attention, at least within the realm of academic study. At the same time, it deflects attention from the fact that we die, and in place of an acceptance of the mortal limits of one's life encourages the scholar to see things, and to value them, from the deathless perspective of the discipline to which he or she belongs. In these ways, the research ideal devalues the elements of inclusiveness and finitude from whose combination the idea of life as a whole derives. It makes the idea of our lives as a whole seem less familiar and compelling. And by doing so, it causes the question of what living is for to seem less urgent, less recognizable even, within the domain in which the modern research ideal holds sway. For however one answers this question, the question itself only comes into view from the vantage point of an idea composed of elements the ideal negates.

This is easiest to see in the case of the first of these elements.

The research ideal insists on specialization. It demands that the researcher select one small corner of his or her field to cultivate exclusively, leaving the rest to others to develop. It asserts that any results of real scholarly value can be achieved only on the condition of such specialization, and condemns the refusal to accept its dictates as a sterile dilettantism incapable of producing anything of intellectual worth.

Specialization is the enemy of inclusiveness—not just in the sense of being incompatible with it, but in the stronger sense of regarding it as irresponsible, as frivolous and self-indulgent, in a word, immoral. The ideal of scholarship as a vocation celebrates the renunciation of all other interests for the sake of one's speciality as a virtue of the highest order. It views specialization as an admirable form of self-sacrifice and elevates it to a moral ideal in accordance with the concept of Bildung which helped its nineteenth-century champions view scholarly specialization as a spiritual value. In any academic discipline in which the research ideal becomes dominant and the requirement of specialization constrains those who wish to be taken seriously in the field, the idea of life as a whole, and hence the question of what living is for, is therefore bound to seem less respectable.

Less obviously, perhaps, but just as insistently, the research ideal draws attention away from the second element of which this idea is composed—the mortality of the researcher himself. No one, scholars included, ever forgets for very long that he must die. But the scholar devoted to the advancement of knowledge in his field is encouraged by the research ideal to consider his own death a non-event, one that lacks significance so far as the work of the discipline itself is concerned. For the researcher who sees the importance of his work in this way, what really matters is the progress of understanding in his field, to which he makes an individual contribution but whose "life," unlike his own, has no boundaries at all. From the perspective of the multigenerational enterprise in which he is engaged, the researcher's own mortality has little or no meaning. Within the realm of academic study, the research ideal devalues death. It deprives death of significance for the scholar who embraces this ideal, and makes any preoccupation on his part with the fact of his mortality seem unprofessional and self-absorbed.

The question of what living is for arises only from the standpoint of the idea of life as a whole. This idea is at once inclusive and bounded. It gathers every aspect of one's life and underscores its mortal limits. Only this combination of inclusiveness and mortality provides the perspective from which the question of the meaning of life comes into view. The modern research ideal attacks both elements of this idea at once. Through its demand for specialization, it discourages inclusiveness. It requires the scholar to concentrate her attention on something much smaller than life as a whole and disdains more inclusive pursuits as a dilettantism with little or no academic value. And through its insistence on the supreme importance of the discipline, of the multigenerational program of discovery and invention in which the individual researcher is engaged and in the context of whose larger life her own mortal career has no meaning, the research ideal minimizes the importance of mortality and promotes an ethic of supersession that condemns the scholar who takes her death too seriously as immature and unprofessional.

The modern research ideal thus compels those who embrace it to concentrate their attention on matters that are, at once, both smaller and larger than their lives as a whole. It discourages, at once, the inclusiveness and the attention to mortality from whose combination the idea of life as a whole derives. It devalues both and deprives the idea of its ethical and spiritual worth. It makes the idea of life as a whole seem childish, ridiculous, unprofessional, self-indulgent. And by doing that, it undermines the credibility and authority of the one point of view from which the question of what living is for arises.

The effect of this, of course, is not to make the question itself disappear, but only to deprive it of legitimacy within the arena of academic work—to push it out of school. Human beings, scholars included, are irresistibly drawn to the question of life's meaning, and there is no reason to expect this will change. But to the extent the modern research ideal systematically devalues the perspective from which this question must be asked, it compels those who would ask it to look outside the academy for answers. It says, to teachers and students alike, "Do not look for answers to the question of life's meaning here. Do not even expect the question to be raised here, for to do so would violate the most basic premises on which modern scholarship is based. If you are interested in the meaning of life, take the question up with your family and friends, with your rabbi or priest, but do not expect that you can give, or will receive, any authoritative guidance in answering it in school—in any academic discipline, the humanities included, that subscribes to the research ideal."

For students, the result is that they are thrown back on their own resources in searching for an answer. For teachers, the result is perhaps even worse. Many college and university teachers devote a large fraction of their waking hours to their careers, and the boundary between their work and the rest of their lives is often quite fluid. What the professional research scholar learns to devalue in school may therefore be especially difficult to honor elsewhere in his life. Even in his private life, the modern scholar who fits his work to the demands of the research ideal may find it harder than others to take seriously the question of life's meaning—a question he remains as eager as anyone to ask, but whose legitimacy the moral and spiritual requirements of his work, and the habits of mind these instill, forbid him even to acknowledge.

The research ideal is today the organizing principle of work in every academic discipline. It defines the culture of professionalism that American graduate students encounter at the threshold of their careers. It sets the standards by which they are taught to judge their work, and in doing so establishes the norms and expectations that govern the world of higher education generally.

The advantages of organizing the production of knowledge in accordance with this ideal are as apparent in the humanities as they are in every other field. Scholars in the humanities have produced vast quantities of research that have profoundly enriched our understanding of their subjects. We know more today about the origin of Homer's poems, the order of Plato's dialogues, the content of Augustine's sermons, the accuracy of Gibbon's citations, and how Ben Franklin spent his time in Paris than we ever knew before. These are real gains—the lasting benefits of specialized research, which has produced impressive results in the humanities as in every branch of academic study.

But the triumph of the research ideal has been for the humanities at most a mixed blessing.

For the benefits it has brought, though real, do not compare with its benefits in the natural and social sciences. And by undermining the authority of secular humanism, the research ideal has deprived the humanities of their most distinctive and valuable possession. It has deprived them of the special authority they once possessed as instructors in the meaning of life and given them, in return, the right to be judged by standards which the natural and social sciences will always be more successful in meeting.

In the natural sciences, the research ideal has proved remarkably fruitful. The new discoveries that pour from our college and university laboratories every year and the clear sense of progressive movement toward an objective understanding of the structure and mechanisms of the natural world testify to the productive fit between the natural sciences and the modern research ideal. The same is true, if to a lesser degree, in the social sciences, especially in those disciplines like economics and political science that make strong and credible claims to possess expanding bodies of objective knowledge about the social world.

In the humanities, by contrast, the benefits of research are less uniform or certain. In some fields, such as history, scholarly research has produced valuable results—an accumulation of discoveries that has deepened our understanding of events and personalities. But in other fields, like literary criticism, it is not at all clear that the sequence of interpretations championed by scholars of succeeding generations constitutes a similarly progressive body of knowledge—as opposed to a cyclical alteration of outlook and values, what Northrop Frye called the spinning of the prayer-wheel of interpretation and a skeptic might describe as the product of fashion or fad.[39] Indeed, to the extent that history is an interpretive discipline and not just a growing repository of facts the same may be said of it too. For viewed in this light, it is less obvious that the competing interpretations of historians of different generations represent a progressive line and not a fashion-driven circle. And in philosophy—a heavily professionalized field now dominated by the research ideal—it can still be claimed without embarrassment that there have been few advances since Plato, a claim whose counterpart in physics or biology or economics would be absurd.

The promise of the research ideal is a steadily growing body of knowledge that approximates ever more closely to the truth about a subject—to the truth about the behavior of subatomic particles, for example, or the dynamics of markets. It is the prospect of such knowledge that motivates and justifies the acceptance of this ideal in any particular field of study. In the natural and social sciences, the goal of an ever-closer approximation to the truth seems entirely reasonable and the appropriateness of a system of specialized research as a means for pursuing this goal appears equally obvious. Its suitability as a means is confirmed by the results of the research itself which moves our knowledge of these subjects forward from one generation to the next in a process of steady accretion.

In the humanities, this is less clear. It is less obvious that the commitment to specialization and multigenerational cooperation that define the modern research ideal is equally well-suited to these disciplines or capable of producing results that confirm its validity with the same undeniable force they do in the natural and social sciences. That is not because the ideas of truth and objectivity have no place in the humanities. Most if not all teachers of history, philosophy, and literature believe there is a truth of the matter about the subjects they study and teach. Indeed, their belief that this is so is a condition of the intelligibility of what they say and do, for there can be no coherent discussion of any subject without an implicit belief in the possibility of discovering the truth about it. What is missing in the humanities is not a commitment to the truth. What is missing is the basis for a confident belief, so palpable in the natural and social sciences, that specialized research and truth are *linked*—that the first is the best, perhaps the only, means for achieving the second. Where the fruits of specialized research accumulate in a growing body of knowledge that moves slowly but surely toward the truth, as they do in the natural and stronger social sciences, a belief of this sort is well-founded. But where the work of scholars, however enlightening, fails to accumulate in the same incremental and progressive way, moving around in a circle instead, this belief is harder to sustain.

That is the case in the humanities. Here the connection between the truth and the modern research ideal is harder to discern and defend. By comparison with the natural and social sciences, where it is obvious and strong, the connection in the humanities is ambiguous and fitful at best. Judged by the results in these other disciplines, research in the humanities is bound to seem less conclusive, less accretive, less fully or finally subject to appraisal in the light of standards scholars consider objectively binding. However valuable the results of their research, teachers of the humanities who judge their work from the standpoint of the research ideal therefore condemn themselves to a position of inferiority in the hierarchy of academic authority and prestige.

At the same time, humanities teachers who judge things from this point of view undermine the unique authority they once enjoyed as guides to the meaning of life. In the modern university, only the humanities have had the inclination and ability to provide such guidance. This sets them apart from the natural and social sciences and defines their special contribution to the work of higher education. It gives the humanities their distinctive authority and a position of dignity and worth in an educational environment dominated by the research ideal. But the values of the research ideal devalue the question of what living is for. They undermine the tradition of secular humanism and sap the confidence that teachers of the humanities once had in their ability to help answer this question. By accepting the imperatives of the research ideal and arranging their work to meet its demands, humanities teachers have therefore traded a valuable and distinctive authority for one based upon values they can never hope to realize to anything like the degree their colleagues in the natural and social sciences can. For the humanities, this has been a very bad bargain indeed. It has left teachers in these disciplines with a sense of inferiority and no way back to their lost authority. It has left them in an anxious void, without a secure sense of their own special role in higher education.

It was into this void that the political ideas of the 1960s and 1970s entered—the ideas of diversity and multiculturalism, and the theory that values are merely disguised acts of power. These took root in the humanities in part because they met with no resistance—because teachers in these fields had lost the self-confidence that would have given them the strength to resist. But more fundamentally, they took root because they seemed to offer an antidote to the emptiness produced by the humanities' own endorsement of the research ideal.

But the cure has proved an illusion. The culture of political correctness that has grown from these ideas has not restored the self-confidence of the humanities but further weakened it instead. It has diminished their authority, not repaired it. It has placed the humanities at an even greater distance from the question of life's meaning—the real source of their most lasting authority—and made it even more imperative that teachers of the humanities recover the wisdom and nerve to ask it.

4

POLITICAL CORRECTNESS

By the early 1970s, the humanities were floundering. Ideological rifts were widening. Traditional ways of teaching had lost much of their authority, and there was worried talk of a "crisis" in the humanities.[1] To many it seemed less clear than it had a quarter century before, when Harvard published its famous report on the aims of liberal education, what the humanities are supposed to do and why their doing it is important.[2]

In this anxious and excited environment, a new set of ideas began to gain currency. The first idea was an outgrowth of the civil rights movement and is associated with the concept of diversity. The second generally goes under the name of multiculturalism, and reflected the deepening suspicion of Western values provoked, in part, by the Vietnam War. The third, which provided philosophical support for the other two, I shall call the idea of constructivism, though its supporters have given it a variety of other names ("post-modernism," "antiessentialism," and the like). Loosely inspired by the work of philosophers as different as Marx, Nietzsche, and Foucault, constructivism affirmed the artificiality of all human values and the absence of any natural standards by which to judge them. It insisted, in particular, that the values of the West have no inherent superiority over those of other civilizations and are merely instruments of power in disguise that must be unmasked and resisted as weapons of colonial oppression. Together, these three ideas are the source of the culture of political correctness that has dominated the humanities for the past forty years.

Each has something to recommend it. Each has a core of good sense with intellectual and moral appeal. And each draws its appeal from a feature it shares with secular humanism, which also acknowledged the diversity of human values and the need to construct one's life by making a choice among them. Together these ideas have helped to maintain the confidence of many in the humanities that they do in fact have something special to contribute to the work of higher education. They have helped define a new and distinctive role for the humanities, organized around attractive moral and political values—one that fills the void that opened up when teachers in these fields abandoned their role as guides to the question of life's purpose and value in favor of the research ideal. And they have done this in a way that appears consistent with the values of secular humanism itself.

But this appearance is a mirage. Secular humanism rested in a balance between the authoritarianism of the antebellum college and the radicalism of the ideas that have dominated the humanities since the 1970s. It occupied an attractive and defensible midpoint between them. The ideas of diversity, multiculturalism, and constructivism exploded this balance. They extended the main principles of secular humanism in ways that do not improve but destroy them, creating an intellectual environment as hostile to secular humanism as the dogmatic classicism of the old-time college had been in a different way. Those who have embraced these ideas have not succeeded in defining a constructive new role for the humanities. They have in fact done just the reverse. They have made their own distinctive authority even harder to recover by casting into deeper doubt the values that once sustained it.

At the same time, they have further weakened the humanities' already vulnerable claim to respect, as measured by the modern research ideal. Diversity, multiculturalism, and constructivism are ideas that have failed to gain even a modest foothold in the natural and strong social sciences. That is because they are antithetical to the scientific ambitions of these disciplines and to their programs of research. Only in the humanities have these ideas attracted a significant following and been embraced as pedagogical values. The result has been to make the humanities appear even less respectable from the vantage point of those disciplines that have had the greatest success in meeting the demands of the research ideal—the principal source of authority and prestige in American higher education today. Today, the humanities are not merely in a crisis. They are in danger of becoming a laughingstock, both within the academy and outside it. Looking to build a new home for themselves, they have instead dug a hole and pitched themselves to its bottom.[3]

The civil rights movement of the 1950s and 1960s was the most important social movement in America in the twentieth century. Its aims were profoundly just and drew for their support on the best in America's legal and political traditions. The first goal of the movement was formal equality before the law. But the achievement of full racial justice demanded a significant redistribution of resources as well. African-Americans had suffered under a regime in which they received far less than their fair share of the basic goods of life. This was a historical injustice that could be repaired only by a compensatory transfer of wealth and opportunities large enough to give the victims of discrimination the resources they needed to take meaningful advantage of their newly won legal protections. Given the importance of education to a person's economic and other prospects, it seemed obvious that any compensatory program of this kind must include a significant redistribution of educational opportunities. At the primary and secondary school levels, this was achieved through busing—the physical transfer of students from one school to another. At the college and university level, the principal instrument of redistribution was "affirmative action."[4]

Affirmative action means giving a preference to minority applicants in a school's admissions process—first and most emphatically to African-Americans and later, as the concept broadened, to other minority candidates as well. In its original conception, affirmative action was a backward-looking program whose aim was to repair the injustice done to victims of past discrimination. Early defenders of affirmative action reasonably argued that this could be done only by giving race a positive weight in admissions decisions to offset the negative weight it had had in the past.[5] But even if the moral legitimacy of such rebalancing seemed clear, a crucial legal question remained. Can a school legally justify its use of race-conscious criteria in the admission of students on the grounds that doing so is necessary to compensate for the racial injustices of the past? In 1978, in the celebrated case of *Regents of the University of California v. Bakke*, the Supreme Court of the United States said no. *Bakke* involved a challenge to the constitutionality of an affirmative action program at the medical school at the University of California, Davis, that reserved a number of places in each entering class for minority applicants. Writing for the Court, Justice Lewis Powell declared that past racial discrimination in the society at large is an insufficient basis for present discrimination based on race in an opposite, compensatory direction and concluded that the Davis program was unconstitutional.[6]

But in his opinion, Justice Powell suggested an acceptable alternative rationale for affirmative action. A scheme of racial preferences is constitutionally permissible, he said, if a school can show (as the University of California had not) that it contributes in a direct and important way to the school's educational program by fostering a diverse student body. This part of Powell's opinion pointed a way to save affirmative action programs—one that did not require a shift in their mechanics but only in their asserted justification. The key to the defense of affirmative action was no longer the idea of compensation for past wrongs. That idea had been ruled out of court. In its place, Powell's opinion forced colleges and universities to substitute the very different idea of diversity as a pedagogical value. To be legally allowable, affirmative action would henceforth have to be linked not to the external goal of promoting racial justice, but to a school's own internal objectives—to the creation of the best possible environment for teaching and learning. For the past quarter-century, the defense of affirmative action has rested entirely on this latter idea, whose legitimacy was recently (if narrowly) reaffirmed by the Supreme Court in a case upholding the University of Michigan's use of a scoring system that gives minority applicants extra points in order to achieve a diverse student body and the educational benefits associated with it.[7]

The claim that diversity promotes learning is, up to a point, uncontroversial. Students surrounded only by others like themselves have a more limited and less challenging exposure to the variety of outlooks and experiences young people bring with them to college. They are more likely to be stimulated and unsettled in the company of others from different backgrounds. For many students, college offers the first opportunity for a sustained encounter with others whose formative experiences, family lives, and religious beliefs are sharply different from their own. This encounter itself has educational value. It plays an important role in the deepening of critical self-awareness and the widening of imaginative sympathy that are crucial elements of moral and intellectual growth.[8]

But this reasonable and innocuous proposition becomes less plausible and its consequences less benign when it is extended from the general culture of a school to the organized work of the class-room—when racial and other forms of diversity are used as criteria for the selection of topics and texts and when they become an important factor in defining the purpose of teaching itself.

The argument for doing this is by now familiar. It starts from the premise that many disciplines call for interpretive judgments that are peculiarly responsive to a person's interests and values. History and literature are good examples. Different people approach these subjects from different points of view, depending on what is of interest and value to them. Honesty requires that these differences be acknowledged, not suppressed, and learning proceeds best in an environment in which they are brought out and the conflicts among them made clear. Among the determinants that shape a person's interpretive judgments, race plays a particularly powerful role, at least in America where race has long been a factor of prime importance in social, political, and cultural life. Gender and ethnicity are factors of near-equal importance. Given the pedagogical value of interpretive diversity and the particularly important role that race, gender, and ethnicity play in the formation of a person's approach to a wide range of interpretive questions, it is educationally appropriate, indeed imperative, that in fields like history and literature teaching materials be chosen, themes and topics selected, and methods of instruction employed with an eye to focusing attention on the ways in which these factors condition a person's interests and values and hence interpretive point of view—whether the person be the author of a text, a participant in a historical event, or a critic attempting to make sense of either.[9]

This argument has not been received with much enthusiasm in the natural and strong social sciences, however. Teachers of physics and economics do not, of course, reject the notion that theirs are interpretive disciplines too. Nor do they deny that competing interpretations in their fields are importantly shaped by a person's value judgments (for example, regarding the choice of topics deemed worthy of study).[10] But they assume that interpretive disputes within their disciplines should be judged from an impersonal point of view that every physicist or economist is able to adopt. And they further assume that a teacher's or student's judgments regarding these disputes are not so closely linked to immutable personal characteristics, like race or gender, that they cannot be revised or overcome in light of considerations that appear compelling from this impersonal perspective. Disciplines like physics and economics reject the assumption of a strong connection—indeed, of any meaningful connection at all—between the interpretive judgments of those in these fields and their race or gender, and therefore reject the pedagogical recommendation that texts be chosen and teaching methods designed for the very purpose of bringing this connection to light, a proposal at war with their own deepest disciplinary ideals.

It is only in the humanities that the connection between interpretation, on the one hand, and race and gender on the other, has been enthusiastically endorsed as a principle of classroom instruction. That this is true as a matter of fact can hardly be doubted. A casual survey of course offerings in the humanities departments of most American colleges and universities today is likely to turn up a fair number whose design reflects the belief that interpretive judgments are strongly shaped by race and gender and that exposing the connection between them is an educational goal of the first importance.[11] But the reason for this is less obvious. Why are courses based on this assumption found with such frequency in the humanities and rarely if at all in the natural and strong social sciences? One answer is a negative one: the absence in the humanities of a compelling ideal of impersonal truth comparable to the one that exists in these other fields and which makes it implausible and inappropriate to suggest that the interpretive judgments of those in these fields are a function of race and gender. But there is another explanation that reflects the special insecurity of the humanities regarding their position in the modern research university and their need to define for themselves some new and useful and distinctive role to fill.

When the Supreme Court declared that racial preferences would henceforth have to be justified on the grounds that they contribute to the advancement of a school's internal educational goals, it gave colleges and universities a powerful incentive to emphasize the link between racial diversity, on the one hand, and the enterprise of teaching and learning on the other. This can be done in a general way by pointing out the broad educational advantages of a diverse student body—the informal opportunities that diversity affords for widening each student's horizon of experience and belief. But for the defense of affirmative action to be as strong as possible, it is strategically useful to show that racial (and eventually, gender and ethnic) diversity contribute to the educational process not only in the unstructured interactions of informal student life, in the dining hall and dormitory, but in the classroom too, where teaching and learning occur in their most explicit and organized form—to establish a connection between racial diversity and classroom instruction and thereby anchor the defense of affirmative action in the very heart of a school's instructional program.

Most college and university administrators, and most teachers too, have felt the need to preserve their schools' programs of affirmative action. They have recognized the remedial justice of these programs and their value in creating opportunities for African-Americans and other historically disadvantaged groups. And given the need to justify affirmative action in the terms the Supreme Court made mandatory in the *Bakke* case, most teachers and administrators have seen the forensic advantage of establishing a strong link between diversity and the instructional work of the classroom. For this places the need for diversity at the point where a school's educational responsibilities are most deliberately focused and its judgments regarding the best ways of meeting them most deserving of judicial respect. But the natural and social sciences cannot acknowledge this link without compromising their own disciplinary ideals. In the humanities, the danger is less apparent. Of all the disciplines, the humanities are therefore in the best position to argue that racial diversity is essential to the work of the classroom and hence to supply in its strongest and least assailable form the connection that Justice Powell's conception of affirmative action demands. They are in fact the only disciplines in a position to endorse the idea of racial diversity as a pedagogical value. The diversity defense, which the Supreme Court in 1978 made the only acceptable justification for affirmative action, thus opened an opportunity for the humanities to reclaim a special place for themselves in the academy. It enabled teachers in the humanities to see themselves as making a distinctive and valued contribution to the work of higher education by protecting their schools' programs of affirmative action in the most effective way possible—something their colleagues in the natural and social sciences were prevented by their own ideals from doing. It helped humanities teachers view themselves as their schools' leading agents in the morally and politically inspiring campaign to correct a great historical wrong and in this way offered, or appeared to offer, an ennobling way out of the directionlessness and self-doubt that overtook their disciplines when they abandoned the tradition of secular humanism and drew themselves into the orbit of the research ideal.

But however compelling the moral and political aims of affirmative action, and however important to its legal defense the claim that in the humanities, at least, interpretive judgments are intimately linked to race and gender, the endorsement of this claim has not strengthened the humanities but weakened them instead. It has compromised their central educational values. And it has widened, not closed, the gap of authority that separates the humanities from the natural and social sciences, where this same idea has been decisively rejected.

The interests and values we have as adults, and the interpretive judgments that flow from them, are importantly shaped by our early experiences. What we care about as grown-ups is to a considerable extent a function of where and how and by whom we were brought up. But we are not prisoners of our upbringings. To varying degrees we are able, as adults, to gain some measure of detachment from the experiences of childhood and to assess them with a critical eye—to reflect on the interests and values that we have inherited from our early lives and to ask whether, on reflection, we wish to continue to endorse them.

Something like this is what a liberal arts education, and the humanities in particular, have always promised. The humanities give young people the opportunity and encouragement to put themselves—their values and commitments—into a critical perspective. They help students gain some distance, incomplete though it must be, on their younger selves and to get some greater traction in the enterprise of living the lives they mean to live and not just those in which they happen by accident to find themselves. No one ever perfectly or permanently achieves a critical perspective of this kind. But its relative enlargement defines the freedom (the "liberation") that a liberal education promises, and the ability of the humanities to help students toward this goal has traditionally been an important source of their authority.

The more our interests and values are assumed to reflect immutable characteristics we inherit at birth, however, the less meaningful the pursuit of this freedom is likely to seem. For if our interests and values are deeply shaped by factors over which we have no control and that can never be changed, the prospect of gaining the independence we need to critically assess them, let alone revise or reject them, is no more realistic than that of jumping over one's shadow. The factors that influence our early experiences fall along a spectrum of mutability. Some are more easily changed than others. How we are brought up is a function, in part, of where we are brought up. As adults, we can choose to live elsewhere. We can even choose to abandon the religion in which we were raised for another or none at all, though this often involves emotional and spiritual turmoil. But some characteristics are fixed at birth and can be changed only with the greatest difficulty, if at all. They lie toward the far end of the spectrum of mutability. Race and gender are characteristics of this kind. Our power to alter or undo them is at a minimum, compared with other characteristics like location, religion, and class. Emphasizing their influence on our interests and values therefore inevitably discourages the hope that with effort one can gain a meaningful degree of independence from these interests and values themselves and be in a position to freely endorse, revise, or reject them. For if my most fundamental attitudes are conditioned by my race and gender, so that I cannot help but see and judge the world from the vantage point they immutably fix, how can I ever hope to escape their orbit, subject these attitudes to critical review, and set myself the goal of living in some way other than the one they prescribe? The more deeply and rigidly my judgments are shaped by race and gender, the more the very idea of pursuing this goal is likely to seem an illusion.

The belief that diversity is a pedagogical value starts with race and with the claim that race is an important and appropriate criterion for the selection of texts and teaching methods. By endorsing this claim the humanities help to strengthen the legal and political case for affirmative action. But their enthusiastic affirmation of a deep connection between judgment and race—the least mutable, perhaps, of all our characteristics—at the same time undermines the pursuit of the intellectual and moral freedom which the humanities once made it their special business to promote. It subjects the goal of self-criticism to tighter restrictions and makes exhortations to reach it less credible. It strengthens the cynical and despairing belief that we can never see the world from any point of view but the one permanently fixed by our racial identities or escape the gravitational pull of the interests and values these create. The claim that gender should play an important role in deciding what and how to teach has a similarly dispiriting effect, for it too is nearly immutable. And even the idea that ethnicity should play such a role tends in the same direction. Ethnic identity is undoubtedly more fluid and changeable than either race or gender. But to the extent that a person's ethnicity is conceived in terms conditioned by these other factors—as being nearly as deep and fixed as they—even it is likely to seem a discouragingly high barrier to the achievement of the freedom the humanities promise.[12]

These effects are often balanced or outweighed by forces pressing in the opposite direction. Diversity is only one factor that today exercises an influence on the way the humanities are taught. Other, more traditional values limit its reach. But at the margin, other things equal, the effect of emphasizing the influence of race and gender on a person's interests and values is to discourage the ambition to gain some critical distance on them. For the more one stresses the depth and pervasiveness of this influence, the more difficult it becomes to believe that one can ever attain a critical perspective of this sort and the harder to sustain the ambition to reach it. The marginal effect of the endorsement of diversity as a pedagogical value is therefore to make this goal more difficult *even to aspire* to attain and by doing so to further compromise the standing of the humanities, whose own special authority has traditionally been tied to the belief that the enhancement of one's self-critical powers, and of the freedom they represent, is a goal that is both worthy and attainable.

The pursuit of this goal has traditionally been described as the search for an individual identity of one's own. But the more students are convinced of the futility of attempting to overcome   the influence of their membership in groups that determine their values and from which they can never escape, the more likely they are to adopt a goal of a different kind. The more likely they are to see themselves as representatives of these groups and to define their task as that of being responsible advocates for them. When individuals exchange views as individuals, they converse. Their exchange is characterized by the flexibility that is the hallmark of every real conversation. This is true even if their views are different or antagonistic. By contrast, when two people meet as representatives, they speak not on behalf of themselves but of the groups to which they belong. It is to the group, not to their interlocutor or to the conversation in which they are engaged, that their loyalty is owed. Betrayal no longer means faithlessness to oneself and to the conversation but to the group on whose behalf one speaks. The individuals exchanging views cease to be individuals, and their exchange ceases to be a conversation. Its personal significance for them declines and its political importance as a negotiation increases.

The more a classroom resembles a gathering of delegates speaking on behalf of the groups they represent, the less congenial a place it becomes in which to explore questions of a personally meaningful kind including, above all, the question of what ultimately matters in life and why. In such a classroom, students encounter each other not as individuals but as spokespersons instead. They accept or reject their teachers as role models more on account of the group to which they belong and less because of their individual qualities of character and intellect. And the works they study are regarded more as statements of group membership than as the creations of men and women with viewpoints uniquely their own—with the depressing result that great works that have been unjustly neglected on account of a shameful discrimination against their creators are finally given their due, but only on the condition that they too be treated as representatives, like the students and teacher in the classroom, and not as individuals whose greatness lies in the singularity of their achievement.

For a classroom to be a productive environment in which to approach the question of what living is for, the students in the class must be personally engaged in the conversation. They must feel free to participate as individuals and not merely as delegates whose first responsibility is to the groups they represent. To the extent they are encouraged to see themselves as representatives instead, the first-personal question of life's meaning is likely to seem less relevant and even, perhaps, self-indulgent. At the same time, they must be open to the possibility that their own ideas about the relative appeal of the different values around which a human life can be arranged may be changed by their encounter with the ideas of their classmates. And for that to be possible, they must view themselves as participants in a shared enquiry, facing the same eternal questions that every human being confronts and struggling together to meet them. These may seem like contradictory requirements—personal engagement and human solidarity. But they represent, in fact, the two sides of a single experience, for it is only on the basis of their common humanity that students from different backgrounds, racial and otherwise, can ever discover or create their shared investment in the intensely personal question of what gives life its purpose and value. The belief that a person's deepest interests and values are irrevocably fixed by immutable characteristics like race and gender, and that the purpose of classroom instruction is to bring this connection to light, undermines both of these conditions at once. It makes it more difficult for students to venture the personal engagement that any serious conversation about the meaning of life demands by encouraging them to adopt the less challenging posture of representatives instead. And at the same time it makes it harder for students to accept the notion of a common human solidarity that transcends the experience of the particular group to which they happen by fate to belong, whose own more limited life forms a horizon beyond which they can never in any meaningful sense aspire to reach.

The argument that supports the use of racial and other forms of diversity as a principle of classroom instruction thus simultaneously undermines both the spirit of personal engagement and the sense of common humanity on which the vitality of the classroom as a forum for the exploration of the question of the meaning of life depends. It does not destroy these conditions completely. No argument has the power to do that. But its tendency is to make them harder to establish and sustain.

Only the humanities have embraced this argument with any warmth. Only they have affirmed that racial and gender diversity is a pedagogical value. The natural and strong social sciences reject this claim completely. But these latter disciplines also make no pretense of addressing the question of what living is for. It is for them no longer a question of any importance. It falls outside their jurisdiction; their own methods demand they ignore it. The sad result of the humanities' use of racial and gender diversity as a criterion for the selection of texts and teaching methods has therefore been to make it harder to pursue the question of life's meaning in the only disciplines in which there is still any chance of asking it.

Secular humanism of course recognized the value of diversity too. It celebrated the plurality of the main forms of human fulfillment and insisted that these can never be ranked in a hierarchy of comparative worth. But the diversity that secular humanism endorsed was a deeper and more challenging one than the shallow version that today's politically and morally inspired defenders of the idea have in view. For the diversity they embrace (of race, gender, and ethnicity) rests implicitly on attitudes and values that everyone is expected to share.

Broadly speaking, these are the values of political liberalism. Today's defenders of diversity assume that, on a range of issues, the interpretive judgments of their students will differ according to their race, gender, and ethnicity. But at the same time they expect their students to share a commitment to the values of political liberalism that support the ideal of racial justice which in turn motivates the programs of affirmative action, to whose defense the contemporary concept of diversity itself is so important. In the humanities today, these values form the bedrock of what solidarity students experience. For however large the differences among their variously conditioned points of view, the legal and moral justification of the educational program in which they are engaged (whose very purpose is to bring these differences to light) presupposes an acceptance of the values of political liberalism and above all of the vigorous and expansive interpretation of equality that lies at its core. Because it rests on these values, the claim that diversity of race and gender should be an organizing principle of classroom instruction itself enforces, openly or covertly, an allegiance to them and to the community of moral and political commitment they represent.

These values may be the best—the fairest and most durable—foundation on which to build a political community. I believe they are. A legal and cultural environment marked by the freedoms and protections that political liberalism affords may be the setting in which institutions of higher education are most likely to flourish. I think it is. But when a presumptive commitment to the values of political liberalism begins to constrain the exploration of the personal question of life's meaning—when the expectation that everyone shares these values begins to place implicit limits on the alternatives that may be considered and how seriously they are to be taken—the enterprise itself loses much of its significance for the students involved and their teachers lose their authority to lead it.

Whatever fails to accord with the values of political liberalism fits uncomfortably within the range of possibilities that the contemporary conception of diversity permits students to acknowledge as serious contenders in the search for an answer to the first-personal question of what living is for. The political philosophies of Plato and Aristotle, with their easy acceptance of the natural inequality of human beings, offend these values at every turn.[13] Likewise, the theological tradition that runs from Augustine to Calvin, with its insistence on church authority and its doctrines of sin and grace. And even much of poetry (all of it, if we believe what William Hazlitt says in his essay on Shakespeare's *Coriolanus*) is motivated by an anti-egalitarian love of beauty and power.[14] All of these ideas and experiences are suspect from the standpoint of the liberal values from which the contemporary ideal of diversity takes its start. None represents the "right" kind of diversity. None fits within the range of acceptable alternatives. None is to be taken in a really serious way, as a live option in the search for an answer to the question of the meaning of life. None is suitable as a basis for political life, and hence—here is the crucial step—none is suitable (respectable, acceptable, honorable) as a basis for personal life either. None provides the least justification for the personal affirmation of illiberal values in a liberal republic. None, in the end, can perform any useful function other than as an example of what to avoid, as an illustration of the confused and intolerant views of those who had the misfortune to be born before the dawning of the light. All of them must be written down, or off, and excluded from serious consideration when exploring the possibilities for answering the question of life's purpose and value in a really serious and responsible way.

By comparison with the diversity that secular humanism affirmed, today's diversity is so limited that one might with justification call it a sham diversity, whose real goal is the promotion of a moral and spiritual uniformity instead. Secular humanism allowed for a much wider palette of possibilities. It had room for the soldier who values honor above equality, for the poet who believes that beauty is more important than justice, for the thinker who regards with disinterest or contempt the concerns of political life—as well as for the moral crusader devoted to liberal values. It had room for Plato's elitism and Augustine's pessimism as well as for more democratic and cheerier views of life. Much of this—most of it, in fact—must be ruled out as archaic or unworthy or worse by those who define the idea of diversity in terms of race, gender, and ethnicity, and who give an overwhelming priority to the system of moral and political values that underlie the ideal of reparative justice for whose sake this conception of diversity has been promoted as a pedagogical norm.

This new conception of diversity may seem to some an improved version of the older one that secular humanism endorsed, which from their perspective looks limited on account of its failure to acknowledge the importance of race and gender in the formation of our values and beliefs. But the politically and legally inspired conception of diversity that has been so influential in the humanities during the past forty years has not produced a widening of the range of human possibilities that may legitimately be considered in reflecting on the question of how one should live. It has produced a contraction instead. The presumption of allegiance to the values of political liberalism that underlie and support the contemporary understanding of diversity in the humanities has reduced the idea of humanity itself to a liberal egalitarian point. Alternative conceptions of value and the ways of life devoted to them have of course not disappeared as subjects of discussion in the humanities departments of our colleges and universities. But they are no longer taken seriously as conceptions one might embrace in one's own life. They are there mainly as examples of how not to live or think. In personal terms—the only terms in which the question of life's meaning can ever be framed— the diversity that today prevails in our humanities classrooms is anemic and misleading. For despite the claim of its defenders to have widened the horizon of student understanding by acquainting them with values and experiences that were previously unnoticed or suppressed, the conception of racial and gender diversity that is so enthusiastically embraced by so many humanities teachers today is in reality driven by an oppressive uniformity of moral purpose from whose perspective the more robust diversity of secular humanism can only seem morally dubious.

Of course, if one starts with the assumption that there is a single right answer to the question of what living is for and that students can be brought to see it, the nature and source of the humanities' authority will be clear. This was the premise on which the program of the antebellum college was based. But secular humanism rejected this assumption and sought to construct an organized approach to the question of life's meaning on non-dogmatic foundations. It recognized the values of plurality, freedom, and choice and claimed for the humanities a new source of authority, the only one available to them so long as we continue to acknowledge these values. By dramatically reducing the range of respectable alternatives that students may consider as personal templates for living, the identification of diversity with race and gender has covertly restored the premise on which antebellum education was founded— the assumption of a single right way of living. It has brought us back full circle to the spirit of moral uniformity with which American higher education began. But the conformist spirit of the antebellum college cannot be restored. Our world is too deeply committed to the values of pluralism and choice for that. We live, and want to live, in a world shaped by these values, and the authority of the humanities today depends on the genuineness of the respect they accord them. The conception of diversity that now enforces a chilling sameness of opinion in many humanities classrooms gives lip service to these values. But it fails to honor them in their deepest and most challenging form. It fails to take them seriously, substituting for a real and disturbing diversity a superficial one whose implicit demand is that everyone think and judge alike. And by doing so it undermines the authority of those who defend the contemporary ideal of diversity, whose own dogmatism about good and bad values, good and bad attitudes, good and bad ways of living, is as out of keeping with the pluralism of our age as the dogmatism of the old-time college.

The authority of humanities teachers to lead their students in an exploration of the question of what living is for is a function of how seriously they take this question themselves. When its investigation is limited to those personal ideals that meet the requirements of political liberalism, the enquiry becomes less demanding. Its urgency and importance and danger and power to change one's life all decrease. It becomes a caricature of a real enquiry. And when this happens, those who are leading it lose their authority to do so. They become the moderators of a conversation in which little of personal consequence is at stake—that is no longer a real conversation at all. The humanities' equation of diversity with race and gender has made the political morality that undergirds it a mandatory premise of the enquiry into the personal meaning of life. It has contracted the range of this enquiry and dramatically reduced its stakes. It has anesthetized the question at its heart and cut teachers of the humanities off from the only source of authority they have to address it in a culture as resolutely pluralistic as ours.

One particularly important expression of this narrowing of outlook is the special weight that today's politically motivated conception of diversity assigns the judgments of the victims of injustice.

Programs of affirmative action rest on the principle of compensatory justice. They start from the morally (and sometimes legally) compelling idea that the victims of injustice should be compensated for their suffering, that those who have mistreated them should restore the balance of justice by making a compensatory payment of some kind. From the vantage point of compensatory justice, victims and victimizers do not stand on the same plane. There is a moral asymmetry between them, and the purpose of the transfer contemplated by every program of compensation is to put the parties back into a more balanced relation—which can only be done by taking something from the victimizers (money, opportunities, etc.) and giving it to their victims.[15]

This basic idea has tremendous force as a principle of moral and legal reasoning. But when it is extended to the classroom and given a pedagogical interpretation—when it is claimed that the insights and perceptions of the victims of injustice have a greater claim to respect than those of their victimizers, that they reflect the realities of the world more accurately than the judgments of their oppressors and hence are truer in some fundamental sense—the result is a contraction of the range of points of view that students are encouraged (or even allowed) to entertain in a serious way. When the moral asymmetry implied by every program of affirmative action is given an epistemic interpretation of this kind, the result is a restriction of diversity.

The idea that the victims of injustice see the world more deeply and clearly than their oppressors is not, of course, a new one. It is a central theme in the prophetic books of the Hebrew Bible and in the Christian gospels. The prophet who sides with the poor and oppressed, the forgotten and abused, with those who lack power and stand outside the circle of worldly authority and respect, sees things from a vantage point that those within this circle cannot reach.[16] For they—the possessors of authority and power—have an interest in the system of oppression from which they benefit that blinds them to it. They cannot see it because they are part of it. But the prophet and his followers are not, and because they are not their eyes are open to things the rich and powerful and contented of the world can never comprehend, things their own privilege prevents them from grasping.

This is a deep and recurrent theme in the sacred writings of Jews and Christians alike, and one of the cornerstones of the Western literary and philosophical tradition. It is an idea that has profound echoes even in our own secular age—in Marx's argument, for example, that among the classes of the capitalist order the proletariat enjoys a privileged position not just in a moral but in an epistemic sense as well, that the structure of the capitalist system can be grasped as a whole only when seen from the perspective of the class on whose exploitation it depends.[17] Perhaps one can even hear an echo of this idea in Freud's insistence on the revelatory power of the most marginal and seemingly insignificant bits of human experience, of slips of the tongue and dreams, which from the privileged position of waking life we tend to dismiss as nonsense.[18] The notion that those who stand outside the established order, with its wealth and privilege and conventional habits of thought, enjoy a special advantage so far as its understanding is concerned, is one of the oldest and most compelling ideas of Western civilization.

But there is a competing and equally venerable idea that must also be given its due in any

open-minded encounter with the traditions of
the West. This is the idea that privilege and good
fortune enable sound judgment rather than
compromise it—that wealth, education, and
other advantages typically help the person who
has them to develop his spirit and mind more
fully and freely. The person who lacks these
advantages is likely, on this view, to be compromised by his lack of them, to be stunted or
deformed intellectually and culturally, so that
however sympathetic we may be to his plight,
we ought not take his judgments as a benchmark of accuracy or wisdom. It is the person of
well-being whose judgments should be our standard instead—the person of comfortable circumstances who has had the leisure to grow into a
rounded, healthy human being. On this view,
ignorance, poverty, and powerlessness are epistemic liabilities, not advantages, even when they
are the products of a political or legal system we
believe to be unjust. This idea plays an important role in Aristotle's account of ethical life, and
in the writings of others who follow his lead.[19]
Nietzsche gives it a particularly dramatic interpretation and emphasizes its conflict with the
epistemic priority that Judaism and Christianity
assign the judgments and values of victims.[20]

The point is not that one or the other of
these is right—that the victims of injustice are
either enlightened or disabled by their exclusion from privilege and power. The point is
that *both* of these ideas are deeply embedded

in the tradition of Western thought, *both* have had articulate champions, *both* retain their plausibility and appeal today, and *neither* can be neglected by any son or daughter of the West who hopes to comprehend the tangled and conflicting skein of beliefs that lie at the heart of the civilization to which he or she is heir.

To say that the conflict between these two ideas is an aspect of the age-old conflict between Athens and Jerusalem is a simplification, but not far off.[21] That conflict is still alive. Indeed, it is hard to imagine how it could ever be settled. To understand the civilization of the West, to become its inhabitant in some personally meaningful sense, one must make this conflict one's own. One must confront it, grapple with it, and make of its competing visions of humanity what one can. Among the diversities of conviction and experience that a person needs to confront in the search for an answer to the question of what living is for, none, perhaps, is more urgent than this.

But today one of these two views has such an overriding presence in the humanities and enjoys so large an authority that its competitor has nearly disappeared from view. The moral and legal priority of the victim, which affirmative action recognizes and properly respects, has been converted in today's classroom into an epistemic priority that always gives decisively greater weight to the judgments of those who can credibly claim to represent the point of view of a group that has been unjustly excluded from wealth and power. The judgments of students who cannot make this claim labor under a disadvantage. They lack the special standing that only the judgments of victims enjoy. Openly to challenge this presumption often requires personal courage in an environment as deeply shaped by the equation of racial justice with epistemic authority as many humanities classrooms now are. And the books and authors who challenge this presumption labor under the same disability too.

To the extent that this equation rules out or renders illegitimate other points of view—and in particular the old Aristotlean association of good judgment with privilege and well-being—it leaves a narrower range of fundamental possibilities to be considered. In place of the real and disturbing diversity that secular humanism acknowledged, it substitutes a superficial diversity, whose own asserted openness to previously excluded points of view conceals the reduction in perspectives it actually promotes and the smothering moral uniformity it encourages. The result is a classroom where the oldest and deepest tensions of Western civilization are no longer felt, where they are no longer allowed to be felt—a classroom in which any word that might give offense to the historical victims of injustice by challenging the epistemic priority of their judgments and perceptions is experienced as a further injustice, as yet another "silencing" of victims who have already been forced to be silent too long. The result is a classroom where everyone, teachers and students alike, feels compelled to tiptoe on eggshells for fear of giving offense, an intellectually and spiritually frozen classroom in which the prospect of honest and passionate debate over matters of deep importance—about which disagreements are bound to be deep too—becomes ever more remote, all under the guise of promoting a more honest confrontation with the facts of racism, sexism, and the like.

However understandable and even admirable the political and moral motives that lie behind the contemporary understanding of diversity, it has compromised the humanities and made them a less promising medium for the exploration of the question of what living is for. The question is perennial and has lost none of its intensity. Today's college and university students—white, black, Hispanic, Asian, male, female—are as gripped by it as students have ever been. But they can no longer look to the humanities for help in answering it. For these have become cautious and fearful fields under the deforming pressure of a great moral ambition that has been forced, by accident of law, into a destructive educational theory.

✦

Multiculturalism affirms the value of different cultures, traditions, and civilizations, especially of those other than the European West. In many ways, it represents the principle of diversity on a global scale. One strong motive for multiculturalism is the belief that the value of Western ideas and institutions has often been overstated, and that their overstatement has helped to legitimate a wide range of unjust and exploitative practices, especially during the centuries of Western colonial expansion: that it has been used to put a good face on behavior driven by racism, xenophobia, and greed. Many therefore regard the idea of multiculturalism as a needed corrective that contributes to a program of moral and political reform by enhancing the dignity and cultural worth of peoples and traditions abused during the period of Western expansion. Like the concept of diversity, the idea of multiculturalism is motivated in significant part by political concerns and functions as an instrument of corrective justice, though the correction it seeks is mainly one of beliefs and values.

Like the concept of diversity, the idea of multiculturalism also has both a benign formulation that few would challenge and a more destructive version. The benign conception starts from the proposition that in today's world, where a variety of economic, technological, and political factors are drawing the peoples of the planet into ever closer contact (a phenomenon usually described as "globalization"), some understanding and appreciation of non-Western cultures is imperative for any young person who hopes to be able to act in this world in an intelligent and responsible fashion. For Westerners, appreciation of this sort was once a luxury—the province of specialists and connoisseurs. Today, it is a necessity. We are all, increasingly, citizens of the planet, confronted with questions and burdened with responsibilities that go far beyond our membership in this or that national community and our accidental, natal allegiance to a particular culture or tradition. Many who hold this view maintain that the education of every undergraduate in America today ideally ought to include a serious and sustained exposure to the art, literature, and historical experience of one or more of the world's non-Western civilizations—of China, for example, or India or Japan or Islam, or the civilizations of South and Central America. Every thoughtful college and university teacher will see the good sense in this proposal, which represents a necessary step toward enlightened and responsible membership in the ecumenical community we now inhabit.[22]

But there is a less innocuous version of multiculturalism which asserts that the ideas and institutions of the West, and the works that embody them, have no more value than those of other, non-Western civilizations. This adds to the recognition of the achievements of these other civilizations an insistence on their moral and intellectual parity. That is the simple, if radical, proposition from which the second, destructive version of multiculturalism starts, and for those who embrace it the denial of its truth can only be the result of a kind of myopia—the natural, if regrettable, tendency of human beings to give greater value to what is near merely because it is familiar and reassuring. For defenders of the stronger version of multiculturalism, this myopia is both an epistemic error and a moral failing. The name they give it is "Eurocentrism," and the remedy they recommend is to become less admiring of the achievements of the West and to cultivate the habit of believing in the equal worth of other civilizations—to lose one's allegiance to the West and replace it with a more expansive allegiance to humanity at large, or the global community of peoples and cultures, or the victims of Western exploitation.[23]

This second version of multiculturalism is driven by a hostility to the ideas and institutions of the West that itself has many sources— the Marxist assault on liberal democratic practices and on the inequalities of wealth and talent that Western societies allow, which communist sympathizers in the West endorsed and that continues to have a moral resonance even today, after the collapse of the Soviet Union and the disaccreditation of the communist movement; the anti-colonial attack on Western values, in the writings of Frantz Fanon and others, that converted the Marxist critique of capitalistic economic exploitation into a cultural and psychological critique of imperial "identity domination"; and the deepening, and partly justified, skepticism about the wisdom and legitimacy of the projection of American power which the Vietnam War provoked and that has shadowed American foreign policy ever since.[24] Together these have encouraged a suspicion of the West, and an antagonism to its values, that has been a powerful force in our colleges and universities for the past several decades. They are the political source of the intellectual outlook expressed by the stronger version of multiculturalism. This is not an outlook that has been embraced with the same enthusiasm in all disciplines, however. Only in the humanities has the politically inspired belief in the equality of Western and non-Western cultures been adopted as a pedagogical principle and made the basis for a range of educational judgments, including the hiring of faculty and the design of courses and curricula. Only in the humanities has the anti-Western animus which these judgments reflect been translated into educational practice, further degrading their authority by undermining values central to the integrity and purpose of the humanities themselves.

This is true, first, with respect to what might be called the humanities' "conversational" values.

The works of non-Western civilizations are lasting and great; only an ignorant fool would deny this. But except occasionally and peripherally, they have not been a part of the conversation that constitutes the civilization of the West.[25] Conversation is a metaphor but it points to something real—to the fact that the great works of Western civilization address each other in complementary and quarrelsome ways. Philo and Augustine grapple with Plato. Hobbes assaults Aristotle. Shakespeare confronts Machiavelli. Spinoza corrects Descartes. Kant answers Hume, Paine condemns Burke, Eliot recalls Dante, Brunelleschi studies the Pantheon, and so on without end. The works and ideas of the West's writers and artists are internally connected. They refer to each other, commending, correcting, disapproving, and building on the works of those who have gone before. It is this internally continuous conversation that the humanities have traditionally studied. By contrast, the works of the world's great civilizations can, with few exceptions, be gathered together only in an external fashion. Each of these civilizations has the same internal connectedness that characterizes that of the West. But the works and ideas of different civilizations can for the most part only be related externally, by setting them up as exhibits for an observer to admire. If they are to be internally connected, if there is to be a conversation among them, it is one the

observer himself must begin, for the works
themselves are not already conversing. They
belong—to extend the metaphor one step
further—to different worlds of speech, each
internally connected but, except in rare and
interesting cases, only externally linked to the
others. If there is to be a conversation in which
these great works meet, and begin to quarrel
or agree, it must be a conversation that the
observer, who surveys them all, creates. It falls
to the observer to start the conversation since
it is not already underway.

Some will say that this is just the point of
multiculturalism: to get this conversation going.
They will emphasize the moral and political
importance of starting such a conversation in
a world that is growing more interconnected
each day. And they will stress that a real conversation cannot begin except on the premise of equality, on the assumption that all the
voices in it, and all the works through which
they speak, are of equal value, and that the
presumed superiority of one (the voice of the
West) is a sure conversation-killer.

But this superficially attractive view has
serious liabilities that its defenders overlook.
First, it underestimates the difficulties of starting a meaningful conversation of the kind they
recommend, for this requires a deep and sympathetic knowledge of all (or at least several)
of the world's great civilizations as well as an
ability to frame questions that link their works

in a conversationally productive way. If these difficulties are not acknowledged, the conversation that results is likely to be a shallow syncretism that never gets beyond the serial and disconnected admiration most museum goers express as they move from one exhibit to the next.

More important, its proponents fail to acknowledge the moral significance of what is lost in the seemingly unobjectionable effort to establish a conversation among the world's cultures and peoples. For something of significance *is* lost, and that is the nuturance of a responsible connection to the past, which comes only with the experience of being brought into a conversation not of one's own making. To have the freedom to begin a conversation from scratch, to create the conversational links among works and ideas that are otherwise only externally related, is to be unconstrained by the limits imposed on those who enter a conversation already underway. It is to be free of the limitations of the past and of the gravitational pull these exert. It is to be in a weightless orbit of one's own. To some, perhaps, this may sound appealing. It may seem a kind of liberation or escape, and if the past from which one was escaping were truly dictatorial, that might be the case. But the past which the conversation of the West conserves and carries forward is hardly dictatorial. It is constraining to be sure. Those who enter it are not free to say or think whatever they wish. They are constrained to respond to what has been said and thought before. But the response which the conversation invites is not one of blind obedience. The conversation of the West invites a free and critical response to the inheritance it conveys. It insists that the past be studied and given the weight it deserves, but demands that one struggle to reimagine its claims in fresh and better ways, in a conversation that is permanently open. To be free of the restrictions one inherits when one joins an ongoing conversation of this kind is not freedom but the illusion of freedom. It is, in fact, a form of irresponsibility, for to think that even with the best of intentions one can create on one's own, with the help of one's contemporaries, a new conversation that will be an adequate substitute for this older one, with all its richness and depth and accumulated links and connections, is to arrogate to oneself immense and immodest powers. It is to cut oneself off from the responsibilities that come with an inheritance and the duty, as a steward, to conserve and improve it. It is to occupy a world that has been extended spatially to encompass the entire planet but flattened temporally to the present moment—a world cut off from the intimate and sobering connection to the past which the experience of being educated in an ongoing conversation, in contrast to the intoxicating experience of creating a new one, affirms as a leading value.

The declared motive for severing this connection is to intensify our sense of community with others, to enlarge the circle of those to whom we feel connected. But its actual effect is to increase one's sense of isolation. For the more independent one is of the past, the less constrained by the tone and substance of a conversation long underway, the closer one approaches a condition of perfect self-sufficiency that resembles nothing so much as that of a divine creator whose powers of invention are limitless and whose loneliness is complete. For a god, perhaps, such weightlessness and freedom are compatible with responsibility. But in the case of human beings they tend to destroy it. For us, responsibility always begins with a rootedness in the past, and the authority it exerts, even if our chief responsibility is to improve on this past in the best way that we can. The new conversation that an egalitarian multiculturalism would have us begin destroys this experience of rootedness. However confident its appeal to the notion of a larger, ecumenical responsibility, it is in truth the enemy of the spirit of responsibility our roots alone can nourish.

What I have just said does not, of course, tilt things in favor of the West. It only affirms the value of having roots in one ongoing conversation or another, and for that purpose any conversation that rises to the level of a civilization will do. There is nothing about the conversation of the West that gives it special value so far as the cultivation of roots is concerned.

It may perhaps be that for those born in the West, its civilization is more conveniently available. But it is certainly possible for a Westerner to adopt another culture or tradition as his or her own, to make its conversation his or her home, and to accept the constraints of its internal connections. The important thing is to be conversationally rooted, for that is crucial to the development of a sense of responsibility. If the strongly egalitarian form of multiculturalism which insists that all cultures and traditions stand on a par, the Western and non-Western alike, were meant merely to encourage such adoptive possibilities by reminding us that every culture provides an equally suitable medium for the growth of roots and that none is in this regard superior to any other—if this were all that multiculturalism affirmed, where, one might ask, is the harm in its passionate denial of the superiority of Western civilization, with its particular (and not always benign) values and institutions?

The harm lies in the disingenuousness of the claim and in the effect it has on the credibility of the disciplines that endorse it.

The emergent global civilization we inhabit today provides the motive for multiculturalism and gives it its plausibility. But while this civilization is respectful—or at least aspires to be respectful—of many different cultures and traditions, acknowledging their distinctive achievements in a spirit of admiring toleration, it does not, at its deepest and most important level, assign equal weight or value to them all. The ideas and institutions that have the greatest prestige in this new global civilization, the ones that have the greatest influence on the individuals and communities striving to join it and that determine most decisively the conditions of everyday life as its inhabitants experience them, from the *favelas* of Rio de Janeiro to the farms of Hunan Province to the suburbs of Los Angeles, are all of Western origin.

The ideals of individual freedom and toleration; of democratic government; of respect for the rights of minorities and for human rights generally; a reliance on markets as a mechanism for the organization of economic life and a recognition of the need for markets to be regulated by a supervenient political authority; a reliance, in the political realm, on the methods of bureaucratic administration, with its formal division of functions and legal separation of office from officeholder; an acceptance of the truths of modern science and the ubiquitous employment of its technological products: all these provide, in many parts of the world, the existing foundations of political, social, and economic life, and where they do not, they are viewed as aspirational goals toward which everyone has the strongest moral and material reasons to strive. To be openly opposed to any of these things is to be a reactionary, a zealot, an obscurantist who refuses to recognize the moral and intellectual authority of this ensemble of modern ideas and institutions and who (fruitlessly) plants his feet against their irresistible tide.

These ideas and practices form the pillars of the global civilization that is taking shape around us, and where they are not already in place, define the direction of reform. Together they condition our everyday practical experience of the world and serve as a normative guide to what is progressive and backward, developed and undeveloped, modern and pre- (or anti-) modern in the world today. No coherent program can be organized on any other basis. The acceptance of these ideas and practices is the hallmark of modernization, which is in turn the defining feature of globalization, and all of them, all of these distinctively modern ideas and institutions, are of Western origin. Globalization *is* modernization, and modernization *is* Westernization. That is perhaps the single most striking fact of life today—a fact of planetary salience for all the peoples of the earth.

This does not mean, of course, that every Western cultural habit, every Western taste, exerts, or should exert, the same irresistible pull as these more basic features of modernization. There is plenty of room within our global civilization for local differences of many sorts, and we have every reason to want them to be preserved and to learn, ourselves, to appreciate and enjoy them, even if only as spectators or (spiritual and cultural) tourists. But their preservation and enjoyment can themselves be secured only within a stable framework of political and economic institutions, and through the practice of a universal tolerance, that are themselves of Western origin.

Nor does it mean that even the most basic and irresistible features of the West are wholly benign. This is plainly not true, for example, of technology, which has a dark side too, in both practical and spiritual terms. But the campaign to contain technology, and to protect what it destroys, is one that itself can only be effectively conducted using other intellectual and moral resources of the West. To resist it from the outside in the name of other, non-Western traditions is a valiant but futile enterprise. Against the tide of technology, the native peoples of the world, whose reverence for the earth the West would do well to imitate, cannot maintain their footing. They are all destined to be swept away too. In this sense, even the fight against the West must be conducted on Western terms.[26]

Nor does it mean that the great generalities of free government and free enterprise, of constitutional security and human rights, admit of only one interpretation. Clearly, they admit of many. The implementation of each requires in every case a choice among alternatives. The constitutions of the world's political communities and the organization of their economies differ in interesting and important ways. But all these differences fall within a range defined by the acceptance of certain basic principles that constitute the permissible space of political and economic variance. And all of these principles, the ones that fix the terms of interpretive debate, are themselves of Western origin.

Nor does it mean that a person's many other identities must all be cancelled in favor of some single new one organized around Western values. We all have many identities. Most of us belong to a family, a linguistic and cultural community, a confessional group, a political association, and so on. We feel, to varying degrees, an allegiance to each and, to varying degrees, identify with them all. Our identities are complex mosaics of overlapping and sometimes conflicting commitments. The Lebanese writer Amin Maalouf describes himself as a Christian Lebanese, from an old and educated family, now living in Paris and writing in French.[27] Maalouf speaks of himself as a person with multiple identities, and his condition is hardly exceptional. The process of globalization has, if anything, made this even more obvious. A fantastic increase in physical mobility combined with the technological ability to maintain relations with others at a great

distance means that many of us today live with
an even more vivid sense of our multiple identities than was the case in the past. Globalization
is helping to make Maalouf's situation our common human condition. It does not produce, or
demand, the elimination of our other identities,
of those that set us apart from one another, and
their replacement by some new master identity based on cosmopolitan values we all share
in common. Quite the opposite: it produces, as
Maalouf and others have observed, a prolifera-
tion of identities and a complex of crosscutting
allegiances. But it does demand that, however
important these allegiances may be, we limit
their authority in our lives by acknowledging
that our relations to others—to all others—must
be governed by a universal respect for their
integrity as human beings. To our other identities, with their more restricted spheres of attachment, globalization adds our membership in an
ecuméne organized on the premise of a universal humanity that transcends all such attachments. And it demands that this last identity
be accorded a decisive primacy over the others
(familial, tribal, religious, even political) in the
sense that its requirements are acknowledged to
constrain theirs. Its primacy is not eliminative.
It does not require that these other identities be
forgotten or abolished. Its primacy is that of a
boundary which limits what may permissibly
be done within the field it defines. This much
globalization *does* demand, and the demand

in question is one that was first accepted as a basis for the organization of human relations on a large territorial scale in the modern West. The idea of tolerance finds support in many traditions, especially religious ones. But only in the modern West did it become—fitfully, hesitantly, but with increasing clarity and determination—an axiom of political life. And while to accept this axiom is not to repudiate one's other identities, it is to fix the limits of what may be done in their name and for their sake. It is, in this sense, to "put them in their place." That is the modest but revolutionary result which the process of Westernization has partly accomplished and, to the extent it has not, that remains an aspirational goal not only for inhabitants of the West but for humanity in general.

Nor, finally, does the process of Westernization mean the triumph of the West in any partisan sense. For though the ideas and practices that are the hallmark of globalization have their historical beginnings in the West, and have been extended to the rest of the world in part through the aggressive and exploitative expansion of Western power, their authority and influence derive ultimately not from the fact of their Western origin, but from their universal validity and applicability. So far as the authority of modern science is concerned, for example, its origin in the West is a purely contingent fact, a historical accident that has no bearing on the truth of modern science itself. That is a function of its commitment to reason and experimental verification, which men and women everywhere accept. The same is true of the ideas of democratic government and human rights. Their Western origins do not contribute one iota to their legitimacy. We acknowledge their authority not *because* they are Western. That has nothing to do with it. We acknowledge their authority because they express the universal moral and political aspirations of all humankind, and though the West has done some terrible things in the name of these aspirations, and has selfishly exploited their appeal, that is no reason to impeach their authority, which rests on transcendent foundations.

"A product of modern European civilization, studying any problem of universal history, is bound to ask himself to what combination of circumstances the fact should be attributed that in Western civilization, and in Western civilization only, cultural phenomena have appeared which (as we like to think) lie in a line of development having *universal* significance and validity."[28] This observation remains as true today as when Max Weber made it in 1920. It has been, we might say, the peculiar fate of Europe to be the homeland of a set of ideas and institutions whose universal validity (to use Weber's term) is no longer conditioned on anything peculiarly European. In that sense, it is not only appropriate but necessary to speak of the privileged position of Western civilization, understanding by this the unique place which the civilization that began in the West but now rests on universal moral and intellectual foundations occupies among the civilizations of the world. The ideas and institutions of the West, liberated from the accidental limits of their historical beginnings, have become the common possession of humanity.

They form the basis of today's planetary civilization, with its startling achievements, great hopes, and glaring failures.

If the strong version of multiculturalism denies this claim, it not only denies the most obvious and basic facts of life, as we experience them everyday, buying coffee, reading the newspaper, riding the bus, engaging in political debate, visiting the doctor. It also denies the ideals we espouse with the greatest strength and conviction—those of human rights and democracy, for example, and of scientific enquiry unfettered by ideological and religious constraints. Outside the classroom, we recognize these facts and endorse these ideals. If the embrace of a multiculturalism that insists on the equality of all the world's civilizations and that denies any claim to priority on behalf of the West requires that we deny these facts and ideals in the classroom, the result will not be that we really give them up. They are too deeply rooted in our experience and belief for that. The result will be that the classroom in which they are denied or disparaged is covered with a pall of self-deception, of disingenuous pretense, and thereby loses its credibility as a forum for the discussion of the deepest questions, which always demand the greatest candor and the courage that candor allows.

Among these is the question of what living is for. To the extent that teachers of the humanities still claim any responsibility for asking this question, and any authority to provide help in exploring it, their enthusiastic embrace of a multiculturalism which in its extreme version asserts the equality of all cultures and traditions makes their classrooms a less credible place to pursue this or any other question of real importance. It puts teachers who embrace this idea at odds with what their students know to be the truth about the world and with their own deepest moral and political convictions. It presents itself as candid talk about the illegitimacy of Western ideas and institutions, but its real effect is to undermine the respect that students have for the candor of those teachers who, in the name of a more rigorous honesty, ask them to deny facts that honesty compels them to acknowledge and values it demands they affirm. This cannot help but make the classroom in which such talk is presented as the truth seem a less honest and serious place. In class, students may enthusiastically affirm the multiculturalism their teachers espouse. They may even feel, for the moment, that they believe it. But underneath they know they don't, and this deeper knowledge undermines the authority of the teachers who defend such ideas and the disciplines on whose behalf they speak.

In disciplines like physics and economics, which are untroubled by the suggestion that the Western approach to their subject-matter is only one among many, inherently no better or truer than any other, no such dissonance exists to compromise their claims to authority. Only the humanities are in this compromised position. Only the humanities have embraced a multiculturalism that drains them of their authority by putting them at war with the experiential and moral worlds their students inhabit outside the classroom. The question of the purpose and value of life demands as much honesty as one can muster. It is a difficult question to ask, let alone answer, in an honest way. But to approach it in any other spirit is already to fail. It is to relinquish the one thing necessary for a meaningful engagement with the question. Through their forced denial of what their students otherwise know and believe, under the influence of a multiculturalism inspired by political and moral ambitions that are themselves of Western origin, teachers of the humanities who deny the priority of the West and of its values forfeit their claim to the honesty that an engagement with the question of life's meaning demands and, with that, their authority to lead their students in the search for an answer to it.

Diversity and multiculturalism are ideas that have been importantly shaped by moral and political events outside the academy. Constructivism, by contrast, is a concept that has its origins in the world of ideas, in intellectual debates about the character and limits of human knowledge—in the branch of philosophical inquiry known as epistemology. Its sources include Kant's transcendental idealism; Nietzsche's perspectivism and his notion of the will to power; Foucault's account of knowledge as a technique of control; Marx's analysis of the "superstructure" of ideas; Wittgenstein's anti-metaphysical philosophy of language; and the writings of the American pragmatists (Dewey and Pierce in particular). Some defenders of constructivism (Richard Rorty, for example)[29] have treated these sources with subtlety and respect. But it is a simpler and less careful version of the concept that has had the greatest influence in the humanities. To those with some knowledge of the history of modern philosophy and a first-hand acquaintance with the texts to which the proponents of this simpler version of constructivism appeal, their ideas are likely to seem a caricature of the more complex ones these texts express. But it is this cruder version that has had the widest currency in the humanities and been most often deployed, with destructive effect, in support of multiculturalism and of the claim that racial, gender, and ethnic diversity is crucial to the work of these disciplines.[30] It is this cruder version of constructivism that has provided the philosophical foundations for the culture of political correctness that has dominated the humanities for the past forty years.

In its simplest form, constructivism asserts that the human world—the whole of reality, including the natural world, insofar as it has any meaning for us at all—is an artifact constructed by the human beings who inhabit it (hence "constructivism"). It therefore regards any claim that some feature of this world exists "by nature" or has an independent "essence" we are bound to respect as necessarily false. For a constructivist, all claims of this sort are projections onto the human world of a false necessity that belies the true generative freedom of the activity of meaning-making from which this world derives its very existence as a realm of meanings.[31]

Constructivism further insists that this activity of meaningmaking receives its motive and direction from a desire to assert power and control over someone or something (oneself, others, or the world). It maintains that the construction of the human world is in this sense always interest-driven and that those who appeal to the false necessity of "nature" and the "essence" of things do so in order to advance the interests that motivate their appeal—which, despite appearances, must itself be understood as just another interest-based construction.

Constructivists claim that the aim of intellectual analysis, in the humanities especially, is to expose these motives, to bring them out of the darkness of falsehood and deception (including selfdeception) and into the light of critical understanding. And finally, they insist that this process of intellectual enlightenment neither depends upon nor yields criteria for ranking the relative worth of the meanings that human beings make or of the desires that drive them to do so.

Defenders of this view of course acknowledge that we judge some human artifacts to be better or more beautiful, even more truthful, than others—that we distinguish among political systems, moral codes, philosophical ideas, and works of art on the basis of their value. Rankings of this sort are unavoidable. It is hard to imagine how we could function without them. But they argue that an enlightened person knows he cannot justify his rankings on the ground that they conform to the "nature" or "essence" of things, and recognizes that even enlightenment itself does not yield a standard by which the value of different human ideas and arrangements can be objectively measured. He knows that his rankings, like those of anyone else, spring from a source outside the process of enlightenment and anterior to it—from his interests, which precede his value judgments and give rise to them, not the other way around. And if enlightenment itself produces some change in a person's interests, that is not because he has attained a vantage point outside them from which their "true" worth can be assessed, but only because he has acquired new (intellectual) interests that modify or displace his old ones. From this it follows that disagreements about the justice or beauty or truth of some feature of the world and what value to assign it can never in reality be anything but a declaration or display of the disputants' interests, which fall outside the domain of argumentative justification and are only concealed (often for strategic reasons) by appeals to reason, nature, and the like.

This connected set of ideas forms the core of the crude version of constructivism that has had so much influence in the humanities, and it is easy to see why it has often been invoked in support of multiculturalism. For if there is no inherent—no "natural"—rank order among the different cultures of the world, then any claim that there is can only be a false and disguised expression of interest whose ability to command assent is a function of the force behind it rather than the reasons to which it appeals. Those, in particular, who make such claims on behalf of the West are only, on this view, engaged in a species of power politics. One must see through their claims to the desires that lie behind them. One must recognize that resistance to the asserted superiority of Western ideas and values is itself a political act that contributes to the larger campaign to rid the world of colonial oppression. For those who hold this view, there can be only one way of treating the world's cultures and traditions, and that is to put them all on a par and to insist that any attempt to rank them is an interest-driven act of self-aggrandizement on the part of those attempting to do so. Multiculturalism is the idea that states the politics of this position and constructivism the theory that provides its philosophical support. The political and moral appeal of the first is an important source of the intellectual attraction of the second, and vice versa.

Constructivism is of course controversial and has often been attacked, especially by defenders of so-called "traditional" values—by those who insist that there are objectively, essentially, naturally better and worse values and institutions.[32] The defenders of traditional values affirm the existence and importance of something that can meaningfully be called human "nature" and generally denounce constructivism as nihilistic, which it is if one understands nihilism to be not the denial that values exist but the denial of the possibility of providing a rational foundation for them, of ever escaping the determining influence of the pre-rational desires that give our values their content and force.

But this line of attack, though it has certainly had many articulate proponents, can always be deflected by a defender of constructivism merely by characterizing the attack itself as just one more act of aggression, motivated by the political or other interests of the attacker, and dressed up in such a way as to conceal its true source by claiming a legitimacy grounded in the nature of things. Every external critic of constructivism invites this response. The result is a predictable back and forth: the critics of constructivism attacking it as a nihilistic doctrine that fails to recognize the truths of human nature, constructivists responding that the attack itself is an interest-driven political act that proves their philosophical point, the critics rejoining that this response is further proof of the depth of their opponents' nihilism, and so on in an endless circle.

The only criticisms of constructivism that cannot be deflected in this way are internal ones—those that seek to show that constructivism is unintelligible on its own terms or supports conclusions different from those its defenders draw.

Let us assume, for example, that the human world *is* an artifact in the sense that constructivism claims—that all the meanings we assign the world are human inventions. Still, the intelligibility of any constructive activity depends on its being carried out in accordance with rules which the person acting is constrained to accept. The employment of these rules—which, were we free to invent and deploy them as we wished, could no longer perform their constraining function—is (to use Kant's formulation) a precondition necessary for the possibility of any such act being intelligible at all, to the actor or anyone else.[33] It is a precondition of our being able to think or say anything whatsoever about it.

But to accept this proposition is to acknowledge that the very freedom of our capacity to create meaning depends for its intel-ligibility— for our recognition of it as an exercise of freedom rather than something else—on a necessity that limits and constrains our freedom from the start, a necessity that is freedom's coeval enabling partner. And to accept this argument, loosely inspired by Kant (or, if you prefer, by Wittgenstein)[34] is to grant a beachhead of necessity in the otherwise boundless realm of creativity that constructivism presumes, from which other enabling conditions of equal necessity may perhaps be derived through a similar process of transcendental analysis. One may even hope that in the end all these conditions can be gathered and harmonized in a philosophical anthropology that restores a measure of legitimacy to the ancient idea of human nature, now expressed in transcendental rather than metaphysical terms.[35] At a minimum, constructivism gives us no reason to think that the hope of doing this is doomed from the start.

Or (to pursue another internal line of attack), even if every value is the expression of an interest, of a pre-rational passion or desire, certain passions, and all those that are most characteristically human, are distinguished by what philosophers call their "ideality." These idealizing passions differ from other, simpler feelings and appetites in a crucial respect. They all include an idea of some sort as one of their components. Anger is an example. The angry person feels rage on account of being mistreated. He is angry because he has not been treated as he should. If he had no notion of how he ought to be treated, he could not be angry. The passion we call anger has built into it as one of its key elements a reference to a standard of proper treatment. This standard is an idea, an abstraction, a thought, and that thought is itself part of what we mean by anger and how we experience it.[36]

Pride is another example. The prideful person takes pleasure in living up to her ideals and in being treated as her status demands. Her pleasure can be conceived only with reference to these ideals. Hope and shame are other idealizing passions. Each of these also refers to an idea that appears as a thought or representation in the mind (or soul) of the person who feels hopeful or ashamed.

The makeup of these passions and desires includes an intellectual component—the imaginative projection of an idea of one kind or another. Indeed, even our most primitive desires typically include a component of this sort, at least in their distinctively human form. Human sexual desire, for example, has an element of fantasy that distinguishes it from the thoughtless sexual appetites of other animals.[37] Animal desires are instinctive. There is (so far as we can tell) no thought in them at all. Some human passions and desires may perhaps be blindly instinctive too, but others, and all the ones that are peculiar to us, are inherently intelligent in the sense that mind—reason, thought, imagination—is a defining feature of them (though a feature that need not be consciously appreciated by the person whose passion or desire it is). And whatever other desires belong to this class of idealizing appetites, the desire a person has to advance his political agenda—the kind of desire that constructivism spies behind all appeals to truth and nature—must surely be included. For every interest of this sort always involves the imaginative projection of some end to be achieved—the anticipatory representation, in the form of an idea, of some institutional scheme, or distributive outcome, or cultural practice, or other political goal. Every political passion is marked by ideality.

This may seem uncontroversial, but its implications for constructivism are large. For constructivism presupposes a domain of interests, of passions and desires, that is anterior to and independent of the world of thought—of ideas, beliefs, and values. The latter can all be reduced, on the constructivist view of them, to interests of one kind or another. Each is the disguised expression of an interest that itself is deaf and dumb—a brute appetite that can be challenged only by another appetite of the same inarticulate kind in a contest of powers that reason cannot adjudicate because there is no reason in it. But for this view to be defensible, for it even to be intelligible, the realms of thought and interest must be entirely distinct, since otherwise the first cannot be reduced to the second in the way that constructivism requires.

To acknowledge the ideality of certain human passions and desires, however, and especially of those that are most distinctively human, is to deny the sharpness and completeness of this very distinction. It is to acknowledge that thinking—the process of imaginative idealization—is a constituent feature of these passions and desires themselves, whose character cannot be described or understood apart from it. And once that is granted, it is no longer clear how the complete reduction of thought to interest that constructivism assumes can be carried out, for the interests to which our thoughts reduce are in many cases themselves already "thoughtful." More important, the acknowledgment that thinking is already present in many of our interests—and certainly in those that relate to the achievement of our moral and political goals—establishes a foothold of thought within the realm of interest and opens the possibility of a reflective, critical review of our passions and desires from a point of view internal to them.[38] Psychoanalysis assumes that even our sexual desires are accessible to an internal review of this kind. If that is true, then surely our political desires, which are even more openly thoughtful, must be subject to internal criticism too.

The constructivist's dismissal of the traditionalist's appeal to reason or nature as just another political move in disguise rests on the assumption that our interests cannot be rationally scrutinized from within, that they are deaf to reason's appeal. It rests on the assumption that reason is, as David Hume remarked, the handmaid of the passions, an "afterthought" that serves our interests and desires but can exercise no influence over them.[39] The recognition that our most characteristically human interests have thought built into them from the start undermines this assumption and clears the way to an internal criticism that wrecks the program of perfect reduction on which the insularity and seeming invulnerability of constructivism depends.

External attacks on constructivism, in the name of reason or nature, are vulnerable to the deflecting response that they beg the question constructivism raises—the question of whether such appeals are ever anything more than expressions of blind interest on the part of those who make them. Internal criticisms, like the two I have just sketched, cannot be deflected in this way. They present a serious, and in the end I think insurmountable, challenge to the crude version of constructivism that has had so many supporters in the humanities. To meet them, constructivism would have to become a philosophically subtler theory. It would have to repudiate the nihilism that denies the possibility of subjecting our interests and desires to rational review. It would have to acknowledge the role of reason in political and moral debate and in disagreements about the relative value of ideas and institutions. It would have to abandon the claim that any attempt to rank the world's cultures is a political act pure and simple.

In particular, it would have to meet the attempt to establish a privileged place for Western ideas with something more than a wave of the hand. It would have to meet the arguments that support this view with counter-arguments of its own. It would have to come to terms with the fact that constructivism is itself a Western invention whose claim to universality reflects the most characteristic feature of the very tradition it rejects, in the name of a critical philosophy that purports to be unhampered by parochial Western ideas. A constructivism that did this might have greater philosophical appeal. But it could no longer supply the strong if mindless support for multiculturalism that the simple version does and would therefore lack the political appeal it has for many humanities teachers today.

The concept of constructivism, even in its crudest form, shares something important in common with secular humanism, just as the contemporary idea of diversity does. In the case of diversity, the common element is a recognition that values are plural. In the case of constructivism, it is the acknowledgment of the role that free invention plays in the creation of meaning and value. Secular humanism acknowledged a flexibility or freedom in our confrontation with the irreducibly plural values that appear before us as options for living. Constructivism, which denies that values are compulsory and insists that we are not forced by "nature" or "reason" to prefer one fundamental value to another, likewise puts choice and freedom at the center of our moral and spiritual lives and underscores that it is up to us to decide what meaning and value the world shall have (though constructivism takes back much of the freedom it grants by reducing the choices we make, and the values we affirm, to the driving force of blind interest).

This similarity in their emphasis on freedom and choice might make it seem that constructivism is merely an extension of secular humanism, and an improving one at that. One might conclude that constructivism merely takes ideas that are central to secular humanism and carries them further, freeing them from their limits and bringing the voluntarist spirit of secular humanism to its proper fulfillment. But that is a mistake. For by radically extending the range and power of our freedom, constructivism destroys the value that freedom possesses within a secular humanist framework and prevents any discipline that adopts a constructivist approach from offering helpful guidance in the search for an answer to the question of what we should care about and why.

From the standpoint of secular humanism, the meaning or value of the choice a person makes about such matters depends upon two interdependent conditions. The first is that it be a genuine choice. To the extent it is dictated by someone else, or compelled by the person's circumstances, to the extent its freedom is compromised or qualified in any of the many ways it can be, its moral and spiritual value is impaired. The second is that it be the choice of something valuable—that it express a commitment to something worthy of commitment. However free a choice, to the extent its object is unworthy of commitment, the choice lacks value and its deficiency cannot be remedied by searching for a way to make the choice freer still. For this second condition to be fulfilled, the worth of the values a person affirms as the cornerstone of his life cannot be a function merely of the fact that he affirms them. They must have a value that is independent of his choice. They must have an intrinsic worth of their own.

It is true that I must choose what to care about in life and that only what I *choose* to care about can have value or meaning for me. But it is also true that what I choose to care about can have value or meaning only if it is valuable or meaningful in its own right, independent of the choice that I make. Secular humanism insists on both these points. It sets two conditions for success in the search for an answer to the question of life's meaning. Between these two conditions there is, of course, a tension. But the tension creates a dynamic within whose vibrant and unstable field we alone can hope to find an answer to this question that is meaningful both on account of its freedom and the worth of what we freely choose.

If the first requirement is suspended, we relapse into an authoritarianism that leaves little or no room for freedom—that conceives right living to be conformity to a single and unambiguously best pattern of life. But if the second condition is suspended, our choices are drained of their meaning and value by being unmoored from what has meaning and value in itself. The tension that gives our choices their meaning goes slack. There is no longer any point to choosing when the entire value of a choice is achieved in its execution, and the subject-matter of the choice—*what* we choose—is treated with indifference.

This is where constructivism leaves us. By insisting that every invocation of nature or reason, every claim that a work or practice or institution possesses an inherent value of its own, is an appeal to a false necessity that enlightened people know is just a way of amplifying the rhetorical power of a choice that has no foundation in the world: by insisting on this, constructivism eliminates the second condition that gives our choices their meaning and value. It deprives us of everything for the sake of which it might be worth having, and exercising, the freedom we possess.

Secular humanism, with its two conditions, occupies a position midway between classicism (where choice plays no role) and constructivism (which denies that there is anything inherently worthy to choose). If one assumes that this midway position is necessarily unstable, that the chronologically later idea of constructivism cures this instability, and that by doing so it advances beyond secular humanism in the same way that secular humanism advances beyond classicism, the line that leads from classicism to constructivism is likely to seem wholly progressive, each stage being an improvement upon the one before. But in reality, it is only secular humanism, with its admitted instability, that gives due recognition to both of the conditions that are required to form a meaningful response to life's most basic question—that it be a free response, and freely embrace something of intrinsic worth. The second of these conditions is lost in the move from secular humanism to constructivism, which eliminates the tension required for the meaningful exercise of freedom and sets our choices about the most important matters loose from the constraints that alone give them purpose and value.

Classicism offered organized instruction in the meaning of life. But its instruction was *too* organized, for it depended on the (no longer credible) assumption of a single right way of living. When secular humanism abandoned this assumption, it was able to continue to offer disciplined guidance in the exploration of life's meaning only because the pluralism of values it recognized was finite and (relatively) fixed. This gave secular humanism a structure that made an organized approach to the question of the meaning of life possible, one that followed an intelligible sequence and explored an agreed-upon range of topics through the study of a more-or-less fixed group of works, all on the assumption that there are certain identifiable ways of life that possess intrinsic value. Among these each of us must ultimately choose and there is no built-in rank order that makes one way of life superior to another. But the choice among them is constrained by the manageable number of such lives and by the continuity of the tradition of great works of literature, philosophy, and art in which they are presented and defended: the core of secular humanism.

Constructivism condemns the idea of intrinsic value as a false "essentialism." It derides the notion of a fixed set of perennial options for living. It mocks the idea of a great conversation. It urges us to liberate ourselves from these primitive and freedom-denying beliefs. But once we do, no limits remain on the possibilities to be explored. The very idea of a limit becomes suspect and any attempt to reimpose one is likely to seem an arbitrary exercise of brute power. Without some limits, however, there can be no agreement among teachers of the humanities as to what to study, in which sequence, and through the examination of which works. And without such limits the search for an answer to the question of what living is for becomes a directionless enquiry that provides no structured environment for the exercise of freedom and hence deprives freedom itself of value. The authority of the humanities to serve as guides in the exploration of the question of the meaning of life depended on their willingness to ask this question when other disciplines had ceased to do so. It also depended on their ability to provide students with some organized help in their search for an answer. The research ideal discouraged teachers of the humanities from asking the question. Constructivism robs them of the means to pursue it in an organized and helpful way.

The ideas of diversity and multiculturalism start from attractive moral and political premises. Each promotes a worthy cause—racial justice in the one case, and responsible global citizenship in the other. By transforming these ideas into principles of pedagogy, teachers of the humanities have been able to reassert their claim to a special and valued role in higher education. They have been able to see themselves as making a distinctive contribution to the moral and political work of their colleges and universities. And by grounding the ideas of diversity and multiculturalism in a constructivist theory of knowledge that emphasizes the depth of human freedom and choice, they have been able to conceive their new role as one that extends a key premise of secular humanism to its fulfilling conclusion.

But all this is a mistake. The real effect of the humanities' endorsement of these ideas has been quite the opposite. It has not restored their authority but further compromised it instead. It has undermined the notion of an old and ongoing conversation that gives each entrant a weighted and responsible sense of connection to the past, and substituted the egotistic presumption that we can start a new and freer conversation on our own, engaging all the works of all the world's great civilizations in a colloquy we invent for ourselves. It has encouraged the fantasy that in our world today, the ideas and institutions of the West have no more significance or value than those of any other civilization. It has wrecked the humanities' claim to be able to provide organized guidance in the exploration of the question of the meaning of life. And it has simultaneously limited the idea of human freedom by tying our powers of judgment too closely to facts about ourselves we cannot change, and expanded the notion of freedom to the point where our choices are emptied of their meaning. In all these ways, the wide acceptance within the humanities of the ideas of diversity, multiculturalism, and constructivism has made it harder for teachers in these fields to acknowledge the legitimacy of the question of what living is for and to approach it in a serious, responsible, and organized fashion.

At the same time, these ideas have hobbled the humanities with beliefs that have little or no credibility in the natural and social sciences. Unburdened by the assumption that our values are irrevocably linked to race and gender, that all civilizations stand on a moral and intellectual par, and that "truth" and "nature" are political fictions in which we should put no trust, the natural and social sciences proceed from strength to strength, as measured by the research ideal. Their standing is secure. They have been untouched by these ideas, which are antithetical to the spirit of objectivity on which the research ideal depends.

None of these developments, of course, has made the question of the meaning of life any less urgent for the young men and women studying in our colleges and universities. The question has simply been forced out of school. Disciplines other than the humanities no longer pretend to address it, and the humanities themselves have lost their willingness and ability to do so—first, by subscribing to the modern research ideal and then, in a failed effort to reestablish some sense of distinctive purpose, by embracing a set of ideas that have made the question even more remote than it was before. Students looking for guidance in their encounter with the question of life's meaning must now look elsewhere for help.

Most students naturally turn to their families and friends. They turn to those with whom they have the most intimate and caring relations. Whatever help one gets from other sources, the affection and support of those one lives with and loves is for most of us essential to maintaining our balance in the face of life's mysteries. But our families and friends are rarely *authorities* in the exploration of life's meaning. They seldom possess a method or organized body of knowledge that enables them to approach the subject in a disciplined way. In any case, that is not what we want from or value about them. What we want is their love, and the fact that they are in no better position than anyone else to provide organized guidance in our investigation of the meaning of life does not decrease the value of their love by an atom. What it does do, however, is give most of us a reason to look elsewhere for such guidance—which, though never a substitute for the love of family and friends, is always a useful and often an essential complement to it.

Our colleges and universities once claimed to possess such authority. One of the reasons that young people went to college—or more accurately, one of the reasons their families sent them to college—was to study the question of life's meaning under the supervision of teachers competent to guide them. This was rarely the only reason for going. There were always other (often clearer and stronger) reasons as well. But the moral and spiritual benefits of a disciplined introduction to the question of what living is for were among the advantages a college education promised. They were part of why one went.

It has never been the case, of course, that our colleges and universities were the *only* institutions purporting to provide authoritative instruction in the meaning of life. Religious institutions in particular have always claimed to do so. The question of life's meaning lies at the heart of every religious tradition. It has always been the central question to which religious thought and the institutionalized forms of religious belief are addressed. For them, the question of life's meaning is constitutive: they could not put it aside, or disclaim the authority to address it, without losing their religious character and becoming institutions of a different kind.

During the first two centuries of American higher education, college and church were nearly synonymous. After the Civil War and during the century that followed, they drew apart and became separate, sometimes competing, centers of authority so far as the provision of instruction in the meaning of life was concerned. When the tradition of secular humanism collapsed and the humanities gave up their claim to such authority, the competitive tension between college and church disappeared, and our churches remained the only institutions still claiming the right and duty to address this question in an authoritative way. Today, if one wants organized assistance in answering the question of life's meaning, and not just the love of family and friends, it is to the churches that one must turn.

The different religious traditions have old, deep, and wellworked-out approaches to the question of life's meaning. These retain, even in a world of increasingly secular habits, an immense reserve of authority and prestige. But these traditions, as different as they are in other respects, share two features that set them apart from the approach to the question of the meaning of life that secular humanism encouraged.

First, no religion can be pluralist in the deep and final sense that secular humanism is. No religion can accept the proposition that there are incommensurably different answers to the question of life's meaning, among which no rank order can be fixed. A religion may be (more or less) tolerant, but every religion must, in the end, answer the question of the meaning of life decisively. It must offer and defend one answer as the best, and however complex that answer is, however insistent that we tolerate the answers others give, it must conceive the variety of human life and human striving from the standpoint of some unitary conception of meaning and value. A religion that denies the very possibility of attaining such a standpoint, as secular humanism does, is no longer a religion at all.

Second, every religion at some point demands a "sacrifice of the intellect." This point may come sooner or later, but every religion eventually reaches it. Every religion insists that at some point thinking is no longer adequate to the question of life's meaning, and that further progress can be made only by means other than thought. All religions recognize the finitude of human reason, as secular humanism does. But in contrast to secular humanism, every religion also affirms the existence and spiritual value of some attitude other than thought that has the power to carry us beyond the limits of reason if we are prepared to adopt it. And all declare that the deepest peace and greatest insight come when we take this step beyond reason's frontiers and open ourselves to the wisdom that "surpasseth understanding."[40]

All religions differ from secular humanism in these two respects: that they cannot accept its ultimate pluralism of values and demand the recognition of spiritual powers that transcend the limits of reason (whether these powers be conceived in mystical, devotional, or other terms). These two features of religious thought and practice are well captured by one of the many meanings of the word "fundamentalist." Today, this word is most often used to distinguish certain religious attitudes from others—to distinguish fundamentalist Islam from non-fundamentalist Islam, fundamentalist Christianity from non-fundamentalist

Christianity, and so on. But there is a more basic sense in which every religion is fundamentalist. For every religion insists, at the end of the day, that there is only one right answer to the question of life's meaning, however tolerant it is prepared to be of the answers others give, either for reasons of convenience or out of a moral respect that itself is anchored in its own answer to this question. Every religion must ultimately insist on a fundament of meaning and value. And every religion must also insist that while reason alone cannot provide a foundation for answering the question of life's meaning—that we cannot, so to speak, argue our way to a demonstrably right answer—something else can. Every religion affirms that there is something else—faith, mystical union with the godhead, the discipline of prayer, something—that can provide us with the fundament we need to secure our answer to the question of the meaning of life against all criticism and doubt. In these two respects, every religion, even the most tolerant, is fundamentalist.

The fact that America's colleges and universities no longer claim the authority to provide organized instruction in the exploration of this question therefore means that the most influential institutions now doing so are religious ones and that nearly all such instruction today starts from the fundamentalist premises on which every religion is based.[41] Our colleges and universities have ceased to be independent centers of authority asserting the right and ability to offer young people guidance in exploring the question of life's meaning from a non-fundamentalist perspective—from the perspective of a secular humanism that acknowledges the ultimate pluralism of values, while insisting on the intelligibility of the idea of human nature and the durability of its most compelling expressions. Our colleges and universities have abandoned this position and by doing so ceded the enterprise of instruction in life's meaning to the religious institutions with which they once shared it in a competitive division of authority. The churches alone now occupy the field. They alone claim such authority and exercise it. Hence, in the organized provision of instruction in the meaning of life, fundamentalism now prevails in America without competitive challenge—fundamentalism not in the narrow sense in which the word is sometimes used to designate particular religious attitudes or orthodoxies but in the deeper and more consequential sense in which every religion, whatever its temper and doctrine, starts from a fundament of belief that secular humanism investigates, interrogates, takes with utmost seriousness, but refuses to embrace.

For a century, the humanities departments of our colleges and universities offered a competitive challenge to fundamentalism, supported by the tradition of secular humanism.

The destruction of that tradition has left those looking for instruction in the meaning of life nowhere to turn but the churches. It has left them with no meaningful alternative to fundamentalism—with a choice between fundamentalism and no instruction at all. When the humanities lost confidence in their capacity to provide such instruction and severed their connection to the question of what living is for, they therefore not only jeopardized their own standing within the academy. They not only cast doubt on their own educational purpose and value. They also caused a dangerous and damaging contraction of intellectual and spiritual possibilities within the culture at large by leaving the question of life's meaning in the nearly exclusive possession of those with fundamentalist beliefs.

Our churches no longer compete with our colleges and universities for the authority to speak to this question. Some undoubtedly view this as a good thing. They believe that such authority belongs only to God's delegates and that once our colleges and universities ceased to be religious institutions themselves, they forfeited the right to claim it. They believe that secular humanism in particular, with its commitment to pluralism and refusal to affirm the power of faith, provides no rightful basis for this claim. They believe that our schools should limit themselves to scholarly research and to the transmission of specialized knowledge in specific fields of study and should leave the question of what living is for to others. They see the absence of this question from the long list of those to which our colleges and universities offer an organized response as a desirable state of affairs that reflects their incompetence to answer it.

What this view ignores is the vital importance of having a credible counterweight to fundamentalism itself—one that takes the question of life's meaning as earnestly as religion does but starts its exploration from premises different from those on which all religiously-inspired instruction is based. For without a spiritually vital alternative to fundamentalism—one that takes the deepest concerns of the human soul with equal seriousness but refuses to concede what every religion demands—our churches become weaker on account of not having to defend themselves against a challenger of consequence. Without such an alternative, our whole culture is spiritually impoverished and debate about matters of ultimate concern degenerates into what it often is today—a shouting match marked by mistrust and incomprehension. Without a real alternative to fundamentalism, those who want some organized help in thinking about the meaning of their lives but, for whatever reason, reject the authority of the churches to provide it, are left to wrestle with the question on their own as best they can. Without the credible counterweight to fundamentalism that secular humanism provides, our spiritual world is flattened and privatized. It becomes shallower and less demanding. And the one question in which we all have an interest—a common human interest—is forced back into the realm of private life for all but those who accept the authority of religion to guide them in their examination of it.

The humanities' embrace of the modern research ideal, the confusion and anxiety this produced, and the desperate search for a new sense of purposefulness organized around a set of politically attractive but intellectually ruinous ideas, has left these disciplines in disrepair, with no clear understanding of the contribution they make to higher education. It has destroyed the confidence they once possessed, and the authority they once exercised, as custodians of the tradition of secular humanism, which for a century after the rise of the American university enabled the humanities to continue, on more pluralistic and skeptical terms, the older tradition of offering instruction in the meaning of life.

For these disciplines themselves, the result has been disastrous. But for the wider culture, which has been deprived of a strong and independent center where such instruction might be sought, and been left with no organized alternative to religious fundamentalism, the consequences are even worse. Today, the restoration of the humanities to a position of authority in our colleges and universities is a matter of signal importance not just for those who teach in these fields, not just for higher education, but for our culture as a whole, whose spiritual vibrancy has been compromised by the self-destruction of the humanities. For our culture to be strong, the humanities must be strong. The tradition of secular humanism must be reclaimed. The question of what living is for must be restored to a respected place in our colleges and universities. And the authority of teachers of the humanities to guide their students in answering this question must be reaffirmed, above all by these teachers themselves.

5

Spirit in an Age of Science

The authority of the natural sciences is today unrivaled. Their intellectual foundations are secure. Teachers and students working in these fields know what they are doing and why it is important. Most social scientists feel similarly about the value of their work. They too believe in its intellectual integrity and practical importance. This is clearest in the case of economics, the most rigorous of the social sciences and the one by which all the others now measure their achievements. In our colleges and universities today, the prevailing mood in the natural and social sciences is thus one of healthy self-regard. Disagreements about methods and aims do from time to time disturb these fields, and even in a discipline like physics there are recurrent uncertainties about the direction the discipline is going.[1] But these disturbances do not upset or challenge the deeper confidence, shared by nearly all those in these fields, that they are making a meaningful contribution to well-understood and valuable goals—to the deepening of our collective knowledge about the structures of the natural and social worlds and to the practical employment of this knowledge for the improvement of the human condition. For teachers and students in the natural and social sciences, this deeper confidence is a fact of professional life. It is something they feel justified in taking for granted. They simply know, in a way that no methodological quarrel or debate about direction can unsettle, that they are making a valued contribution to the work of higher education and feel secure in their entitlement to intellectual respect and to a share of the money and honor their schools have to bestow.

The mood in the humanities, by contrast, is one of insecurity and doubt. Talk of a "crisis" of purpose—a loss of direction, an absence of aims, a failure of nerve, a collapse of traditions— has been widespread in these disciplines since the 1960s and continues unabated today.[2] The lack of self-confidence that such talk reflects remains a pervasive fact of professional experience for teachers and students of the humanities. To some, perhaps, looking at the situation superficially, these doubts will seem unwarranted. After all, the worth of the humanities is regularly reaffirmed by college and university presidents and ritually endorsed by curriculum committees reviewing their schools' programs, as it recently was at Yale.[3] Humanities classes continue to be taught. Humanities departments continue to make appointments. No one is calling for their abolition. On the surface, their position appears as secure as that of the natural and social sciences. But the reality is that teachers of the humanities, unlike their counterparts in these other fields, do not share a clear and confident understanding of the contribution they make to higher education. They do not have a buoyant, collective sense of the distinctiveness and worth of what they do. They lack today, as they have for the better part of the past half-century, the relaxed and easygoing confidence in the value of their work that scientists of all sorts share. And while those in the natural and social sciences often express a conventional respect for the humanities, their real attitude is frequently one of bemusement or even contempt for these disciplines, whose paroxysms of political correctness have made them appear increasingly ridiculous to those who value the norms of objectivity, impersonality, and coordinated, accretive discovery that lie at the heart of the modern research ideal. In the hierarchy of academic authority and prestige, the humanities today stand at the bottom.

As I have tried to show, this is the result, in part, of developments internal to the academy. It is a consequence of the humanities' own self-destructive embrace of the research ideal and of the even more destructive culture of political correctness that has gripped these disciplines for the past forty years. But it is also a consequence of developments outside the world of higher education which, in a parallel and complementary fashion, have undermined the authority of the humanities and cast doubt on their value.

The most important of these is the immense authority of science in the world at large.

Science is today the greatest authority in our lives—greater than any political or religious ideal, any cultural tradition, any legal system. We depend on science and defer to it as we do to nothing else. Politics, culture, religion, and law: in all these areas of life, different conceptions of truth and legitimacy compete. In none are the ideas of truth and objectivity accepted in the same nonpartisan spirit they are in the realm of science. Today, our very understanding of what these ideas mean is a function of their meaning in science. The truth and objectivity of science set the standard by which their more limited availability in other domains is measured. Many things claim our respect and demand our allegiance. But nothing in the world now does so with the same insistence as science. The preeminent authority of science is the central fact of our age and the collapse of the authority of the humanities within our colleges and universities is in part a consequence of the authority that science possesses outside them.

✦

In practical terms, the authority of science begins (though it does not end) with technology.[4] Our lives today are conditioned to an unprecedented degree by the powers of technology, which for the most part we unthinkingly accept as a desirable and in any case inescapable fact of life. Virtually every aspect of human life is now shaped by technology, and our dependence on it and deference to it instill a respect for science at the deepest and least articulate level of lived experience. Today we live surrounded by an array of ingenious gadgets on which, in the developed world at least, the lives of even moderately well-to-do people are hopelessly dependent. There are the cooking and other appliances that have transformed the nature of housework; the telephones that put us in immediate touch with others around the world; the trains, planes, and automobiles that have obliterated the real and imagined distances that once separated the peoples and places of the earth and that have turned the dangers of travel into mere inconveniences; the televisions that provide an endless stream of images of events around the planet, at the very moment they occur; the computers, which simplify and accelerate countless tasks and place at our fingertips a world of information larger than the real world itself; and beyond all these, beyond the gadgets themselves, the stupendous interlocking web of plants and wires that produces the energy that drives them all.

If, for the most part, we are no longer amazed by any of these things but simply take them for granted, that is because they have become such familiar elements of our material civilization that we hardly notice their existence. But the technologies in whose midst we live are now indispensable to us. Every day our dependence on them grows. Every day it becomes harder to imagine life without them. Every day our acceptance of them deepens and our deference to their powers increases. And when we contemplate the future, all we can imagine (barring a catastrophe great enough to wreck the world, at whose prospect imagination fails) is a further expansion of these powers themselves. All we can imagine is more technology: new and better gadgets that permit us to do what we want at greater speed and lower cost. That is for us today the only imaginable future, and we embrace it both because we want it and because we believe it is inevitable.

Technology is a tool and the countless gadgets on which we now depend are at bottom nothing more than an accumulation of tools. Every tool is a device for increasing our power to reach some end or perform some task. In this respect, our modern technologies are no different from earlier, more primitive tools. But their vastly greater power constitutes a difference of kind, not merely degree. It sets them apart and gives birth to ambitions undreamt of before.

Modern technological tools increase our power exponentially. They give us the power to control what human beings have never been able to control before. They allow us to extend or avoid limits that earlier generations had to accept as their fate. Today, we control the temperature in our homes with furnaces and air-conditioning units. We correct our vision with laser surgery. We extend our lives with pacemakers and chemotherapy. And everyday conveniences, like airplanes, telephones, and cameras, make it possible for us to overcome once-fixed limits of time and space. They make these limits less of a hindrance to our desire to go where we want, speak with whom we wish, and recall the past with the vividness of present perception. Modern technology expands the limits of human action to an unprecedented extent and in doing so reveals with greater clarity at every step the ambition that lies behind the modern technological order as a whole— the ambition to eliminate every constraint that prevents us from doing as we please.

Even the most enthusiastic admirer of technology is unlikely to think we can reach this goal. Some limits will always remain. Our actions will always be subject to constraints of one kind or another. But even if the goal of a life without limits can never be reached, it remains the end that technology strives to attain. It is the guiding purpose that gives technology its meaning and value. A technological advance has meaning and value *because* it carries us further in this direction, and the limits that at any given moment confine our freedom to live and do as we wish are, from a technological point of view, merely a challenge to be overcome through some new and better technology that will enable us to supersede them.

Technology is in this sense an anti-fatalistic force, the greatest the world has ever known. For its defining aim is to transform fate into freedom—to change what we must accept into something our powers permit us to accept or not as we choose. The goal of technology is the completion of this transformation. This is not a goal we can attain. But it is a meaningful goal nonetheless, since we can approach it ever more closely over time. The purpose of technology, and hence its meaning, lies in the pursuit of this meaningful if unattainable goal.

Our dependence on technology and the authority it possesses in our lives are a consequence of our deep attraction to this goal. For the desire to push back the boundaries of fate is one of our oldest desires and the fantasy of erasing these boundaries completely one of our deepest dreams. But while the desire itself is primordial, the opportunities that modern technology affords for its satisfaction are entirely unique. Technology gives us grounds to be increasingly impatient with anything that frustrates the fulfillment of this desire. The promise of technology is that we can now for the first time confidently plan on making steady progress toward the age-old human dream of a perfect freedom from fate, with no end of further progress in sight. The new inventions that appear every day give this promise credibility. They confirm that at last we are in a position to do what we have wished to do from the start. They promise to release us from the prison house of fate in which our ambitions have been confined. The authority of technology in our lives today is as deep as the archaic desire for control whose fulfillment it brings within reach. That we cannot imagine our lives without technology and do not wish to do so is more than a sign of its authority. It is that authority itself.

The authority of technology extends backward to the science that lies behind it, though again not always in ways that we notice. Few of us understand much of the science that underlies the technology we use every day. None of us grasps it all. In this sense, we live surrounded by devices on which we depend and whose operation we do not comprehend. But we also know that someone somewhere understands how each of these things works, that each, though perhaps not comprehensible to you or me or anyone we know, is comprehensible to the human mind.[5] And we also know that this comprehension is based on a knowledge of how the world works, of its structure and laws, and that it is this knowledge of the world that makes it possible for human beings to create the technical devices we employ in our everyday lives. And if these technologies work as well as they do, that can only be because the scientific knowledge on which they depend is accurate and true. The technologies whose practical utility we recognize thus validate the theoretical understanding of the world from which they spring. They validate the truths of science. They derive from these truths and give us reason to accept them. The authority that technology possesses in our lives and over them thus flows backward to the science whose truth is confirmed by the effectiveness of the technology its discoveries enable us to produce.

In speaking of "science," I have in mind first and most emphatically the modern sciences of nature that emerged from the intellectual revolution of the sixteenth and seventeenth centuries. The contemporary sciences of the natural world all derive from methods and ideas first formulated in the revolution that began with Copernicus and ended with Newton. These had important medieval and early modern precursors, and their views have been substantially revised by later thinkers. But it was during the century and a half that separated the most famous works of these two thinkers that the science of nature assumed the form, and acquired the authority, it possesses today.[6]

Many factors contributed to this development. Some were conceptual, such as the new theory of motion that replaced the old Aristotlean idea of natural place and prepared the way for Cartesian, and later Newtonian, mechanics.[7] The invention of new tools of observation played a role as well. With the telescope, study of the heavens was no longer limited, as it had been before, to what can be seen with the "naked" eye. And with the clock, periods of motion, and hence rates of change, could be measured with previously unattainable precision.[8] The development of mathematical techniques that permitted the formalization of basic concepts like acceleration and that allowed for the creation of a unified world picture expressible in abstract formulae made an essential contribution too.[9]

Another factor of great importance was the refinement of the experimental method, a uniquely fruitful technique for aligning theory and observation.[10] An experiment is a controlled experience that has been artificially shaped to isolate certain of its features. The purpose of an experiment is to expand our ability to reason about the experiences we have. If we had to take our experiences as they come, as "lump sums" whose elements cannot be isolated and independently scrutinized and whose causal significance can therefore not be separately assessed, our capacity to reason about them would be severely constrained. The experimental method is a technique for liberating our powers of reasoning from the limits to which sense experience otherwise confines them, while at the same providing a mechanism for testing the soundness of reason's abstractions against experience itself.

By freeing reason from its dependence on the given facts of experience while simultaneously creating a means to check our theories in a systematic way against a novel set of artificially created facts, the experimental method made the idea of limitless progress toward a perfect understanding of the natural world seem more plausible than it had ever been before. It made it an idea that scientists could confidently adopt as their goal. The experimental method enabled scientists to redescribe the world in rational terms of the greatest possible abstraction and at the same time to demonstrate that their description of it accurately depicts the world as it truly is—to undertake the fusion of mathematical and empirical truth, the mathematization of reality, that has been the hallmark of all scientific knowledge ever since.

The truths of modern science, expressed in mathematical terms, are thus arrived at by a manipulative method that permits us both to use our experience and to transcend it—using experience to confirm what we think while freeing us from all experiential limits on our power to think about it. These scientific truths, which are the product of our intellectual manipulation of the world, in turn enable us to construct tools for its practical manipulation. They provide us with the knowledge we need to increase our practical powers of control and many have seen in the expansion of these powers the motive and goal of science itself.

Francis Bacon, for example, famously observed that we seek knowledge for the sake of power— that knowledge *is* power.[11] There is considerable truth in this. We want to know how the world works because we want to know how to make it work as we wish, and the great technological powers that modern science places in our hands not only confirm the truths of science but supply one of the principal motives for seeking them in the first place. But Bacon's famous dictum leaves something important out of the account. It is true, but only a half truth. For while modern science has vastly increased our practical powers of control and enjoys the authority it does in part because its discoveries provide the foundation on which these powers rest, its authority has another source as well. Science today enjoys the authority it does not only on account of the practical inventions that flow from it and from their capacity to satisfy our desire for control, but because it satisfies more fully than any other form of knowledge we possess a second elementary desire, the desire to understand.

We want to know how the world works for the sake of such knowledge itself, apart from any practical benefits it yields. The desire to understand is a distinct, and distinctively human, desire. It is not the same as the desire for control. But it is as old and as deep, and the authority of modern science is a function not only of the practical powers it puts in our hands, but also of its capacity to satisfy our desire to understand the world for the sake of the pleasure that such understanding affords.

"All men by nature desire to know," Aristotle remarks in a matter-of-fact way at the beginning of the *Metaphysics*.[12] He compares the pleasure we take in the satisfaction of this desire to the pleasure of sight. We enjoy looking at things, he says, not just because it is useful to do so—because we must look at them to find our way about—but because it is intrinsically delightful as well. According to Aristotle, the pleasure we take in understanding the world is like this too.

Many animals might be said to be "curious" about the world—cats famously so. But except in the case of human beings, animal curiosity is limited to the surface of things. Is there a mouse behind the chair? Or a bird behind the song in the garden? Human beings are curious about these things too, but they are also, and uniquely, curious about something else as well. They are curious about the organizing structure of the world that lies beneath its surface. We want to know not only *whether* something is the case—is there a deer in the woods?—but also *why* it is the case—why do deer appear at certain times and not others? This latter, distinctively human curiosity seeks a knowledge of the causes or reasons for things.[13] And while a knowledge of causes and reasons can be put to practical use, the possession of such knowledge is also, Aristotle says, intrinsically rewarding. Among the animals, we alone are moved to investigate the structure of the world, and we alone experience the understanding this produces as something delightful in itself.

If our study of the world is motivated, as both Plato and Aristotle say, by "wonder,"[14] by our human curiosity about the reasons and causes for the world's being as it is, the pleasure in which our investigations culminate might be described as a kind of wonder too—as our astonishment that the world has a structure that explains it and that we are able to comprehend this structure ourselves.[15] The human study of the world thus both begins and ends in wonder, and the wonder it produces is a state we enjoy for its own sake and independently of the utility of the discoveries that fill us with astonishment—independently of what these discoveries are good *for*.

Science is the name we give to our study of the world. It begins in ignorance and the desire to understand why things are as they are. It starts with amazement, which the dictionary defines as being filled with wonder. Science aims to replace ignorance with understanding, puzzlement with comprehension. But its goal is not to make our wonder at the world disappear. Science does not seek to eradicate wonder, in the way that other activities, like eating and drinking, eradicate the states (of hunger and thirst) that provide their motivation. It transforms the nature of our wonder, from wonder *about* things to wonder *at* them, to amazement at the structure of things and our capacity to grasp this structure ourselves.

The first kind of wonder is characterized by the absence of understanding. That is what gives rise to the search for knowledge. The second is characterized by the presence of understanding, which is its very source. One kind of wonder is therefore defined by the presence of precisely what is missing in the other. They are related in the way that the beginning and end of all developmental processes are, in Aristotle's view, always related, the beginning being marked by the absence of and longing for what the end actually possesses.[16] Every such process is therefore a fulfillment and not just an interval between two different states. Science is in this sense a fulfillment too. For the states of wonder in which science begins and ends are related as longing to achievement, privation to possession, and the movement from one to the other is the realization of a uniquely human potential whose attainment brings us, Aristotle says, a pleasure distinct from the useful powers it yields.

It may seem implausible that this old, Aristotlean way of thinking should have any relevance to science today. After all, the scientific revolution of the sixteenth and seventeenth centuries began by repudiating Aristotle's conception of nature, with its "entelechies" and other vital powers, and by replacing his picture of the world with a strikingly different one in which all causes are mechanical and mathematically measurable. Moreover, for Aristotle, the knowledge in which our study of the world concludes, and our curiosity about it is fulfilled, consists in the understanding of what he calls "being *qua* being" and the contemplation of God—in metaphysics and theology.[17] Modern science rejects these completely, as it also rejects the assumption, so important to Aristotle's thought, that the world has a fixed and final structure which the human mind can grasp completely. Today, we know that science is an endless process with no final terminus yielding ultimate and unsurpassable knowledge. We know it is an inquiry that is forever probing deeper into the structure of the world without exhausting the questions that remain to be asked. We know that science is a series of defeasible discoveries, each destined to be displaced by those that follow, in the way that classical mechanics has been displaced by quantum theory and Mendel's understanding of genetics by molecular biology.

These are fundamental differences between our conception of scientific knowledge and Aristotle's. But his claim that we take pleasure in such knowledge for its own sake and pursue it, among other reasons, for the intrinsic satisfaction it affords, remains as true today as when Aristotle made it. The character and content of science change from one age to the next. But the desire to understand the world is ageless, and the pleasure we take in the satisfaction of this desire is perennial too.

Today, the modern sciences of nature surpass all other modes of human knowledge—religious, philosophical, historical, and literary—in their capacity to satisfy our desire to understand. From this knowledge, great powers flow and these powers satisfy to an unprecedented extent the human desire for control. But quite apart from its utility, which is manifest in the expanding arsenal of modern technologies on which we all depend, our scientific under-standing of the world commands the authority it does in our civilization because it satisfies more fully than any other kind of knowledge our desire to understand. The natural sciences now have a near monopoly on wonder. They have by far the greatest power to pro-duce in us that condition of amazement that is the result of every successful investigation of the world. We defer to the natural sciences and admire them on account of their unri-valed capacity to produce this condition, and if we sometimes lose sight of the intensity of the pleasure we take in the satisfaction of our desire to understand, that is only because it is almost always accompanied by the equally intense pleasure we take in the expansion of our powers of control.

Our deep dependence on the modern technological order, outside of whose web of power-enhancing gadgets few today venture, even in imagination; our recognition that the marvels of modern technology have all been wrung from the world by the deepening knowledge of its structure that the natural sciences afford; and the capacity of these same disciplines to provoke, even among those with no scientific training at all, a sense of wonder at the intelligibility of the world and our ability to grasp it—an experience that once only other forms of knowledge could produce: all these today conspire to give the natural sciences and their practical products an incomparable authority in the world at large. The natural sciences validate themselves with the useful results of their discoveries. They set the standard by which the solidity and objectivity of other forms of knowledge must be measured. They illuminate the world and bring it under our control. They gratify our desire for control and our desire to understand, and their capacity to satisfy so powerfully both of these desires at once is the source of the unique authority the natural sciences possess in the world today. Theirs is the dominant authority of our age.

The same is true, though in a more limited way, of the social sciences. The knowledge that is produced by the social sciences does not, of course, manifest itself in practical inventions of the same indisputable utility as those that flow from the discoveries of the natural sciences. But we now look to the social sciences for objective guidance in solving an ever wider range of social and political problems and rely to an increasing degree on the technologies of management their methods and ideas allow.

Modern political societies are no longer administered through a combination of statesmanship and personal allegiance and on the basis of common sense and anecdotal knowledge. These may have been adequate for the polities of the past. But for the modern nation state, whose political, legal, and administrative apparatus touches virtually every aspect of human life and regulates many in exquisite detail, more systematic and impersonal forms of knowledge are required.[18] Much of this apparatus is today in the hands of experts whose authority derives from their possession of a rigorous and objective understanding of the structures and systemic forces that condition the work of politicians and administrators. Indeed, these very structures are themselves typically the product of what is sometimes called "social engineering" or "institutional design"—of a process deliberately directed toward the achievement of specific functional goals and guided by a methodical understanding of the means required to reach them, which the experts who possess and apply this understanding look to the social sciences to supply.

Every political society is always, to some degree, an inheritance as well as an artifact. It is always, to some degree, a product of history and chance as well as of self-conscious design. But the political societies of the modern world are, to an extent unprecedented in the whole of human history, artifacts constructed according to a plan. They are the products of decisions made by experts relying on systematic and impersonal knowledge—on social science as opposed to the wisdom of the statesman—and requiring for their administration the continuing application of such knowledge to the challenges of social and political life.

Those who live in these societies understand this condition intuitively. They know that the organization of their societies depends upon a managerial expertise that is sufficiently reliable to give those responsible for maintaining the complex machinery of social life the guidance they need to do so. And they understand, confidently if not always clearly, that the expertise in question is the fruit of the social sciences, which in this way come to possess a powerful authority themselves.

The authority of the social sciences manifests itself in countless ways. Today, for example, elected officials in many countries rely on opinion-testing devices to frame positions and develop strategies, and their constituents depend on these same devices to judge the performance of those in office. The effectiveness of prisons in achieving the goals of criminal punishment and the relative utility of other methods for preventing crime; the design of a process for approving new drugs that strikes an optimal balance between safety and speed; the creation of a plan for sustainable fisheries; the choice among alternative systems of health care; the setting of speed limits for automobiles and the placement and timing of stoplights; the reform of social security; the definition of property rights in ideas: these and an endless stream of other issues that modern societies face are today debated by experts who look to the social sciences for instruction and guidance.[19]

The social sciences cannot always settle these debates decisively. Intractable differences of value and opinion often remain. But the knowledge they provide plays a crucial role in the formulation of the issues involved and in the evaluation of the solutions that different experts propose. Indeed, it is increasingly difficult to think of *any* problem in the expanding universe of tasks for which the modern administrative state has assumed responsibility to whose solution the social sciences are not now expected to make some contribution. In many cases, we can no longer even describe these problems, or imagine a means of addressing them, without relying on the methical understanding of human society which the social sciences provide.

This is clearest in the case of economics. The discipline of economics plays a larger role in modern public life than any other social science. Legislators, administrators, and even judges today routinely use the vocabulary and methods of economics to frame the issues they confront and the solutions they propose.[20] In some areas of administration it is today nearly inconceivable that a question could be approached from any other point of view, and nowhere is it surprising to find an issue formulated in economic terms. One might without exaggeration say that economics is today *the* science of administration and policy-making—that every weighing of costs and benefits in pursuit of the greatest good (which is what policy-makers are expected to do) is either a form of economic analysis or an ad hoc judgment with no discipline at all.

Of course, even with the instruments of economic and political power which the social sciences now place at our disposal, our capacity to control our social, political, and economic circumstances is limited. The progressive income tax is a device for softening disparities of wealth, but birth still makes an enormous difference so far as our life chances are concerned. More of what politicians do is subject to review, but much is still done in the dark. And though our power to control the market and to adjust for its systemic effects (the degradation of the environment, for example) is greater than ever before, the market itself remains a force that is unpredictable and uncontrollable in important respects—a fate that shapes our lives in ways we must simply accept.

But were it not for the technologies of social and political control which the modern social sciences enable us to employ, our lives would be more deeply and decisively determined by fate than any of us could accept or even imagine. The essential meaning of the powers with which the social sciences equip us is therefore the same as the meaning of the powers the natural sciences provide. Our modern technologies of communication, transportation, and medicine are all devices for defeating, or at least extending, the fateful limits within which we would otherwise be cabined. The modern technologies of economic and political control do the same. Their results may not be as dramatic or their powers as complete. But they press in the same direction. They are motivated by the same ambition. And we value them for the same reason too. We value them because they satisfy our desire to rid the world of fate, which takes a social and economic form (the position of the families into which we are born, the anonymous powers of the market, etc.) as well as a purely physical one (our inability, without technological help, to speak with those thousands of miles away or live with diabetes).

Like the natural sciences, the social sciences enjoy the authority they do for another reason as well, because they enable us to understand the social world we inhabit with a precision and thoroughness never before attainable—an understanding that is a source of satisfaction in its own right, quite apart from the practical powers it yields. The nature and workings of human society were of course topics of observation and analysis long before the rise of the modern social sciences in the eighteenth and nineteenth centuries. Philosophers, historians, politicians, and others, from Plato to Tocqueville, explored these subjects in detail. But the practitioners of the new social sciences possessed something their predecessors lacked: a set of methods that enabled them for the first time to explore these ageold subjects in a rigorous fashion, to study human societies systematically and to express their laws in quantitative terms, much as the new sciences of nature had found the means to do two centuries before.

These new methods rested upon a number of simplifying assumptions about the sources and character of human motivation (the counterpart of the simplifying assumptions about the motion of physical bodies on which classical mechanics was based) and made use of novel techniques for the gathering and analysis of large volumes of information about the behavior of people in society, which in turn permitted the laws of social action to be framed and tested on the basis of something more reliable than anecdotal knowledge.[21] The philosophers and others who, in earlier ages, had written about the nature and workings of society had had nothing to go on but their own, unsystematic experience of the social world and their personal judgments about it. The pioneers of the new social sciences relied instead on surveys and statistics, and their contemporary descendants make use of more advanced techniques like those of econometrics. In this way, the social sciences were able to reorganize the study of social behavior along lines resembling those already well-established in the natural sciences. Rigor, objectivity, impersonality, a reliance on quantitative methods, the framing of hypotheses that are vulnerable to empirical disconfirmation—the hallmarks of understanding in the natural sciences—all these now became for the first time achievable in the study of human affairs as well.

It may be unreasonable for the social sciences to hope to attain a level of precision comparable to that of the natural sciences. The more limited extent to which they can make use of the experimental method; the relatively less refined instruments of observation they employ; and the inherently purposive nature of the human actions they study (which introduces a special kind of indeterminacy the natural sciences do not confront) all constrain the social sciences in their pursuit of precision and objectivity. But despite these limitations, the social sciences have sought from the beginning to emulate the natural sciences, in so far as this is possible, by defining the laws of social action with a degree of exactness greater than any attained before. This is what distinguishes the social sciences as a family of disciplines from the older, less rigorous traditions of study to which they succeeded, and together they have gone far enough in realizing this ambition to justify their claim to have put the study of human society on a scientific footing for the very first time.

If, for example, one compares Aristotle's brief remarks on the economics of the household with Alfred Marshall's analysis of the firm or contemporary models of general equilibrium theory; if one contrasts Rousseau's comments about the role of public opinion with the latest study of polling techniques; if one places Madison's account of political factions side by side with any recent discussion of the dynamics of coalition formation, one is led in each case to conclude that however engaging the first, the second treats its subject with incomparably greater rigor and advances our understanding from anecdote and speculation to a deeper form of knowledge.[22] It is hard to resist the conclusion that we are approaching more closely an objective understanding of how the social world actually works. And even though this understanding can never rival in its exactness our knowledge of the natural world, it satisfies, so far as such satisfaction is attainable at all, our desire to understand the mechanisms of human society for the sheer pleasure of such understanding itself.

Today, the natural sciences satisfy our desire for understanding to a unique degree. But the social sciences have a share in this as well, just as they have a share in the creation of the modern technological order that gives us such immense powers of control over our social and natural environments. From their twofold satisfaction of our desires for understanding and control, the social sciences derive the large authority they now enjoy, like the even greater authority of the natural sciences which draws on these same two sources.

Outside the academy, the natural and social sciences are valued for the powers they produce and the knowledge they provide. This naturally causes us to assign a special value to the areas of academic research from which these powers and knowledge derive. Indeed, even this way of putting things fails to express how close the connection is between the position of the sciences outside our colleges and universities and their standing within them. For viewed as academic disciplines, as subjects of instruction and fields of research, the natural and social sciences *belong to* the larger system of practices and beliefs that gives our world as a whole its dominantly scientific character. They do not support this system from without, as an adjunct to it. They are part of it. They are nodes within it. The prestige which the natural and social sciences today enjoy in the realm of higher education is thus merely a local expression of the tremendous authority that science and its products enjoy in our civilization generally.

The humanities, by contrast, do not share in this authority. They are not part of the system of science and make no contribution to it. They neither add to its practical powers nor participate in its intellectual progress. And because of this they are cut off from the most potent source of authority in the world today.

The disciplines that comprise the humanities are of course connected in a variety of ways to activities and institutions outside the realm of higher education. They are connected, most directly, to the sphere of "culture"—to museums and movies and orchestras and publishing houses. Many people make their living in this sphere, and its products are a familiar and valued part of most people's lives. We enjoy the works of culture and would be desperately impoverished without them. But however much pleasure and fulfillment they provide, the world of culture lacks the authority that today science alone possesses.

The technological products of science affect us in decisive ways and change our lives in a common direction. Technology is in this sense a force of convergence. Even as it expands our powers of choice, it makes our lives more alike. It brings us more and more completely into a community of shared experiences, habits, and expectations. The science that lies behind technology is a force of convergence too. Its truths are ones that we are all compelled to recognize, and our recognition of them moves us steadily and irresistibly toward a community of shared belief, one that transcends all other differences of outlook and opinion.

Culture, by contrast, is neither uniform nor progressive. It tends to be a force of separation more often than one of convergence. It sets us apart, according to taste and tradition, and however meaningful its products, however much enjoyment they afford, the claim that some cultural object or activity reveals in a decisive way the universal and incontestible truth about the world is a claim we often find hard to accept, in contrast to the unreflective ease with which we accept similar claims when made on behalf of a new scientific discovery. In this sense, culture lacks the authority that science possesses, and the humanities—the academic disciplines that belong to the sphere of culture, that form nodes within it in the way the natural and social sciences form nodes within the realm of science—lack such authority too.

From the wondrous achievements of science, from its engorging powers and commanding discoveries and hence from the authority of science itself, the humanities are almost completely cut off. We do not need the humanities for technology. They cannot satisfy our desire to understand with the same decisive clarity as the natural and social sciences. What, then, do we need them for? What can their purpose and value be?

The answer is that we need the humanities to meet the deepest spiritual longing of our age, whose roots lie in the hegemony of science itself. At the very heart of our civilization, with its vast powers of control, there is an emptiness that science has created and cannot fill. It is an emptiness that many people feel and a cause of much anguish and yearning. It is the nursery bed of that great upwelling of religious feeling, of the surge of fundamentalist belief, that is such a striking feature of life today, in America and the world at large. To this yearning, which many in our colleges and universities wrongly dismiss as a kind of mindless obscurantism, the humanities offer the best response we have. Our need for them is as great as the spiritual emptiness our immense powers have bequeathed us. Once this need is named and acknowledged, the humanities will be seen to be our most durable source of wisdom in responding. Their purpose will again be clear and their authority patent. The nature and value of their contribution to higher education will once more be transparent. And the way will be opened to the restoration of the question of life's meaning to a respected place in our colleges and universities and to the reaffirmation of secular humanism.

The spiritual emptiness of our civilization has its source in the technology whose achievements we celebrate and on whose powers we all now depend.

Technology relaxes or abolishes the existing limits on our powers. There is no limit to this process itself. Indeed, every step forward is merely a provocation to go further. This might be called the technological "imperative." The greater our powers become, the more aware we are of the limits to which they are still subject and the more anxious to overcome them. If planes fly fast, we want them to fly faster. If medicines work well, we want them to work better. The result is a process of technological improvement that goes on forever. The end of this process, could it be attained, would be the expansion of our powers to omnipotence, the abolition of our finitude. This end of course cannot be reached. But it functions as a regulative ideal against which all technological progress is measured and from whose vantage point it is considered progress as such.

But there is a problem with the pursuit of this goal that has nothing to do with its unattainability. It arises from the fact that our powers have meaning for us only within the limits of human life. Their value and meaning are conditioned by our mortality. However great they may be, our powers have the meaning they do only because they are not unlimited, because we are not perfectly powerful, because we are finite beings who possess and exercise these powers subject to certain binding constraints. That we must die is a fate no human being can escape, though technology permits us to extend the length of life and to exert ever greater control over how and when we die. But it is only because we are mortal that the powers we possess have value for us and their use any meaning at all.[23]

If we lived forever, our powers, however great, would have no significance. How could it possibly matter whether we exercised them one way or another, sooner rather than later? This can matter to us only within the framework of a lifetime, that is, within the boundaries of a mortal existence. That we sometimes imagine (or think we imagine) that we want to have and use limitless powers in a limitless life is an illusion that always depends on our covertly smuggling into our imagined picture of such an existence some essential feature of the human mortality we can never escape. In reality, the idea of immortality is for us quite unimaginable. It remains an empty abstraction. All we ever know and all we can imagine is the mortality that forms the widest horizon of our speculations and that fixes the fateful frame within which everything we have and do, including our powers and the uses to which we put them, alone has meaning for us.

In fact, we are limited in many ways. None of us, for example, can stay awake all the time. Technology helps us control when, where, and for how long we sleep. But no one can do without sleep altogether. The respite it offers from living is essential to the tiring work of life itself. Nor can any human being share the routines of everyday life in an intimate way with more than a limited number of others. Technology helps us keep in touch with family members when we are separated from them, and it certainly alters in profound ways the patterns of domestic life. But it can never enable to us to have a family relationship, or friendship, with every other human being. Perhaps if we were immortal we could do this, by rotating from one family and friend to the next, assuming that everyone else was immortal too. In that sense, it might be more accurate to say that our mortality is not merely the most impressive of our limits but the condition or sum of them all.

Mortality, so understood, is our destiny or fate. It sets a limit to what we do. On the one hand, we want to push this limit further and further back. We always want to have greater control over ourselves and the world, to be less dependent on fate. We would like not to be subject to fate at all. We have a desire for control that can never be satisfied by any degree of control we actually achieve. We always want more. The desire for more control is inscribed in the human soul. And yet on the other hand, the meaning of all the powers we possess is dependent upon their location within a fateful limit without which the exercise of our powers would be pointless. They are not pointless only because they are directed toward the achievement of various ends, and these ends themselves would not—could not—exist for us if our lives themselves were endless. An immortal existence can have no purpose, in the strict sense of the word, and the longing we sometimes think we have for immortality is not a longing for a life in which all our purposes might finally be achieved, but for an existence that is free of the burdens of purposefulness that are the mark of our humanity—for an existence that is no longer human.

Our situation is therefore, in an elementary way, selfcontradictory. For it is characterized by a longing for the abolition of the very limits that give all our longings their meaning—limits whose final abolition, were it actually attainable, would not be the fulfillment of our deepest ambition but the elimination of the ground of our having any ambitions at all, and therefore of living lives that possess any meaning whatsoever. This is the human condition, which is characterized by our subjection to fateful limits that we can neither tolerate nor do without. This is the truth about who we are.

Of course, the longing to abolish fate can never be fulfilled. Technology can extend life but it cannot cancel death. Hence it always leaves in place the limits that ground the meaningfulness of our ambitions, including the ambition for ever greater control over the circumstances of life itself. It might therefore seem that technology is consistent with the truth about our self-contradictory nature.

But this is wrong in one crucial respect. For the most important thing about technology is not *what* it does but what it *aspires* to do. It is true that technology always has limits. But from the standpoint of technology itself, these limits are an affront—something to be overcome. Technology encourages us to believe—or to think that we believe—that the abolition of fate should be our goal. It devalues the fateful features of human existence. It encourages us to view them as *nothing but* an obstacle, a challenge, something to be erased, and promotes the habit of regarding whatever limits remain on our powers of control at any given level of technological development as a wholly negative fact, one that only compromises the purposefulness and hence meaning of human life and in no way contributes to its achievement.

Technology discourages the thought that our finitude is a condition of the meaningfulness of our lives. It makes this thought appear backward and stupid. It deprives it of intelligibility. It causes us to forget the connection between mortality and meaning. It makes the effort to recall our limits and to reflect upon them seem less valuable and important. It obscures the imaginative space in which this happens, or might happen. It makes it harder for us to find this space and to inhabit it, or even to recall that it exists. Technology suppresses as a subject of contemplation and wonder the very condition on which the powers of technology themselves depend for their meaning.

Our civilization is characterized by its unprecedented powers of control. It is also characterized by its unparalleled repression of the mortal facts and this, too, is a consequence of technology. Technology obscures the truth about us. In place of the full truth, it gives us a half-truth that recognizes our limitless desire for control but denies all value to the limits on which the meaning of this desire depends. It encourages a partial knowledge of humanity and invites us to think that this is all there is worth knowing. It encourages a kind of ignorance, and not about a trivial thing. For the ignorance that technology encourages is an ignorance about ourselves, the most important thing we could ever want to understand. It promotes an ignorance of the worst and most troubling sort, the kind we should be most eager to avoid. And yet it is precisely this worst of all forms of ignorance that is the hallmark of our civilization with its immense powers of control and its systematic devaluation of the fateful limits of human life—apart from which nothing in our lives, and least of all the powers we possess, can ever have any meaning or value for us. Increasingly today we live in ignorance of the human condition.

The devaluation of these limits is the source of the spiritual crisis that motivates the inspired religious movements that have large and growing followings in the United States and elsewhere today. Some of these movements preach peace and others war. Some approve the separation of church and state; others abhor it. Some demand submission to church leadership. Others emphasize the saving power of individual conscience. But all condemn human arrogance and pride. All insist that we are not fully in control of our lives, that we depend on powers other than our own, that we are subject to limits we can never exceed—and all demand humility in the presence of these limits. All of these movements derive their energy and appeal from their opposition to the secular morality of the civilization that most of their followers comfortably inhabit most of the time—from their opposition, above all, to the morality of choice that regards the expansion of freedom, of the power to do as we choose, as the preeminent if not exclusive human good. To this morality, the fundamentalist Protestant churches in America, the jihadist wing of Islam, and the Pope all oppose a morality of humility and submission, of acquiescence in our lack of control and grateful acceptance of the power of God, on which we depend and must never foolishly arrogate to ourselves. All seek to revalue the limits of human life, to turn these from something we view as an obstacle and to which we can only assign a negative value, into something we accept and whose existence is an occasion for gratitude rather than rebellion.[24]

Different religions express this thought in different ways and draw on different traditions to do so. But the thought itself is common to the movements that comprise the religious revival we are witnessing today. It is what sets these movements in opposition to the morality of our technological civilization, even as they exploit the powers it provides. And it is what attracts their followers, who increasingly experience the devaluation of mortality that technology implies as an emptiness in which these powers themselves lack all meaning and value. The result is a spiritual crisis of large proportions. The religious movements that today call for humility and acquiescence in place of arrogance and pride are the most visible and influential response to this crisis. Their common goal is the restoration of meaning to mortality, and with that to the lives we live within the fateful frame of birth and death.

These movements offer a common diagnosis of the crisis of our age. They say it is a consequence of the "death of God" and of man's appropriation of God's place, of man's assertion of the right and power to be the self-sufficient ground of his own life, the master of his fate and hence subject to no fate at all. They call this the "godlessness" of the modern world and identify the death of God as the source of the loss of meaning that has come with the hypertrophic expansion of our human powers. And for this "disease"—which is how they see it—these movements all propose a common cure: the restoration of God to His rightful place, and the demotion of man who has usurped it. Only in this way, their prophets and preachers say, can the spiritual crisis of modernity be overcome. This is the common thread of advice that all the religious movements of our day, the militant and peaceful alike, offer their followers, and there are many who are prepared to hear and follow it.

Cosmopolitan observers, especially in our colleges and universities, tend to view such advice with bemusement and scorn. They consider it shallow and mindless. They look down on those who give and receive it. They consider them naive and possibly dangerous. But their smugness prevents them from grasping the source and magnitude of the crisis of meaning these religious movements address, and from seeing that it is a crisis in which they too are caught, along with those whose spiritual yearnings they mock.

This crisis has its source, as the leaders of these movements understand, in the devaluation of mortality that defines the powerful but pointless age we inhabit. Genuine comprehension, as opposed to the facile dismissiveness that often takes its place in our colleges and universities, begins with the acknowledgment that the crisis is real. But there is another, better response to it than the one these movements recommend. For the crisis we face is not the result of the death of God. There have been other ages, that of classical antiquity most famously, from which the love of God as these movements conceive it—the love of a personal, transcendent Creator God to whom one gratefully submits—was absent, but in which the bond between mortality and meaning was recognized with a force and clarity we have forgotten. The crisis of spirit we now confront is a consequence not of the death of God, but of man. It is the forgetfulness of our own humanity, of the contradictory condition of the gloriously self-defeating animal we are, marked by a striving for infinite powers whose pursuit has meaning only within the framework of mortality, that has given rise to this crisis and to the emptiness that millions of men and women now experience in their everyday lives.

These are religion's eager recruits, for whom the call to remember God has such appeal. But it is not God that needs to be remembered. It is man. Only the recollection of humanity is an adequate response to the meaninglessness that haunts our technical powers. It is the love of man that needs to be restored: the love of the amusing, tragic, contradictory creature who yearns to be the master of his fate and transforms the world in pursuit of that ambition, but to whom, as Sophocles says, death comes in the end regardless—the inescapable end, foreshadowed from the start, which alone confers meaning on the doomed but magnificent campaign to overcome it.[25] Not the technological fantasy that devalues our mortality and encourages the forgetfulness of man, not the submission to a being greater than ourselves that religion recommends as the alternative (to a being who *is* that infinitely powerful creature that technology invites us to think we may reasonably hope to become), but the recollection of our humanity, the restoration of the love of man, the distressed and affectionate reaffirmation of the human condition that technology obscures and religion would have us surrender: this, and only this, has any real promise of leading us out of the spiritual crisis in which we find ourselves today.

To find our way out of this spiritual crisis, we must learn to attend once more to our mortality. We must learn to value the meaning it confers on what we do and think, on our human loves and labors and ambitions and failures. The natural and social sciences, which we badly need in other ways, cannot help us do this. So far as understanding of this kind is concerned, the natural and social sciences are part of the problem, not its solution. It is to the humanities that we must turn for help in this regard. For the humanities are the record of our encounter with mortality, and their common subject is the very thing that technology eclipses: the fateful limits that constrain our longing for control, and the pathos of yearning and defeat that colors all our human works.

Every living thing is moved by desire. But only human beings are moved by the desire to be different than they are, to transcend their own condition through absolute knowledge, complete power and perfect self-control.[26] Only human beings yearn to escape the orbit of their natural condition, and this yearning for transcendence is as much a part of who we are as the impossibility of its fulfillment. The yearning and its inevitable defeat, the longing for transcendence and the fateful horizon of mortality within which it arises: this *is* our human nature, unique among the natures of all the creatures of the earth in its disquietude.

The humanities study this nature. They represent it. They meditate on its meaning. They bring it into view and concentrate our attention on it. They invite—they compel—us to confront the truth about ourselves and help us to inhabit with greater understanding the disjointed condition of longing and defeat that defines the human condition. Achilles' reflections on honor and memory and the fleeting beauty of youth; Shakespeare's defense of love against the powers of "sluttish time"; Kant's struggle to put our knowledge of certain things on an unchallengeable foundation so as to place the knowledge of others forever beyond reach; Caravaggio's painting of the sacrifice of Isaac, which depicts a confusion of loves that defeats all understanding; and so on endlessly through the armory of humanistic works: the subject is always the same. The subject is always man, whose nature it is to yearn to be more than he is. Technology invites a forgetfulness of mortality that hides this subject away. Only the humanities, whose subject this has always been, can help us recover it. Only they can restore the wonder which those who have glimpsed the human condition have always felt, and which our scientific civilization, with its gadgets and discoveries, obscures through the production of a different kind of wonder that blinds us to our mortality and encourages us to forget who we are.

The science on which technology depends has the authority it does because it gratifies at once our desire for control and our desire to understand for the sake of understanding itself. But this knowledge is not only incomplete, as it must of course be at every stage of its development. It is also the cause of an important kind of ignorance *precisely because* it satisfies so fully our desire to be in ever greater control of our circumstances. Science supports the technological imperative and encourages the devaluation of mortality this implies. But in doing so, it promotes the forgetfulness of humanity that technology invites. Hence just because it satisfies as powerfully as it does our archaic desire for control, science frustrates the equally deep desire for understanding, so far as the understanding of ourselves is concerned. In this one important department of understanding, science does not satisfy both of our most elementary desires at once. It satisfies one and frustrates the other. It frustrates our desire to understand *because* it satisfies our desire for control to such an extraordinary degree.

In other areas of knowledge, perhaps, this conflict does not exist. But with respect to our knowledge of humanity it does. Our scientific knowledge of the world is today greater than ever before. But earlier ages knew more about humanity than we do. By comparison with their steady attention to the human condition, and the great works this produced, our attention is fitful and anemic at best. We have not gained ground in our understanding of humanity, as we have in our knowledge of the physical world. We have lost ground instead.

And the very science which has advanced our knowledge of the physical world and produced technological wonders beyond number, has at the same time diminished our understanding of the human condition itself. Only the study of mortality can combat the ignorance that science and technology breed and satisfy our longing to know who we are. Only in this way can we meet the spiritual crisis of our age, born of the forgetfulness of man, on terms that are adequate to it.

We need the humanities to help us remain alert to the human condition in an age that obscures it from view. We need them because without the humanities we lose the only perspective from which the demon of meaninglessness can be met—a real demon to whom the contemporary revival of religion is a real response. We need the humanities because they offer a better response than religion does, with its promise of redemption through submission to a perfect power that fulfills by other means the technological fantasy of perfect control. And we are motivated to affirm the response the humanities offer by one of our oldest and deepest desires. For the desire to understand, even when the truth is hard, is as deep as our desire for control and, if anything, more distinctively human.

It is a desire that can be frustrated but never lost. We can never cease to want to understand for the sake of understanding itself. But today this desire *is* frustrated with respect to the understanding of ourselves. Science blocks the way to such understanding. Only the humanities can help us recover it. Only they can gratify our desire to understand the peculiar nature of the yearning and doomed creature we are, ennobled by our own self-defeat. Only the humanities can help us meet the need for meaning in an age of vast but pointless powers and satisfy our desire to understand for the intrinsic pleasure such understanding affords, in the branch of knowledge where the frustration of that desire today is most complete.

Nothing, therefore, could be further from the truth than the claim that we do not need the humanities in the way, or to the degree, we now need the natural and social sciences. The truth is just the opposite. The truth is that our need for the humanities is desperate; that it is anchored in a real crisis to which others are responding with real effect; and that the recovery of the humanities, and of the space of observation and reflection they afford, is driven by a desire of the deepest and most durable kind which only the humanities can meet.

The position of the humanities in our colleges and universities today is discouraging. They stand at the bottom of the hierarchy of authority and prestige. They lack the obvious value, and easy self-confidence, that the natural and social sciences possess. But anyone who grasps the depth of our need for the humanities; who understands the magnitude of the crisis that gives rise to this need; who appreciates the potency of our frustrated desire to understand the terrible and inspiring truth about ourselves and who recognizes that the humanities alone can fulfill it, must conclude that forces outside the academy, far from working to keep the humanities in their present position of low esteem, press in exactly the opposite direction and exert a tremendous pressure on their behalf.

Outside our colleges and universities one finds the needs and motives to inspire a revival of the humanities and their restoration to the position of authority and self-confidence they once enjoyed. All that is required is a recognition of the depth of the crisis of meaning our civilization confronts, of the humanities' unique ability to help us respond, and of the close connection between— indeed, the identity of—the question which this crisis has brought to the fore with such urgency for so many people and the question to which the authority of the humanities has always been tied: the question of what living is for.

The technological imperative that rules our lives imprisons the devout and their bemused critics alike. It has created a crisis of meaning in which both are caught. In this crisis lie the occasion and incentive for a revival of the humanities and for the restoration of their lost authority. For the humanities' loving but unsentimental study of the mortal facts represents a more honest and honorable response to the crisis than either the churches or their critics can offer. These both run away from the crisis—the churches by promising salvation if only one makes the humbling sacrifice of human spirit this demands, and their critics by glibly denying there is any crisis at all. Only the humanities give us the resources to face this crisis with the self-respecting composure in the presence of danger that we commonly call courage. Whether those now teaching the humanities in our colleges and universities seize the opportunity to do this remains to be seen, but the prospects seem brighter at the present moment than even a decade ago.

I say this for several reasons. First, the rising tide of religious fundamentalism has given questions of a spiritual nature increasing prominence in the culture at large, among the opponents of religion as well as its supporters. To take one recent example, the question of whether students in public schools should be taught that intelligent design is a respectable alternative to the theory of evolution has stirred a debate about the relation between science and religion in which those on both sides have been forced to clarify their views of man's spiritual needs and of the capacity of science to meet them.[27] The debates over abortion and euthanasia, and the appropriate use of medical technology generally, have had a similar effect. Here, too, the question of whether and how our spiritual nature sets limits to the power of science has been forced into the open. Questions of this sort are increasingly at the center of our cultural attention. The fundamentalists have done us all a service by putting them there. But while they also know how these questions should be answered, there are others who are less certain. There are many who recognize the importance of the questions the fundamentalists ask but reject the answers they give, and who hunger for a serious spirituality of a non-fundamentalist kind.[28] At the moment, however, there are few places for them to look to satisfy their hunger. Our colleges and universities in particular seem unresponsive. The revival of the humanities, and of the tradition of secular humanism, would be for them a welcome development. It would give them a way to reclaim their commitment to the human spirit without the dogmatic assumptions that religion demands. It would give them a platform from which to launch a vigorous and spiritually serious counter-offensive against the fundamentalist movements of our day, which at the moment represent the only serious response to the crisis of meaning whose pervasive presence in our technological civilization makes itself manifest in the debates about religion and science that stir such passions today. The appetite for an alternative to fundamentalism; the longing in the culture at large for an undogmatic rebirth of spiritual concern; the perplexity and confusion of those who recognize the seriousness of the questions the churches ask but reject the answers they offer: these set the stage for a revival of the humanities and provide the energy to sustain it. The hunger is there and only the humanities—the custodians of the tradition of secular humanism—have what it takes to feed it.

Second, the culture of political correctness that has deformed the humanities for the past forty years and been an obstacle to the revival of secular humanism inspires a declining enthusiasm today. The excitement that accompanied the ideas of multiculturalism and constructivism in their early days has subsided. The period defined by their dominance is coming to a close. A spirit of exhaustion now prevails in the humanities, of waiting for these old ideas to play themselves out and for something new to replace them. For most of the second half of the twentieth century, the culture of political correctness has made an appreciation of the values of secular humanism impossible. It has put these under a cloud of disrepute and made them seem more the instruments of partisan oppression than a treasured common possession. But the cloud is lifting. Resistance to their affirmation is decreasing. And as it does, as the culture of political correctness loses its power to chill and discourage, the willingness to reassert these values, to put them forward as a source of spiritual help at a time when we badly need it, and to reclaim the tradition of secular humanism as a confident and credible alternative to the fundamentalism of the churches, will have a smaller hurdle to overcome. It will be easier for those who feel this way to say so, and to represent their point of view as the genuinely progressive one that holds the greatest promise of leading the humanities forward out of their present malaise.

Third, many students in our colleges and universities today would, I think, welcome the chance to explore the question of life's purpose and value in a more disciplined way. Students today enjoy a nearly limitless freedom in choosing what to study. Most schools of course have some nominal divisional or other requirements that impose a superficial order on their under-graduate programs. But these requirements are typically so broad and flexible as to create no meaningful direction at all. In practice, students are almost entirely free to study what they wish, selecting their courses according to taste and ambition from a sprawling array of alternatives. Many will tell you they need this freedom to prepare for the careers they intend to pursue after school. But this is not true and the students themselves know it. There are few careers that require more than a handful of undergraduate courses as pre-professional training. Medical school requires a half-dozen; law school none at all.

Nor is the freedom students enjoy to design their own course of studies always a source of personal gratification. As often, it produces anxiety and regret. A disturbingly large number of today's undergraduates, even at our best colleges and universities, spend four years sampling courses with little or no connection, moved by fancy and curiosity but guided by no common organizing principle or theme. Their freedom leaves them with a transcript that is a patchwork of disconnected bits and scraps, except for whatever modest structure the choice of a major supplies. Too many graduates today view their college years—the most leisurely years of their lives, until they wash up on the far shores of retirement—as a wasted opportunity, squandered in pursuit of a disorganized and idiosyncratic program of study. They view it with regret, as a lost chance to explore the question of what living is for before the demands of life take hold and they become too busy to ask it.

This is not a recipe for happiness and many students know it, as do their parents who understand even more acutely than they how urgent the question of life's meaning is and what a precious, unrepeatable opportunity their children have to explore it. For many students, the reassertion by teachers of the humanities of their competence to guide them in a non-authoritarian but organized examination of this question would be a happy development. It would be responsive to a need that many of them feel but recognize too late and are reticent to express on account of the culture of political correctness, which chills them too—a need which the combination of specialization and free election that now defines most under-graduate programs fails miserably to meet. And it would cheer their parents as well, who want their children's education to be something more than a bit of vocational training supplemented by a random sampling of courses with no organized center, and who hope that their children will have a chance, on the threshold of adulthood, to stock their souls with the greatest and most lasting images of human striving and fulfillment, as guides to the choices they must face in the years ahead and as a fund of perennial inspiration.

These are all reasons to be hopeful about a revival of the humanities and the reassertion of their authority to lead students in exploring the life of the human spirit with the limited but real confidence that secular humanism allows. But there is one factor pulling strongly in the other direction. That is the continued dominance within the humanities of the modern research ideal.

Like their colleagues in other fields, today's humanities teachers are, with rare exceptions, graduates of Ph.D. programs at large research universities. They thus begin their careers having already internalized the research ideal. It colors their understanding of professional success and conditions their view of what is important and valuable in the disciplines to which they belong. It defines their prospects for advancement, which depend upon the volume and quality of the research they produce. The research ideal shapes their professional judgments and fixes the terms of their material and reputational success, just as it does those of other college and university teachers today. But from the standpoint of this ideal, and of the values it reveres and rewards, the question of the meaning of life is not a professionally respectable subject. It is not a question that a research specialist can pursue without appearing to be a self-absorbed dilettante, which is just what the research ethic condemns most harshly. So long as the research ideal continues to define the attitudes and ambitions of teachers of the humanities, any attempt to restore the question of what is living for to an honored place in these disciplines must therefore contend with a professional culture that is hostile to this question itself.

This is a real impediment to the revival of secular humanism but not an insurmountable one. If a reaffirmation of the values of secular humanism demanded a full-scale repudiation of the research ideal, the prospects would indeed be bleak, for the continued dominance of this ideal within the humanities is for the foreseeable future an inescapable fact of life. But a repudiation of this sort is neither necessary nor desirable. In the first place, research in the humanities has produced results of lasting value. It has added importantly to our understanding of the historical, literary, artistic, and philosophical subjects with which the humanities deal. Research in these fields may lack the clearly cumulative character that it has in the natural and social sciences and its connection to the truth may be less evident or stable than in these other disciplines. But its value is indisputable. No one is calling—or should call— for a halt to research in the humanities or a repudiation of its value, and the revival of secular humanism certainly does not require that we do so.

Nor does it require that the values at the heart of the research ideal—the celebration of originality, the demand for specialization, the ethic of supersession—be rejected across the board, that their legitimacy be attacked root and branch. That would be not only impractical but unwarranted, since the problem with these values is not their illegitimacy *tout court* but their tendency to occupy the whole of the humanities and to dictate the exclusive terms on which the worth of everything that is done in them is measured. *That* is what must be resisted if the question of what living is for is to be restored to a place of respect in the humanities and again become a subject to which those teaching in these fields may honorably devote some fraction of their time and energy. What must be resisted is the imperial sprawl of the research ideal, its expansive tendency to fill every corner of each discipline in which it takes hold and to color the expectations and judgments of teachers in these disciplines regarding all they do. Admittedly, this is asking a lot. The modern research ideal is deeply entrenched in the habits of the humanities, and its authority rests on a morally inspired conception of scholarship that casts doubt on the respectability of everything that falls outside the range of questions and pursuits it values, and on the question of the meaning of life in particular. But it is not asking for something impossibly large. It is not asking that teachers of the humanities give up their attachment to the research ideal, repudiate the values it enshrines, and turn the clock back to a time before the research ideal swept the field of all competition. It is merely asking for a somewhat greater degree of humility on the part of those in the humanities whose first allegiance is to this ideal—for a recognition that there is something else of value that teachers in these fields are uniquely equipped to do, and that can be done with honor and respect only if the values that underlie the research ideal are humbly acknowledged to have their limits too.

I suspect that for some teachers of the humanities this acknowledgment would be a liberation. It would give them the professional freedom to take up questions with their students that might otherwise seem both too large and too intimate to be pursued without apology or embarrassment. By "professional" freedom I mean freedom from the inhibiting influence of a professional culture whose devotion to specialization and impersonal research condemns most ventures of this kind. For it is this condemnation that most discourages teachers of the humanities from making their classrooms a forum, some of the time at least, for exploring the question of the meaning of life.

In a formal sense, most college and university teachers, including teachers of the humanities, already enjoy an immense amount of freedom in the classroom. What and how to teach is, to a considerable degree, up to them. The exercise of this freedom is of course constrained by a teacher's own sense of its professionally appropriate uses, and so long as these are defined to rule out the sort of general but personal inquiry that secular humanism endorsed, fewer teachers will have the confidence to undertake it than otherwise might. Lifting this inhibition will liberate more of them to do so. It will give them the freedom to return to the question of life's purpose and value, which even today is what first draws many teachers of the humanities to their fields; to regard the examination of this question as a professionally responsible use of classroom time; and to view the help they give their students in fashioning their own answers to this question as a high, if not the highest, duty they owe the students in their charge.

The freedom of the classroom is immense. The teacher whose freedom it is does not need the permission of a dean or department chair to use as he or she thinks best. With this freedom comes enormous responsibilities. Every serious teacher feels this deeply, and that is entirely as it should be. What is needed in the humanities today is not a relaxation of the teacher's sense of responsibility. What is needed is its reconnection to questions and modes of inquiry that secular humanism honored but the modern research ideal devalues. Even a young teacher, concerned about his or her prospects for promotion and mindful of the fact that these depend on scholarly production, can affirm this connection again, without risk to reputation or career, if given the professional freedom to do so. Nothing is standing in the way but a culture that equates professionalism with the research ideal, and even a modest separation of the two will create the space, for some teachers of the humanities at least, to reaffirm the dignity of secular humanism and their dedication to the ideal of teaching associated with it. If this were to happen, even on a modest scale, it would represent a sea change in the humanities, and the remarkable and inspiring truth is that it lies in the power of individual teachers to bring this about, on their own, one by one, simply by exercising the freedom they already possess. What is needed is not more freedom, or permission from on high. What is needed is relief from the inhibitions of the research ideal, whose internalized authority—which recognizes no limits and demands that all work in the humanities be judged by its standards—is the greatest obstacle to the revival of secular humanism today.

For those who are moved to reclaim the tradition of secular humanism and to reassert its authority against the tidal pull of the research ideal, there are models to follow. The tradition of secular humanism has never died out completely. At a number of schools there are still programs in which its spirit remains alive. The required freshman course in the humanities at Reed College is an example. The five course sequence at St. Olaf's known as "The Great Conversation" and the Directed Studies program at Yale are others. The core curriculum at Columbia is perhaps the best-known example. Many of these programs were established years ago, at a time when the tradition of secular humanism was still strong, and they have retained their original character. Their continued existence is encouraging to anyone who hopes for a wider revival of this tradition and helpful to those looking for suggestions as to how this might be done.

Yale's Directed Studies program, in which I teach, is the model I know best. It was established in 1947, at the same time as Harvard's General Education program and with a similar aim—to provide undergraduates with an organized introduction to the ideas and values of the civilization in whose defense the Second World War had been fought and to prepare them for life in the free and democratic society that was expected to follow. Over the years, Directed Studies has undergone various changes. Today, it is a one-year freshman program in the humanities. Students in Directed Studies take three courses—in literature, philosophy, and history and politics. They hear a lecture a week in each of their subjects, and meet twice a week in groups of eighteen with their teachers in each class. The classes are taught by a mix of junior and senior faculty. The reading list is the same for all the students in the program, and the faculty teaching each subject meet weekly to discuss the assigned material themselves. Students write a paper a week. In addition, there are occasional symposia on topics related to the common readings (the "ancient quarrel" between philosophy and poetry, the status of the Bible as literature, the philosophical origins of the idea of human rights, and so on).

In the literature course, the fall readings start with Homer and end with Dante. In the spring term, the readings begin with Cervantes and conclude with T. S. Eliot. In philosophy, the readings run from Plato to Aquinas in the fall, and Descartes to Wittgenstein in the spring. In history and politics, students start in the fall with Herodotus and then read Thucydides, Plato, Aristotle, Livy, Polybius, Tacitus, Augustine, and Dante. They continue in the spring with Machiavelli, Locke, Hobbes, Rousseau, Kant, and Marx. Modest additions and deletions are made each year, but the reading list has remained largely unchanged for some time. I have included a complete description in an appendix.

The Directed Studies program is elective. Admitted Yale freshmen may apply to the program and must be accepted into it. Last year, 120 students were admitted from a larger applicant pool. The small size of the classes and the large number of faculty required to teach them make the program expensive to run. Staffing is also a perennial challenge. Those teaching in the program enjoy it, but some view it as a distraction from their research interests and hence as a cost in professional terms. Yet despite these difficulties, Directed Studies remains a wonderfully vital program whose popularity among students continues to grow and that regularly attracts to its faculty some of Yale's most distinguished scholars.

At the heart of the program is the question of what living is for. Students read a range of texts that express with matchless power a number of competing answers to this question. They consider the different ways of living that have been held up by different authors at different times as the best life a human being can live. They are encouraged to consider each with interpretive generosity—to enter as deeply as they can into the experiences, ideas, and values that give each its permanent appeal. They are helped to see the tensions that exist among these possibilities and to understand why some of these tensions can never be dissolved. They are invited to consider which alternatives lie closest to their own evolving sense of self. And they are supported in their effort to do this by being welcomed into a conversation whose participants have been arguing about these matters for thousands of years.

This is the spirit of secular humanism. It is the spirit of Directed Studies and of similar programs at other schools. No one of these programs is a model to be copied with mechanical precision. Each has its limits and flaws. None is perfectly adapted to the circumstances of every school that might wish to establish a program of this kind. But their mere existence is proof that even in the age of the research university it is possible for the humanities to address the question of the meaning of life in an organized way, and their details suggest ways to do this. For those who would follow, encouraging examples exist and nothing prevents them from following except their own internalized doubts about the legitimacy of the unspecialized and intensely personal inquiry these programs invite. That is a high hurdle to overcome. But internal doubts are also peculiarly within our own power to dissolve. The spiritual emptiness of our scientific civilization; the receding authority of political correctness; the discontent of many students and their parents with the current system of undergraduate education; the need only to modestly resist the sweeping imperialism of the research ideal in order to clear a place for secular humanism; and the ready availability of models to follow: none of these guarantees that the internal doubts that represent the greatest obstacle to the revival of secular humanism will lose their potency and be overcome to any significant degree, but together they suggest that one who hopes for this has grounds to be cautiously optimistic.

✦

Secular humanism was born at a moment of doubt. When the pieties of the antebellum college began to lose their power and a culture of diversity and doubt took their place, the tradition of offering instruction in the meaning of life—on which American higher education had been based from the start—could survive only in an altered form. Secular humanism made this possible. It offered a way of keeping the question of life's meaning at the center of academic attention and of pursuing it in a disciplined way, while recognizing the pluralistic and skeptical beliefs that had undermined the authority of the old order and the credibility of its principal premise: that there is a single right way to live in God's ordered and intelligible world. The doubts that brought this older order crashing down made it seem to some that no school could now claim the authority to do what every school before had done, to instruct its students in the meaning of life. But secular humanism showed how this was still possible. It was a source of confidence in an age of doubt and for those teachers who embraced it, a new kind of faith, the only one allowed them in the disenchanted world they now inhabited.

Today we need secular humanism for the opposite reason, not as a bulwark against doubt but as a solvent of our certainties. We need it to help us challenge the pieties that condition our lives in deep and unnoticed ways. The revival of secular humanism is needed to help us be doubtful again.

Instead of enforcing a deadening uniformity of opinion, as the humanities' culture of political correctness now does, a revitalized humanism would put the conventional pieties of our moral and political world in question. It would compel students to consider whether justice is a higher good than beauty, whether democracy has room for nobility, whether our reverence for human beings should be qualified by a recognition of original sin. It would force them to confront a wider and more disturbing diversity of opinion than the one they now do in their college and university classrooms. It would disrupt their confidence and deepen their doubts. Today, just the opposite is the case. What doubts students have about these matters are rejected and repressed. They are denied expression. They are barely acknowledged and when they are, they are generally condemned. The revival of secular humanism would turn this culture upside down.

It would convert certainties to doubts and convictions to questions. It would bring the moral and political beliefs that condition our lives into view and give us the chance to inspect them. It would bring what is hidden into the open—the highest goal of the humanities and the first responsibility of every teacher.

It would do this in a second way as well. Students today come to college believing that the most important choice they face is that of a career. Many are undecided about which career to pursue. But nearly all assume that a fulfilling life can be lived only within the channels of a career, which defines a pathway with more or less fixed expectations and rewards. The challenge, as they see it, is to get into the right channel—the right groove—so they can be steered by its demands. The pressures of specialization push students in this direction, and they can hardly be faulted for going along. But a career—any career—has a horizon narrower than that of the life of the person whose career it is. However important, however absorbing, however rewarding, a career is only part of life. Questions always remain about how a person's career fits into his or her life as a whole. These are questions that come more to the fore the longer one lives and become acute toward the end of life, when one again confronts the need to live outside the bounds of one's career. But they are not questions that can be answered from within the horizon of a career. They arise, and can be answered, only from the vantage point of one's life as a whole. But that is a point of view which the anxious search for a career discourages students from adopting, or even recognizing, and which their teachers' commitment to the research ideal systematically devalues.

However urgently students feel pressed to choose a career, to get in a groove and start moving along, their college years are their last best chance to examine their lives from this wider perspective and to develop the habit, which they will need later on, of looking at things from a point of view outside the channels of their careers. This is precisely what secular humanism encourages. In doing so, it runs against the grain of the belief most students share that there is no point of view outside these channels. That a life *is* a career is for them an article of faith. Secular humanism puts this piety in doubt by insisting on the importance of the idea of life as a whole. For a young person on the threshold of a career, nothing could be more disturbing or helpful.

More deeply rooted even than the dogma of career is our addiction to technology and the equation of truth with science. We live today in a narcotized stupor, blind to the ways in which our own immense powers and the knowledge that has produced them cuts us off from the knowledge of who we are. We take these powers for granted and fail to see how the restless drive to expand them devalues the mortal limits within which our lives alone have meaning. We equate this knowledge with truth and fail to see how it obscures the truth about us. Nothing has a tighter hold on us today than technology and science. They fix our values and define the limits of our imagination. They cover the human condition in forgetfulness. Secular humanism is a force for recollection. It seeks to bring us back to our humanity. It does this by reminding us of what our world would have us forget: that we are dying animals, fastened to bodies and fated to pass away, who yet yearn for something more. Our world has reduced death to an inconvenience and robbed us of our humanity. That technology can cancel death is the great orthodoxy of our age. It is the piety by which we live. Secular humanism recalls us to the mortal facts. It helps us remember who we are. But it does this by sowing doubts where certainties exist and by putting into question the answers our scientific civilization invites us to take for granted.

In the early years of the twentieth century, in the great research universities that already had become the dominant force in American higher education, some new way had to be found to educate students in the art of living. Amidst the unprecedented freedoms of the elective system and the growing specialization of faculty departments, teachers of the humanities were forced to invent a new way to do what America's colleges had done from the start, without relying on dogmas that had lost their credibility. Secular humanism pointed the way. It suggested how this might be done. It secured the idea of an art of living in an age of skepticism and doubt.

Today, this idea is not threatened by doubts. It is threatened by pious conviction. Its real enemy is the new faith which prescribes the orthodoxy to which so many students subscribe—the culture of political correctness that strangles serious debate, the careerism that distracts from life as a whole, the blind acceptance of science and technology that disguise and deny our human condition. It is these that now put the idea of an art of living at risk and undermine the authority of humanities teachers to teach it. But these same pieties make it essential that this authority be reclaimed. The secular humanism that once saved us from our doubts must now save us from our convictions. It must rescue the question of life's meaning from the forces that belittle and obscure it and restore the openness and wonder that will always accompany any authentic effort to ask it.

America's colleges and universities are today the leading centers of research in the world. But we have the right to expect something more. We have the right to expect that they offer their students an education in the meaning of life. Once they did, and will again, when the tradition of secular humanism, which has been misplaced but can never be lost, is recovered and put to work as a lever to dislodge the orthodoxies that now blind us. That this will happen I am hopeful. The conditions are encouraging, and the need is great. For the desire to understand is eternal, and in an age of forgetfulness, when our humanity is concealed by the powers we possess and the question of life's meaning is monopolized by the churches, to whom our colleges and universities have relinquished all authority to ask it, the revival of secular humanism offers a spiritual alternative to the fundamentalists who invite us to give ourselves up and to the science that invites us to forget who we are. With wonder and sobriety and the courage to face our mortal selves: let our colleges and universities be the spiritual leaders they once were and that all of us, teachers, students, parents, citizens of the republic, need for them to be again.

Appendix

FALL 2005
Literature

Homer, *Iliad*

Homer, *Odyssey*

Aeschylus, *Oresteia*

Sophocles, *Oedipus the King*

Sophocles, *Oedipus at Colonus*

Virgil, *Aeneid*

Ovid, *Metamorphoses*

The Hebrew Bible (selections)

The New Testament (selections)

Dante, *Divine Comedy* (selections)

History and Politics

Herodotus, *The History*

Thucydides, *History of the Peloponnesian War*

Plato, *Republic*

Aristotle, *Politics* (selections)

Livy, *The Rise of Rome*

Polybius, *The Rise of the Roman Empire*

Tacitus, *The Annals of Imperial Rome*

Augustine, *City of God* (selections)

Dante, *Monarchy*

Brian Tierney, *The Crisis of Church and State, 1050–1300*

Philosophy

Plato, *Euthyphro*

Plato, *Phaedo*

Plato, *Symposium*

Plato, *Republic*

Aristotle, *Nicomachean Ethics* (selections)

Aristotle, *Physics* (selections)

Aristotle, *Categories* (selections)

Aristotle, *De Anima* (selections)

Aristotle, *Metaphysics* (selections)

Sextus Empiricus, *Outlines of Pyrrhonism*

Aquinas, *Summa Theologica* (selections)

Epictetus, *Handbook*

Augustine, *On Free Choice of the Will*

SPRING 2006

Literature

Petrarch, *Rime Sparse*

Shakespeare, *The Sonnets* (selections)

Cervantes, *Don Quixote*

Shakespeare, *King Lear*

Milton, *Paradise Lost*

Blake, *Songs of Innocence and of Experience*

Wordsworth, *Selected Poems and Prefaces*

Goethe, *Faust: Part One*

Flaubert, *Madame Bovary*

Dostoevsky, *The Brothers Karamazov*

Eliot, *The Waste Land*

History and Politics

Machiavelli, *The Prince*

Luther, *On Christian Liberty*

Hobbes, *Leviathan* (selections)

Locke, *Second Treatise of Government*

Rousseau, *The First and Second Discourses*

Rousseau, *The Social Contract*

Burke, *Reflections on the Revolution in France*

Hamilton, Madison, and Jay, *The Federalist Papers* (selections)

Tocqueville, *Democracy in America* (selections)

Mill, *On Liberty*

Emerson, *Self Reliance*

Marx, *The German Ideology; The Jewish Question; The Communist Manifesto*

Nietzsche, *Uses and Disadvantages of History for Life*

Arendt, *Origins of Totalitarianism* (selections)

Philosophy

Descartes, *Meditations on First Philosophy*

Leibniz, *Philosophical Essays ("Primary Truths," "Discourse on Metaphysics," "Monadology")*

Berkeley, *Three Dialogues Between Hylas and Philonous*

Hume, *Enquiry Concerning Human Understanding*

Hume, *A Treatise of Human Nature* (selections)

Kant, *Critique of Pure Reason* (selections)

Kant, *Grounding for the Metaphysics of Morals*

Mill, *Utilitarianism*

Kierkegaard, *Fear and Trembling*

Nietzsche, *On the Genealogy of Morals*

Wittgenstein, *On Certainty*

Notes

INTRODUCTION

1. Tom Hayden, *The Port Huron Statement: The Visionary Call of the 1960s Revolution* (New York: Thunder's Mouth Press, 2005).

CHAPTER ONE. WHAT IS LIVING FOR?

1. See, e.g., Ludwig Wittgenstein, *Tractatus Logico-Philosophicus* (London: Routledge and Kegan Paul, 1922), 6.52–6.521 ("We feel that even if *all possible* scientific questions be answered, the problems of life have still not been touched at all. Of course then there is no question left, and just this is the answer. The solution of the problem of life is seen in the vanishing of the problem."). For a variety of thoughtful perspectives on "questioning the question" of the meaning of life, see E. D. Klemke, ed., *The Meaning of Life*, 2nd ed. (New York: Oxford University Press, 2000), 207–294.

2. Woody Allen, *Getting Even* (New York: Random House, 1966); *Monty Python and the*

Meaning of Life, DVD, directed by Terry Jones and Terry Gilliam (1983; Los Angeles: Universal Studios, 2003).

3. Gina Kolata, "At Last, Shout of 'Eureka!' in Age-Old Math Mystery," *New York Times*, June 24, 1993; Gina Kolata, "Flaw Is Found in Math Proof, but Repairs Are Under Way," *New York Times*, December 11, 1993; Gina Kolata, "How a Gap in the Fermat Proof Was Bridged," *New York Times*, January 31, 1995.

4. Jason Socrates Bardi, *Calculus Wars: Newton, Leibniz, and the Greatest Mathematical Clash of All Time* (New York: Thunder's Mouth Press, 2006); Gottfried Wilhelm Leibniz and Samuel Clarke, *Correspondence*, ed. Roger Ariew (Indianapolis: Hackett, 2000); A. Rupert Hall, *Philosophers at War: The Quarrel Between Newton and Leibniz* (Cambridge: Cambridge University Press, 1980); Alexandre Koyré, *From the Closed World to the Infinite Universe* (Baltimore: Johns Hopkins University Press, 1957), 235–272.

5. François duc de La Rochefoucauld, *Maxims*, trans. Stuart D. Warner and Stephanie Douard (South Bend: St. Augustine's Press, 2001), 8.

6. Compare Heidegger's discussion of angst in *Being and Time*, trans. Joan Stambaugh (Albany: State University of New York Press, 1996), Sec. 40.

7. T. S. Eliot, "The Lovesong of J. Alfred Prufrock," in *Collected Poems 1909–1935* (New York: Harcourt, Brace, 1936), 17.

8. Johann Wolfgang von Goethe, *The Sorrows of Young Werther*, trans. Elizabeth Mayer and Louise Brogan (New York: Modern Library, 1993); Thomas Mann, *Death in Venice*, trans. Kenneth Burke (Avon, Conn.: Heritage Club, 1972).

9. In what follows, I have been much influenced by the deep and thoughtful work of Harry Frankfurt. See especially, Harry G. Frankfurt, "The Importance of What We Care About," in *The Importance of What We Care About: Philosophical Essays* (New York: Cambridge University Press, 1988), 83.

10. Aristotle, *Nicomachean Ethics*, in *The Basic Works of Aristotle*, ed. Richard McKeon, trans. W. D. Ross (New York: Random House, 1941), 1145a 15–1151a 28; Sigmund Freud, *Introductory Lectures on Psychoanalysis*, trans. and ed. James Strachey (New York: Norton, 1966), 286–302.

11. Bernard Williams, *Moral Luck: Philosophical Papers, 1973–1980* (Cambridge: Cambridge University Press, 1981).

12. Ludwig Wittgenstein, *Philosophical Investigations*, trans. G. E. M. Anscombe (Malden, Mass.: Blackwell, 1977), 38.

13. Aristotle, *Nicomachean Ethics*, 1155a–1163b.

14. Compare Max Weber's famous distinction between those religious virtuosi who think of themselves as the "instruments" of God and those who conceive of themselves as "vessels" of the divine. Max Weber, "The

Sociology of the World Religions," in *From Max Weber*, ed. H. Gerth and C. W. Mills (New York: Oxford University Press, 1946).

15. Spinoza, *Ethics* V., Prop. XLI, Scholium.

CHAPTER TWO. SECULAR HUMANISM

1. In April, 2006, the Council for Higher Education recognized 6,814 institutions accredited either by it or by organizations approved by the United States Department of Education. Council for Higher Education Accreditation, "Fact Sheet #1: Profile of Accreditation," http://www.chea.org/pdf/fact_sheet_1_profile.pdf (accessed June 9, 2006).

2. For a general survey, see *American Universities and Colleges*, 16th ed., ed. James J. Murray III (New York: Walter de Gruyer, 2001), 1: 3–26; Arthur M. Cohen, *The Shaping of American Higher Education: Emergence and Growth of the Contemporary System* (San Francisco: Jossey-Bass, 1998), 300–319; *The Chronicle of Higher Education*, "The Almanac of Higher Education, 2005–6," http://chronicle.com/free/almanac/2005/ (accessed June 11, 2006).

3. For a discussion of the difficulty of "quantifying the creation and marketing of knowledge," see Michael Mandel, "Why the Economy Is a Lot Stronger Than You Think," *Business Week*, February 13, 2006, 63.

4. For a classic statement of the importance of education to a democracy, see John Dewey,

Democracy and Education (New York: Macmillan, 1916), 115 ("A society which makes provision for participation in its good of all its members on equal terms and which secures flexible readjustment of its institutions through interaction of the different forms of associated life is in so far democratic. Such a society must have a type of education which gives individuals a personal interest in social relationships and control, and the habits of mind which secure social changes without introducing disorder."). Before Dewey and after him, pronouncements concerning the links between higher education and the health of the Republic have been issued at regular intervals. See, e.g., "The Yale Report of 1828," in *American Higher Education: A Documentary History*, ed. Richard Hofstadter and Wilson Smith (Chicago: University of Chicago Press, 1961), 1: 275–291, 289 ("Our republican form of government renders it highly important, that great numbers should enjoy the advantage of a thorough education."); Gail Kennedy, ed., *Education for Democracy: The Debate Over the Report of the President's Commission on Higher Education* (Boston: D. C. Heath, 1952), v ("In a modern democracy education has a unique function. It must not impress conformity but create attitudes that foster independence. It must rear the young to exercise freedom and accept responsibility."); Alexander W. Astin, "Liberal Education and Democracy: The Case for Pragmatism," in *Education and Democracy:*

Re-imagining Liberal Learning in America, ed. Robert Orrill (New York: College Entrance Examination Board, 1997), 207–223, 219 ("In short, we in the higher education community not only have helped to create the problems that plague U.S. democracy, but we are also in a position to begin doing something about them."); Amy Gutmann, *Democratic Education* (Princeton: Princeton University Press, 1999), 174 ("Control of the creation of ideas—whether by a majority or a minority—subverts the ideal of *conscious* social reproduction at the heart of democratic education and democratic politics. As institutional sanctuaries for free scholarly inquiry, universities can help prevent such subversion.").

5. Meiklejohn, "College Education and the Moral Ideal," *Education* 28 (1908), 554.

6. See, e.g., Harvard University, "Handbook for Students 2006–2007," http://webdocs.registrar.fas.harvard.edu/ugrad_handbook/current/ugrad_handbook.pdf (accessed August 5, 2006), 2; Bates College, "Mission Statement and By-Laws," http://www.bates.edu/mission-statement.xml (accessed June 14, 2006). Williams College describes its mission by quoting from the inaugural addresses of its past and present leaders, including President John E. Sawyer, who in 1961 declared: "The most versatile, the most durable, in an ultimate sense the most practical knowledge and intellectual resources which [students] can now be offered

are those impractical arts and sciences around which the liberal arts education has long centered: the capacity to see and feel, to grasp, respond and act over a widening arc of experience; the disposition and ability to think, to question, to use knowledge to order an ever-extending range of reality; the elasticity to grow, to perceive more widely and more deeply, and perhaps to create; the understanding to decide where to stand and the will and tenacity to do so; the wit and wisdom, the humanity and the humor to try to see oneself, one's society, and one's world with open eyes, to live a life usefully, to help things in which one believes on their way." Williams College, "Williams College Mission," http://www.williams.edu/home/mission.php (accessed June 14, 2006).

7. As the famous Harvard report of 1946, *General Education in a Free Society*, makes clear.

8. Perry Miller, *Errand into the Wilderness* (Cambridge, Mass.: Belknap Press of Harvard University Press, 1956).

9. Quoted in Samuel Eliot Morison, *The Founding of Harvard College* (Cambridge, Mass.: Harvard University Press, 1995), 3.

10. For more on the curriculum at Oxford and Cambridge in the sixteenth and seventeenth centuries, see Laurence Brockliss, "Curricula," in *Universities in Early Modern Europe (1500–1800)*, ed. Hilde de Ridder-Symmons, vol. 2 of *A History of the University in Europe*, ed. Walter Rüegg (Cambridge: Cambridge University Press,

1996), 563–620; Kenneth Charlton, *Education in Renaissance England* (London: Routledge and Kegan Paul, 1965), 131–168; Mark H. Curtis, *Oxford and Cambridge in Transition, 1558–1642: An Essay on Changing Relations Between the English Universities and English Society* (London: Oxford University Press, 1959), 83–125.

11. Morison, *Founding of Harvard College*, 40.

12. Quentin Skinner, *Reason and Rhetoric in the Philosophy of Hobbes* (New York: Cambridge University Press, 1996), 45–46.

13. Jean-Jacques Rousseau, *Emile: Or, On Education*, trans. Allan Bloom (New York: Basic Books, 1979), 168; John Dewey and Evelyn Dewey, *Schools of Tomorrow* (New York: Dutton, 1962), 102–104.

14. Miller, *Errand into the Wilderness*.

15. Frederick Rudolph, *The American College and University: A History*, 2nd ed. (Athens: University of Georgia Press, 1990), 62–63; Cohen, *Shaping of American Higher Education*, 64–65; Lawrence A. Cremin, *Traditions of American Education* (New York: Basic Books, 1976), 86, 101.

16. Quoted in Rudolph, *American College and University*, 63.

17. For details see, "The Yale College Curriculum, 1701–1901," *Educational Review* 22 (June 1901): 1–17.

18. "Yale Report of 1828," in Hofstadter and Smith, eds., *American Higher Education*.

19. Laurence R. Veysey, *The Emergence of the American University* (Chicago: University of Chicago Press, 1974), 142–143.

20. Brooks M. Kelley, *Yale: A History* (New Haven: Yale University Press, 1974), 178.

21. George P. Schmidt, *The Old Time College President* (New York: Columbia University Press, 1930), 110.

22. Ibid., 94.

23. Schmidt, *Old Time College President*, 79.

24. Rudolph, *American College and University*, 97.

25. E. J. Dijksterhuis, *The Mechanization of the World Picture* (London: Oxford University Press, 1961), 490–491; Koyré, *Infinite Universe*, 273–276; Edwin Arthur Burtt, *The Metaphysical Foundations of Modern Physical Science* (Garden City, N.Y.: Doubleday, 1954), 297–298.

26. Quoted in Rudolph, *American College and University*, 226.

27. For more on efforts to expand and reform the curriculum before the Civil War, see Cohen, *Shaping of American Higher Education*, 73–83; John S. Brubacher and Willis Rudy, *Higher Education in Transition: A History of American Colleges and Universities, 1636–1976*, 3rd ed. (New York: Harper and Row, 1976), 100–111; Stanley M. Guralnick, *Science and the Ante-bellum American College* (Philadelphia: American Philosophical Society, 1975); Rudolph, *American College and University*, 110–135; Elbert Vaughan Wills, *The*

Growth of American Higher Education (Philadelphia: Dorrance, 1936), 166–185.

28. Schmidt, *Old Time College President*, 140.

29. Rudolph, *American College and University*, 274–275 ("For the acceptance of revealed religious truth the new university in Baltimore substituted a search for scientific truth. For preparation for life in this world it substituted a search for an understanding of this world. . . . In time the spirit of Johns Hopkins would penetrate everywhere."); Allan Nevins, *The Emergence of Modern America, 1865–1878*, vol. VIII of *A History of American Life*, Arthur M. Schlesinger and Dixon Ryan Fox, eds. (New York: Macmillan, 1935), 286 ("The clash between scientific-minded young men and their theological-minded elders rapidly extended over a broad front. . . . As was to be expected, the principal struggle centered largely in the colleges."). Such clashes were a far cry from the vision of harmony offered by Cardinal Newman in 1859. See John Henry Newman, *The Office and Work of Universities* (London: Longman, Green, Longman, and Roberts, 1859), 24.

30. See "A Southerner Argues for a 'Southern Education' in the Hedrick Case, 1856," in Hofstadter and Smith, eds., *American Higher Education*, 1:466–469 ("Southern fathers are beginning to feel the necessity of educating their sons south of Mason and Dixon's line."); Charles F. Thwing, *A History of Higher Education in America* (New York: D. Appleton, 1906),

252–253 ("The aggressiveness of the abolition movement was regarded as an insult to the South. . . . As a result the expediency of sending the sons of southern families into northern colleges for their education was questioned.").

31. See Veysey, *Emergence of the American University.*

32. Daniel Fallon, *The German University: A Heroic Ideal in Conflict with the Modern World* (Boulder: Colorado Associated University Press, 1980), 51; Charles E. McClelland, *State, Society, and University in Germany, 1700–1914* (Cambridge: Cambridge University Press, 1980), 171–174.

33. Carl Diehl, *Americans and German Scholarship, 1770–1870* (New Haven: Yale University Press, 1978).

34. Rudolph, *American College and University*, 261.

35. Quoted in Rudolph, *American College and University*, 252. See also Earl D. Ross, *Democracy's College: The Land-Grant Movement in the Formative Stage* (Ames: Iowa State College Press, 1942), 47; Edward Danforth Eddy, Jr., *Colleges for Our Land and Time: The Land-Grant Idea in American Education* (New York: Harper, 1957), 27–30.

36. See Rudolph, *American College and University*, 291–293.

37. R. Freeman Butts, *The College Charts Its Course* (New York: McGraw-Hill, 1939), 210–211.

38. Ralph Waldo Emerson, "Intellect," in *Emerson's Essays* (New York: Harper and Row, 1926), 229–245, 233; Henry David Thoreau, "Walking," in *Walden and Other Writings of Henry David Thoreau*, ed. Brooks Atkinson, 597–632, 626 (New York: Modern Library, 1950).

39. See generally W. B. Carnochan, *The Battleground of the Curriculum* (Stanford: Stanford University Press, 1993).

40. Veysey, *Emergence of the American University*, 183.

41. For details, see Rudolph, *American College and University*, 399– 402.

42. Ibid., 396. See also Donald W. Light, "The Development of Professional Schools in America," in *The Transformation of Higher Learning, 1860–1930: Expansion, Diversification, Social Opening and Professionalization in England, Germany, Russia and the United States*, ed. Konrad H. Jarausch (Stuttgart: Klett-Cotta, 1982), 345–365, 353; John S. Brubacher and Willis Rudy, *Higher Education in Transition: A History of American Colleges and Universities, 1636–1976*, 3rd ed. (New York: Harper and Row, 1976), 195–196.

43. For more on the historical roots of this phenomenon, see Koyré, *Infinite Universe*; Burtt, *Metaphysical Foundations*.

44. Peter T. Manicas, *A History and Philosophy of the Social Sciences* (Oxford: Basil Blackwell, 1987); Theodore M. Porter, *The Rise of Statistical Thinking, 1820–1900* (Princeton: Princeton

University Press, 1986); Thomas L. Haskell, *The Emergence of Professional Social Science: The American Social Science Association and the Nineteenth-Century Crisis of Authority* (Urbana: University of Illinois Press, 1977); Robin M. Williams, Jr., "Sociology in America: The Experience of Two Centuries," in *Social Science in America*, ed. Charles M. Bonjean et al. (Austin: University of Texas Press, 1976), 77–111.

45. Max Weber, "The Meaning of 'Ethical Neutrality' in Sociology and Economics," in *The Methodology of the Social Sciences*, ed. and trans. Edward A. Shils and Henry A. Finch (New York: Free Press, 1947).

46. Veysey, *Emergence of the American University*, 128, 132–135, 173– 174. See also Laurence Veysey, "The Plural Organized Worlds of the Humanities," in *The Organization of Knowledge in Modern America, 1860–1920*, ed. Alexandra Oleson and John Voss (Baltimore: Johns Hopkins University Press, 1979), 51–106, 54.

47. See Cohen, *Shaping of American Higher Education*, 74 ("The organizing principles for this growth in curricular variety can be traced to the separation of philosophy from religion, the rise of the scientific method, and a breakdown in the notion of privilege. . . . One mode of thought was not being superseded by another; all was additive. . . . Inside the colleges and in the community in general, people were learning to allow religion and different patterns of thought to coexist.").

48. Louis Menand, *The Metaphysical Club: A Story of Ideas in America* (New York: Farrar, Straus and Giroux, 2002).

49. Op. cit., 554.

50. Samuel P. Cowardin and Paul Elmer More, *The Study of English Literature* (New York: Henry Holt, 1939), 10.

51. William James, "The Sentiment of Rationality," in *Essays in Pragmatism* (New York: Hafner, 1948), 25.

52. Meiklejohn, "College Education and the Moral Ideal," 557.

53. Roland G. Usher, "The Fundamentals of an Education," *North American Review* 210 (December 1919): 782–784.

54. Veysey offers an illustration: "Aesthetic influences must always reflect themselves in human action, declared a professor at Lafayette College in 1892. They must prompt the student 'to think beautiful thoughts, to utter beautiful words, to do beautiful acts, to become a beautiful person, to construct for himself a beautiful environment.' " Veysey, *Emergence of the American University*, 187.

55. Quoted in Brian C. Lambert, ed., *The Essential Paul Elmer More* (New Rochelle: Arlington House, 1972), 19.

56. James, "Sentiment of Rationality," 25.

57. See Veysey, *Emergence of the American University*, 28–29, 114, 161, 186–187.

58. Ibid., 113–118, 188–191.

59. "The Spirit of Learning," in *College and State: Educational, Literary and Political Papers (1875–1913)*, eds. Ray Stannard Baker and William E. Dodd (New York: Harper and Brothers, 1925), 2: 110.

60. Irving Babbitt, *Literature and the American College* (Washington, D.C.: National Humanities Institute, 1986), 116.

61. Paul Kurtz, *In Defense of Secular Humanism* (Buffalo: Prometheus Books, 1983); Vito R. Guistiniani, "Homo, Humanus, and the Meanings of 'Humanism,'" *Journal of the History of Ideas* 46 (April– June, 1985): 167–195.

62. Alan Trachtenberg quotes nineteenth-century essayist E. L. Godkin's jeremiad against "a kind of mental and moral chaos, in which many of the fundamental rules of living, which have been worked out painfully by thousands of years of bitter human experience, seem in imminent risk of disappearing totally." Alan Trachtenberg, *The Incorporation of America: Culture and Society in the Gilded Age* (New York: Hill and Wang, 1982), 157. See also Geoffrey Blodgett, "Reform Thought and the Genteel Tradition," in *The Gilded Age*, 2nd ed., ed. H. Wayne Morgan (Syracuse: Syracuse University Press, 1970), 55–76, 55 (explaining that in the 1890s "careful social relativism replaced the sweeping commands of immutable moral authority"); Robert H. Wiebe, *The Search for Order, 1877–1920* (New York: Hill and Wang, 1967), 42–43 ("As the network of relations

affecting men's lives each year became more tangled and more distended, Americans in a basic sense no longer knew who or where they were. The setting had altered beyond their power to understand it, and within an alien context they had lost themselves.").

63. Hannah Arendt, *The Origins of Totalitarianism*, 2nd ed. (New York: Harcourt, Brace, and World, 1966), 478–479 ("But there remains also the truth that every end in history necessarily contains a new beginning; this beginning is the promise, the only 'message' which the end can ever produce. Beginning, before it becomes a historical event, is the supreme capacity of man; politically, it is identical with man's freedom. *Initium ut esset homo creatus est*—'that a beginning be made man was created' said Augustine. This beginning is guaranteed by each new birth; it is indeed every man.") [footnote omitted].

64. Max Weber, "Science as a Vocation," in *From Max Weber*, ed. H. Gerth and C. W. Mills (New York: Oxford University Press, 1946); Isaiah Berlin, "The Pursuit of the Ideal," in *The Crooked Timber of Humanity: Chapters in the History of Ideas*, ed. Henry Hardy (New York: Knopf, 1991).

65. Rudolph, *American College and University*, 245.

66. Edmund Burke, *Reflections on the Revolution in France*, ed. Conor Cruise O'Brien (1790; New York: Penguin, 1970), 281–282. See also

Hannah Arendt's discussion of the "modern concept of process." Hannah Arendt, *Between Past and Future* (Cleveland: Meridian Books, 1963), 63–68 ("To our modern way of thinking nothing is meaningful in and by itself, not even history of nature, and certainly not particular occurrences in the physical order or specific historical events. There is a fateful enormity in this state of affairs. Invisible processes have engulfed every tangible thing, every individual entity that is visible to us, degrading them into functions of an over-all process.").

67. Ernst Cassirer, *The Individual and the Cosmos in Renaissance Philosophy*, trans. Mario Domandi (Oxford: Basil Blackwell, 1963), 56 ("We have already seen how much this link to the language and terminology of the Middle Ages limited the free unfolding even of [Nicholas] Cusanus' original thoughts. . . . But now, the Italians who take up and develop his thoughts are free of this limitation. They—the mathematicians, the technicians, and the artists—reject not only the content but also the form of traditional knowledge. They want to be discoverers, not commentators."); Ernst Cassirer, *The Philosophy of the Enlightenment*, trans. Fritz C. A. Koelln and James P. Pettegrove (Boston: Beacon Press, 1951), 49 (explaining that the Enlightenment "finished . . . what the Renaissance had begun; it marked off a definite field for rational knowledge within which there was to

be no more restraint and authoritative coercion but free movement in all directions.").

68. Michael Oakeshott, "The Voice of Poetry in the Conversation of Mankind," in *Rationalism in Politics and Other Essays* (Indianapolis: Liberty Fund, 1991).

69. Alvin Kernan, *In Plato's Cave* (New Haven: Yale University Press, 1999); Carnochan, *Battleground of the Curriculum.*

70. Roger Kimball, *Tenured Radicals: How Politics Has Corrupted Our Higher Education* (New York: Harper and Row, 1990).

CHAPTER THREE. THE RESEARCH IDEAL

1. Max Weber, "Scholarship as a Vocation," in *From Max Weber*, ed. H. Gerth and C. W. Mills (New York: Oxford University Press, 1946).

2. For the characteristics of community-college faculty, see Kent A. Phillippe, ed., *National Profile of Community Colleges: Trends and Statistics*, 3rd ed. (Washington, D.C.: Community College Press, 2000). See also John S. Levin et al., *Community College Faculty: At Work in the New Economy* (New York: Palgrave Macmillan, 2006); Michael Scott Cain, *The Community College in the Twenty-First Century: A Systems Approach* (Lanham, Md.: University Press of America, 1999), 41–76; George A. Baker III, ed., *A Handbook on the Community College in America: Its History, Mission,*

and Management (Westport, Conn.: Greenwood Press, 1994), 397–435.

3. Adam Smith, *The Wealth of Nations: Books I–III* (New York: Penguin, 1999), 110.

4. Karl Marx and Frederick Engels, *Collected Works* (New York: International Publishers, 1975), 3: 220, 308, 321.

5. See Jacques Le Goff, *Intellectuals in the Middle Ages*, trans. Teresa Lavender Fagan (Cambridge, Mass.: Blackwell, 1993), 154–166; Charles Van Doren, *A History of Knowledge: Past, Present, and Future* (New York: Birch Lane Press, 1991), 127–167; William Kerrigan and Gordon Braden, *The Idea of the Renaissance* (Baltimore: Johns Hopkins University Press, 1989), 83–153; Robert E. Proctor, *Education's Great Amnesia: Reconsidering the Humanities from Petrarch to Freud* (Bloomington: Indiana University Press, 1988), 3–83.

6. Diarmaid MacCulloch, *The Reformation: Europe's House Divided, 1490–1700* (New York: Allen Lane, 2003), 97–105.

7. See, e.g., Isaac Newton, *Philosophical Writings*, ed. Andrew Janiak (Cambridge: Cambridge University Press, 2004); Marsilio Ficino, *Meditations on the Soul: Selected Letters of Marsilio Ficino*, ed. Clement Salaman, trans. Language Department of the School of Economic Science, London (London: Shepheard-Walwyn, 2002); Michael Sean Mahoney, *The Mathematical Career of Pierre de Fermat* (Princeton: Princeton University Press, 1973).

8. Carl Diehl, *Americans and German Scholarship, 1770–1870* (New Haven: Yale University Press, 1978), 36.

9. Walter Isaacson, *Benjamin Franklin: An American Life* (New York: Simon and Schuster, 2003), 138–144.

10. Paul Oskar Kristeller, *The Philosophy of Marsilio Ficino*, trans. Virginia Conant (New York: Columbia University Press, 1943), 16–17; Matthew Stewart, *The Courtier and the Heretic: Leibniz, Spinoza, and the Fate of God in the Modern World* (New York: Norton, 2006).

11. Desmond M. Clarke, *Descartes: A Biography* (Cambridge: Cambridge University Press, 2006); Stephen Gaukroger, *Descartes: An Intellectual Biography* (Oxford: Clarendon Press, 1995); Jack Rochford Vrooman, *René Descartes: A Biography* (New York: G. P. Putnam's Sons, 1970).

12. Max Weber, "Scholarship as a Vocation," in *From Max Weber*, 129–156, 131.

13. Mark Goldie and Robert Wokler, *The Cambridge History of Eighteenth Century Political Thought* (New York: Cambridge University Press, 2006).

14. Isaiah Berlin, *The Roots of Romanticism*, ed. Henry Hardy (Princeton: Princeton University Press, 1999).

15. Isaiah Berlin, "Montesquieu," in *Against the Current: Essays in the History of Ideas*, ed. Henry Hardy (New York: Viking, 1979).

16. Alexander Nehamas, *The Art of Living* (Berkeley: University of California Press, 1998); Friedrich Nietzsche, *The Gay Science*, trans. Walter Kaufmann (New York: Random House, 1974), 299; Michel Foucault, "On the Geneaology of Ethics: An Overview of Work in Progess," in *The Foucault Reader*, ed. Paul Rabinow (New York: Random House, 1984), 350.

17. See Nehamas, *Art of Living*, 6–10, for the history of the idea of life as a work of art. See also Ernst Cassirer, *The Individual and the Cosmos in Renaissance Philosophy*, trans. Mario Domandi (Oxford: Basil Blackwell, 1963), 83–86.

18. Isaiah Berlin, "Vico and the Ideal of the Enlightenment," in Hardy, ed., *Against the Current*; Wilhelm Dilthey, *Introduction to the Human Sciences* (Princeton: Princeton University Press, 1989).

19. Friedrich August Wolf, *Prolegomena to Homer*, 1795, trans. Anthony Grafton et al. (Princeton: Princeton University Press, 1985).

20. Nietzsche belonged to this tradition of philological research. See James Whitman, "Nietzsche in the Magisterial Tradition of German Classical Philology," *Journal of the History of Ideas* 47 (July–September 1986): 453–468, 468.

21. Alexandre Koyré, *From the Closed World to the Infinite Universe* (Baltimore: Johns Hopkins University Press, 1957).

22. Immanuel Kant, *Critique of Pure Reason*, trans. and ed. Paul Guyer and Allen W. Wood

(New York: Cambridge University Press, 1998), 520–521.

23. Exemplary is this remark of nineteenth-century German chemist Justus von Liebig to his friend Friedrich August Kekule: "If you wish to become a chemist, you must be prepared to sacrifice your health. Whoever does not ruin his health by studying will not amount to much in chemistry these days." Ralph E. Oesper, *The Human Side of Scientists* (Cincinnati: University of Cincinnati, 1975), 108. Joseph F. Mulligan, editor of a collection of writings on the eminent German physicist Heinrich Rudolph Hertz, suggests that Hertz's death at the age of thirty-six may have resulted not only from his generally frail state of health but also from his insistence on returning to a laboratory where potentially unsafe conditions prevailed: "If . . . Hertz's health improved when he was away from the Institute, and deteriorated when he returned to it, why did he not do something about this destructive situation? Was it an excessive sense of duty that kept him at the Institute even when it was undermining his health?" Joseph F. Mulligan, ed., *Heinrich Rudolph Hertz: A Collection of Articles and Addresses* (New York: Garland Publishing, 1994), 78.

24. Max Weber, *Economy and Society: An Outline of Interpretive Sociology*, ed. Guenther Roth and Claus Wittich, trans. Ephraim Fischoff (New York: Bedminster Press, 1968), vol 3., ch. 11.

25. Karl Marx, *Capital: A Critique of Political Economy*, trans. Ben Fowkes (New York: Penguin, 1981), 3: 349–375; Max Weber, *The Protestant Ethic and the Spirit of Capitalism*, trans. Talcott Parsons (New York: Scribner, 1958).

26. Quoted in W. H. Bruford, *The German Tradition of Self-Cultivation: Bildung from Humboldt to Thomas Mann* (New York: Cambridge University Press, 1975), vii.

27. Ibid.

28. Goethe, in this respect, was an outlier. For a comprehensive account of his diverse achievements, see Nicholas Boyle, *Goethe: The Poet and the Age* (Oxford: Clarendon Press, 1991).

29. Aristotle, *Nicomachean Ethics, in The Basic Works of Aristotle*, ed. Richard McKeon, trans. W. D. Ross (New York: Random House, 1941), 1097a–1098b. See also Sarah Broadie, *Ethics with Aristotle* (New York: Oxford University Press, 1991), 26.

30. Bruford, *German Tradition*, 22–23, 70–71; John Kekes, *Art of Life* (Ithaca: Cornell University Press, 2002), 33–34.

31. Bruford, *German Tradition*, 72–73.

32. Diehl, *Americans and German Scholarship*, 115.

33. Roger L. Geiger, "The Crisis of the Old Order: The Colleges in the 1890s," in *The American College in the Nineteenth Century*, ed. Roger Geiger (Nashville: Vanderbilt University Press, 2000), 264–276, 267; Philip Lindsley, "Philip

Lindsley on the Inadequacy of Preparatory Schools," in *American Higher Education: A Documentary History*, ed. Richard Hofstadter and Wilson Smith (Chicago: University of Chicago Press, 1961), 1:328–334, 331; Guralnick, *Science and the Ante-bellum College*, 14.

34. Diehl, *Americans and German Scholarship*, 102–108, 117.

35. Laurence R. Veysey, *The Emergence of the American University* (Chicago: University of Chicago Press, 1974), 173–177 ("The closing years of the nineteenth century saw the rhetorical allegiance to science by professors in most of the disciplines reach giddy heights."). See also Proctor, *Education's Great Amnesia*, 87–96 (describing "the degeneration of the original humanities into pure scholarship"). For a rich discussion of the state of scholarship in the humanities between 1865 and 1920, see Laurence Veysey, "The Plural Organized Worlds of the Humanities," in *The Organization of Knowledge in Modern America, 1860–1920*, ed. Alexandra Oleson and John Voss (Baltimore: Johns Hopkins University Press, 1979).

36. For an elegant statement of the notion that we are the custodians of our civilization, see George Kennan, *The Nuclear Delusion: Soviet-American Relations in the Atomic Age* (New York: Pantheon Books, 1976), 205 ("This civilization we are talking about is not the property of our generation alone. We are not the proprietors of it; we are only the

custodians. It is something infinitely greater and more important than we are. It is the whole; we are only a part. It is not our achievement; it is the achievement of others. We did not create it. We inherited it. It was bestowed upon us; and it was bestowed upon us with the implicit obligation to cherish it, to preserve it, to develop it, to pass it on—let us hope improved, but in any case intact—to the others who were supposed to come after us.").

37. See Weber, "Scholarship as a Vocation."

38. *Economy and Society: An Outline of Interpretive Sociology*, ed. Guenther Roth and Claus Wittich, trans. Ephraim Fischoff et al. (Berkeley: University of California Press, 1978), 1: 217.

39. Northrop Frye, *Anatomy of Criticism* (Princeton: Princeton University Press, 1957), 11.

CHAPTER FOUR. POLITICAL CORRECTNESS

1. Roger Kimball, *Tenured Radicals: How Politics Has Corrupted Our Higher Education* (New York: Harper and Row, 1990), 1 ("It is no secret that the study of the humanities in this country is in a state of crisis."); Allan Bloom, *The Closing of the American Mind: How Higher Education Has Failed Democracy and Impoverished the Souls of Today's Students* (New York: Simon and Schuster, 1987), 346; Walter Kaufmann, *The Future of the Humanities* (New York: Reader's Digest Press, 1977), xii ("The humanities are in deep trouble."). But for some useful

cautionary remarks on talk of a crisis, see W. B. Carnochan, *The Battleground of the Curriculum* (Stanford: Stanford University Press, 1993). See also Geoffrey Galt Harpham, "Beneath and Beyond the 'Crisis in the Humanities,' " *New Literary History* 36 (2005): 21–36; Joan W. Scott, "The Rhetoric of Crisis in Higher Education," in Michael Bérubé and Cary Nelson, eds., *Higher Education Under Fire: Politics, Economics, and the Crisis of the Humanities* (New York: Routledge, 1995), 293–304; Stephen A. McKnight, "Is There a 'Crisis' in the Humanities?," in *The Crisis in the Humanities: Interdisciplinary Responses*, ed. Sarah Putzell-Korab and Robert Detweiler (Madrid: Studia Humanitatis, 1983), 21–30.

2. Harvard University, *General Education in a Free Society* (Cambridge, Mass.: Harvard University Press, 1945). For an endorsement of the vision articulated in the Harvard Report as against that expressed in Bloom's *Closing of the American Mind,* see Martha C. Nussbaum, "Undemocratic Vistas," *The New York Review of Books*, November 5, 1987. A briefer and less illuminating treatment of the relevance of the humanities to higher education appears in Yale University, *Report on Yale College Education* (2003).

3. Criticism of the humanities by natural and social scientists is a time-honored tradition. In 1861, Herbert Spencer remarked: "Sad, indeed, is it to see how men occupy themselves with

trivialities, and are indifferent to the grandest phenomena—care not to understand the architecture of the Heavens, but are deeply interested in some contemptible controversy about the intrigues of Mary Queen of Scots!—are learnedly critical over a Greek ode, and pass by without a glance that grand epic written by the finger of God upon the strata of the Earth!" Herbert Spencer, *Education: Intellectual, Moral, and Physical* (Syracuse, N.Y.: C. W. Bardeen, 1894), 78–79. More recently, Moody Prior observed that "there has probably never been a time when the humanities have not been the object of some kind of criticism. . . . Today, however, the protest which seems to carry the most weight is that which comes from science." Moody E. Prior, *Science and the Humanities* (Evanston, Ill.: Northwestern University Press, 1962), 45. Some practitioners of the humanities have turned the tables by attacking the sciences, prompting angry rejoinders: "The academic left is embedded in a nearly inviolable insularity, which extends and intensifies that of the traditional humanists. The classicists and historians of whom C. P. Snow spoke famously in *The Two Cultures and the Scientific Revolution* were excoriated for their self-satisfied ignorance of the most basic principles of science. Today we find ourselves, as scientists, confronting an ignorance even more profound—when it is not, in fact, simply displaced by a sea of misinformation. That ignorance is now conjoined with a startling eagerness to judge and condemn in the scientific realm. A respect for the larger intellectual community of which we are a part urges us to speak out against such an absurdity." Paul R. Gross and Norman Levitt, *Higher Superstition: The Academic Left and Its Quarrels with Science* (Baltimore: Johns Hopkins University Press, 1994), 7.

4. For more on the early history of affirmative action, see Terry H. Anderson, *The Pursuit of Fairness: A History of Affirmative Action* (Oxford: Oxford University Press, 2004); Jo Ann Ooiman Robinson, ed., *Affirmative Action: A Documentary History* (Westport, Conn.: Greenwood Press, 2001); Lincoln Caplan, *Up Against the Law: Affirmative Action and the Supreme Court* (New York: Twentieth Century Fund, 1997); Robert J. Weiss, *"We Want Jobs": A History of Affirmative Action* (New York: Garland, 1997).

5. Ronald Dworkin, *Taking Rights Seriously* (Cambridge, Mass.: Harvard University Press, 1977), 223–239.

6. *Regents of the University of California v. Bakke*, 438 U.S. 265 (1978).

7. *Gratz v. Bollinger*, 539 U.S. 244 (2003). Briefs for respondent.

8. See the briefs submitted by the University of Michigan in the *Gratz* case, which emphasized the educational value of diversity. Respondents' Brief at 2–3, 21–29, *Gratz v. Bollinger*, 539 U.S. 244 (2003).

9. For a thoughtful discussion of some of these themes, see Henry Louis Gates, Jr., *Loose Canons* (New York: Oxford University Press, 1992). See also John R. Maitino and David R. Peck, eds., *Teaching American Ethnic Literatures: Nineteen Essays* (Albuquerque: University of New Mexico Press, 1996), 11 ("What we want to do in this volume is to help the scholarship catch up with the ethnic literature that is increasingly becoming a central part of the American literary tradition—to translate for students and teachers alike the cultural assumptions and values that lie just beneath the surface of these important works."); James Robert Payne, ed., *Multicultural Autobiography: American Lives* (Knoxville: University of Tennessee Press, 1992), xviii ("At the present scholarly-critical moment, it is not really possible for a single critical voice to put forth a credible, full-scale study of American autobiography if American cultural diversity is to be acknowledged and if American autobiographies are to be studied as specific 'cultural narratives' as well as 'individual stories,' as [Albert E.] Stone rightly proposes."); Houston A. Baker, Jr., ed., *Three American Literatures: Essays in Chicano, Native American, and Asian-American Literature for Teachers of American Literature* (New York: Modern Language Assoc., 1982), 7 ("Literature both expresses and helps to achieve cultural identity. . . .").

10. See Max Weber, "Objectivity in Social Science and Social Policy," in *The Methodology of the Social Sciences*, ed. and trans. Edward A. Shils and Henry A. Finch (New York: Free Press, 1947), 49–112.

11. A sampling of humanities offerings from the course catalogues of major American universities and colleges illustrates the point: Gay Autobiography, Comparative Fictions of Ethnicity (Stanford); The Borderlands: Latina/o Writers in the United States, Colonial and Postcolonial Masculinities (Dartmouth); Central European Jewish Writers, Dreams of a Common Language: Feminist Conversations Across Difference (Harvard); The Female Literary Tradition (Princeton). Stanford University, *Stanford Bulletin 2005–06*, http://www.stanford.edu/dept/registrar/bulletin/bulletin05-06/index.html (accessed August 17, 2006); Dartmouth College, *Course Descriptions and Departmental Requirements*, http://www.dartmouth.edu/reg/courses/desc/(accessed August 17, 2006); Harvard University, *Current Courses of Instruction*, http://www.registrar.fas.harvard.edu/fasro/courses/index.jsp?cat=ugradandsubcat=courses (accessed August 17, 2006); Princeton University, *Course Offerings Fall 2006–2007, Listed by Race, Ethnicity, and Cross-Cultural Encounter*, http://registrar1 .princeton.edu/course/upcome/RaceEthnicityCourses.pdf (accessed August 17, 2006).

12. See Joseph F. Healey and Eileen O'Brien, eds., *Race, Ethnicity, and Gender: Selected Readings* (Thousand Oaks, Calif.: Pine Forge Press, 2004); Ronald Takaki, ed., *Debating Diversity: Clashing Perspectives on Race and Ethnicity in America,* 3rd ed. (New York: Oxford University Press, 2002); Ida Susser and Thomas C. Patterson, eds., *Cultural Diversity in the United States: A Critical Reader* (Malden, Mass.: Blackwell, 2001).

13. See Anthony T. Kronman, "The Democratic Soul," in *Democratic Vistas: Reflections on the Life of American Democracy,* ed. Jedediah Purdy (New Haven: Yale University Press, 2004), 16–35.

14. William Hazlitt, "Coriolanus," in *Characters of Shakespear's Plays,* 2nd ed. (London: Taylor and Hessey, 1818), 69–82.

15. Aristotle, *Nicomachean Ethics, in The Basic Works of Aristotle,* ed. Richard McKeon, trans. W. D. Ross (New York: Random House, 1941), 1132a 5–10. See also Jules L. Coleman, *The Practice of Principle: In Defense of a Pragmatist Approach to Legal Theory* (Oxford: Oxford University Press, 2001); Jules L. Coleman, *Risks and Wrongs* (Cambridge: Cambridge University Press, 1992).

16. Max Weber, *Ancient Judaism,* trans. and ed. Hans H. Gerth and Don Martindale (Glencoe, Ill.: Free Press, 1952), 267–296.

17. Georg Lukács, *History and Class Consciousness*, trans. Rodney Livingstone (Cambridge, Mass.: MIT Press, 1971).

18. Sigmund Freud, *Interpretation of Dreams*, trans. and ed. James Strachey (New York: Science Editions, 1961); *Jokes and Their Relation to the Unconscious*, trans. and ed. James Strachey (New York: Norton, 1963).

19. Aristotle, *Nicomachean Ethics*, 1098 a–b; 1099b.

20. Friedrich Nietzsche, *On the Genealogy of Morality*, trans. Carol Diethe and ed. Keith Ansell-Pearson (Cambridge: Cambridge University Press, 1994).

21. See Leo Strauss, "Jerusalem and Athens: Some Preliminary Reflections" (lecture, The City College, New York, March 13 and 15, 1967).

22. See Derek Bok, *Our Underachieving Colleges: A Candid Look at How Much Students Learn and Why They Should Be Learning More* (Princeton: Princeton University Press, 2006), 225–254, 226 ("Clearly colleges have a responsibility to try to remove such ignorance [of world affairs] and prepare their students adequately for lives increasingly affected by events beyond our borders."); Richard C. Levin, *The Work of the University* (New Haven: Yale University Press, 2003), 99–105, 100 ("When I speak of becoming a global university, I envision a curriculum and a research agenda permeated by awareness that political, economic, social, and cultural phenomena in any part of

the world can no longer be fully understood in isolation."); Martha C. Nussbaum, *Cultivating Humanity: A Classical Defense of Reform in Higher Education* (Cambridge: Harvard University Press, 1997), 50–84, 63 ("The task of world citizenship requires the would-be world citizen to become a sensitive and empathetic interpreter. Education at all ages should cultivate the capacity for such interpreting.").

23. See Rajani Kannepalli Kanth, *Against Eurocentrism: A Transcendent Critique of Modernist Science, Society, and Morals* (New York: Palgrave Macmillan, 2005); Molefi Kete Asante, *The Painful Demise of Eurocentrism: An Afrocentric Response to Critics* (Trenton, N.J.: Africa World Press, 1999); Arthur B. Powell and Marilyn Frankenstein, eds., *Ethnomathematics: Challenging Eurocentrism in Mathematics Education* (Albany: State University of New York Press, 1997); Ella Shohat and Robert Stam, *Unthinking Eurocentrism: Multiculturalism and the Media* (London: Routledge, 1994); Edward W. Said, "The Politics of Knowledge," in *Debating P.C.: The Controversy over Political Correctness on College Campuses*, ed. Paul Berman (New York: Dell, 1992), 172–189; Molefi Kete Asante, "Multiculturalism: An Exchange," in *Debating P.C.*, 299–311; Martin Bernal, *Black Athena: The Afroasiatic Roots of Classical Civilization* (New Brunswick, N.J. : Rutgers University Press, 1987), 1: 215–223.

24. See Maurice Merleau-Ponty, "Concerning Marxism," *Sense and Non-Sense*, Pt. II, Ch. 9, trans. Hubert Dreyfus and Patricia Dreyfus (Evanston: Northwestern University Press, 1964); Jean-Paul Sartre, *Search for a Method*, trans. Hazel Barnes (New York: Knopf, 1963); Frantz Fanon, *The Wretched of the Earth*, trans. Constance Farrington (New York: Grove Press, 1963); Frantz Fanon, *Studies in a Dying Colonialism*, trans. Haakon Chevalier (New York: Monthly Review Press, 1965); Lorenzo M. Crowell, "The Lessons and Ghosts of Vietnam," in *Looking Back on the Vietnam War: A 1990s Perspective on the Decisions, Combat, and Legacies*, ed. William Head and Lawrence E. Gritner (Westport, Conn.: Greenwood Press, 1993), 229–240; Adam Yarmonlinsky, "The War and the American Military," in *The Vietnam Legacy: The War, American Society and the Future of American Foreign Policy*, ed. Anthony Lake (New York: New York University Press, 1976), 216–235. More recently, with regard to American power, the wars in Iraq and Afghanistan have spawned a new round of doubts and misgivings. See Stephen M. Walt, *Taming American Power: The Global Response to U.S. Primacy* (New York: Norton, 2005); Andrew J. Bacevich, *The New American Militarism: How Americans Are Seduced by War* (Oxford: Oxford University Press, 2005).

25. Islam is an important and interesting exception, especially during the period of the

great flourishing of Al-Andalus. See Maria Rosa Menocal, *The Ornament of the World: How Muslims, Jews, and Christians Created a Culture of Tolerance in Medieval Spain* (Boston: Little, Brown, 2002). Another sometime exception is China. See D. E. Mungello, *The Great Encounter of China and the West, 1500–1800* (Lanham, Md.: Rowman and Littlefield, 1999); Jonathan D. Spence, *The Search for Modern China*, 2nd ed. (New York: Norton, 1990); Wolfgang Franke, *China and the West*, trans. R. A. Wilson (Oxford: Basil Blackwell, 1967).

26. Among the most promising strategies for protecting the Amazon rain forest, for example, is a technique derived from modern finance: the debt-for-nature swap, whose application in Amazonia was the brainchild of biologist Thomas Lovejoy. Thomas E. Lovejoy 3d, "Aid Debtor Nations' Ecology," *New York Times*, October 4, 1984, A31 ("Stimulating conservation while ameliorating debt would encourage progress on both fronts."). For a closer analysis of the technique, see Robert T. Deacon and Paul Murphy, "The Structure of an Economic Transaction: The Debtfor-Nature Swap," *Land Economics* 73 (February 1997): 1–24. For general background on the clash between technology and nature, see Bronislaw Szerszynski, *Nature, Technology, and the Sacred* (Malden, Mass.: Blackwell Publishing, 2005); Roger S. Gottlieb, ed., *This Sacred Earth: Religion, Nature, Environment*, 2nd ed. (New York: Routledge,

2004); Jerry Mander, *In the Absence of the Sacred: The Failure of Technology and the Survival of the Indian Nations* (San Francisco: Sierra Club Books, 1991); Andrew Revkin, *The Burning Season: The Murder of Chico Mendes and the Fight for the Amazon Rain Forest* (Boston: Houghton Mifflin, 1990); Alex Shoumatoff, *The World Is Burning* (Boston: Little, Brown, 1990); Bill McKibben, *The End of Nature* (New York: Random House, 1989).

27. Amin Maalouf, *In the Name of Identity: Violence and the Need to Belong*, trans. Barbara Bray (New York: Arcade Publishing, 1996). See also Amartya Sen, *Identity and Violence: The Illusion of Destiny* (New York: Norton, 2006).

28. "Introduction," Max Weber, in *The Protestant Ethic and the Spirit of Capitalism*, trans. Talcott Parsons (New York: Scribner, 1958), 13.

29. Richard Rorty, *Philosophy and the Mirror of Nature* (Princeton: Princeton University Press, 1979).

30. For examples, see Dinesh D'Souza, *Illiberal Education: The Politics of Race and Sex on Campus* (New York: Free Press, 1991), 182–193; Kimball, *Tenured Radicals*, 219 ("The denunciation of Western civilization as inextricably racist, sexist, elitist, and patriarchal; the efforts by college administrations to enforce speech codes on college campuses; the blatant rewriting of history text books to soothe wounded ethnic feelings: all are transforming the nature of American society."); David Barn-heiser,

"A Chilling of Discourse," *St. Louis University Law Journal* 50 (Winter 2006): 361–423, 367 ("Cloaked in its claim of representing a higher social morality because of its deconstructive critique of the biases inherent within the existing political order, multiculturalism is a device to limit the power of those who have traditionally possessed it.").

31. See Roberto Unger, *Politics: The Central Texts*, ed. Zhiyuan Cui (New York: Verso, 1997).

32. Alvin J. Schmidt, *The Menace of Multiculturalism: Trojan Horse in America* (Westport, Conn.: Praeger, 1997); Kimball, *Tenured Radicals*; William J. Bennett, *The De-Valuing of America: The Fight for Our Culture and Our Children* (New York: Simon and Schuster, 1994).

33. Immanuel Kant, *Critique of Pure Reason*, trans. and ed. Paul Guyer and Allen W. Wood (New York: Cambridge University Press, 1998), 121, 126.

34. Ludwig Wittgenstein, *Philosophical Investigations*, trans. G. E. M. Anscombe (Malden, Mass.: Blackwell, 1977), 241–318.

35. Martin Heidegger, *Being and Time*, trans. Joan Stambaugh (Albany: State University of New York Press, 1996), Sec. 5.

36. Jonathan Lear, *Love and Its Place in Nature: A Philosophical Interpretation of Freudian Psychoanalysis* (New York: Farrar, Straus and Giroux, 1990); Martha C. Nussbaum, *The Therapy of Desire: Theory and Practice in Hellenistic Ethics* (Princeton: Princeton University

Press, 1994). Aristotle, *Nicomachean Ethics*, 1105b–1106b.

37. Of Freud's theory of the human sexual drive, Jonathan Lear has observed: "An *Instinkt*, for Freud, is a rigid innate behavioral pattern, characteristic of animal behavior: e.g., the innate ability and pressure of a bird to build a nest. . . . A *Trieb*, by contrast, has a certain plasticity: its aim and direction is to some extent shaped by experience. To conceive of humans as powered by *Triebe*, as Freud did, is in part to distinguish humanity from the rest of the animal world." Jonathan Lear, *Love and Its Place in Nature*, 123–124. See also Sigmund Freud, *Three Essays on the Theory of Sexuality*, trans. James Strachey (New York: Basic Books, 1962), 100 ("The fact that the onset of sexual development in human beings occurs in two phases, i.e. that the development is interrupted by the period of latency, seemed to call for particular notice. This appears to be one of the necessary conditions of the aptitude of men for developing a higher civilization, but also of their tendency to neurosis. So far as we know, nothing analogous is to be found in man's animal relatives.").

38. See Stuart Hampshire, "Spinoza and the Idea of Freedom," in *Spinoza and Spinozism* (Oxford: Oxford University Press, 2005), 175–199.

39. *A Treatise of Human Nature*, ed. L. A. Selby-Bigge, 2nd ed., revised by P. H. Nidditch (Oxford: Clarendon Press, 1978), 415.

40. Max Weber, "Social Psychology of the World Religions" and "Rejections of the World and Their Directions," in *From Max Weber*, ed. H. Gerth and C. W. Mills (New York: Oxford University Press, 1946), 267–301, 323–359.

41. See, e.g., Oral Roberts University, *Vision and Mission Statement*, http://www.oru.edu/aboutoru/missionstatement.html (accessed August 23, 2006) ("It is the mission of Oral Roberts University—in its commitment to the Christian faith and to the University's Founding Vision—to assist students in a quest for knowledge of and relationship to God, humanity, and the universe."); Regent University, *Mission Statement*, http://www.regent.edu/general/about—us/mission—statement.cfm (accessed August 23, 2006) ("Our vision, through our graduates and scholarly activities, is to provide Christian leadership in transforming society by affirming and teaching principles of truth, justice and love as described in the Holy Scriptures, embodied in the person of Jesus Christ, and enabled through the power of the Holy Spirit."); Liberty University, *Statement of Purpose*, http://www.liberty.edu/index.cfm?PID=6899 (accessed August 23, 2006) (describing Liberty University's mission as "to develop Christ-centered men and women with the values, knowledge, and skills essential to impact tomorrow's world").

CHAPTER FIVE. SPIRIT IN AN AGE OF SCIENCE

1. Dennis Overbye, "Science Panel Report Says Physics in U.S. Faces Crisis," *New York Times*, April 30, 2006.

2. See, e.g., Pauline Yu, "Comparative Literature in Question," *Daedalus*, March 22, 2006, 38; Stanley N. Katz, "Liberal Education on the Ropes," *The Chronicle of Higher Education*, April 1, 2005, 6; Richard Byrne, "A Crisis in Academic Publishing Gives Way to a Crisis in the Humanities," *The Chronicle of Higher Education*, January 15, 2005; Lindsay Waters, "Bonfire of the Humanities," *The Village Voice*, September 7, 2004, 46.

3. Yale University, *Report on Yale College Education*, 2003, www.yale.edu/yce/report/ (accessed August 17, 2006). See also, e.g., Lawrence H. Summers, "Remarks at the 20th Anniversary of the Humanities Center," Harvard University, October 10, 2004, http://www.president.harvard.edu/speeches/summers/2004/humanities.html (accessed August 18, 2006) ("We have no more important obligation as a university than to make certain that the study of the humanities . . . is strengthened from generation to generation."); *Report of the Presidential Humanities Commission: Executive Summary*, University of California, 2001, www.ucop.edu/research/news/uchcexecsumm.pdf (accessed August 18, 2006) ("No university can

be truly great without a rich and multifaceted environment for the humanities.").

4. My discussion of technology owes much to Martin Heidegger's treatment of the subject. See Martin Heidegger, *The Question Concerning Technology*, trans. William Lovitt (New York: Harper and Row, 1977).

5. Max Weber, "Science as a Vocation," in *From Max Weber*, ed. H. Gerth and C. W. Mills (New York: Oxford University Press, 1946), 139.

6. See E. J. Dijksterhuis, *The Mechanization of the World Picture* (London: Oxford University Press, 1961).

7. Edward Casey, *The Fate of Place: A Philosophical History* (Berkeley: University of California Press, 1997).

8. See David S. Landes, *Revolution in Time* (Cambridge, Mass.: Harvard University Press, 1983). References to the telescope and Galileo's work.

9. Otto Toeplitz, *The Calculus: A Genetic Approach*, trans. Luise Lange (Chicago: University of Chicago Press, 1963); Alfred W. Crosby, *The Measure of Reality: Quantification and Western Society, 1250–1600* (New York: Cambridge University Press, 1997).

10. See generally Hans Reichenbach, *The Rise of Scientific Philosophy* (Berkeley: University of California Press, 1956); M. B. Foster, "The Christian Doctrine of Creation and the Rise of Modern Natural Science," *Mind* vol. 43 (October 1934): 446–468; M. B. Foster,

"Christian Theology and Modern Science of Nature," *Mind* vol. 45 (January 1936): 1–27.

11. *The Great Instauration,* in *The Works of Francis Bacon,* ed. J. A. Spedding, R. L. Ellis, and D. D. Heath (London: Longman, 1858), 4: 32.

12. Aristotle, *Metaphysics,* 980a 22.

13. Aristotle, *Physics,* 192b ff.

14. Plato, *Theaetetus,* 155d.

15. See Jonathan Lear, *Love and Its Place in Nature: A Philosophical Interpretation of Freudian Psychoanalysis* (New York: Farrar, Straus and Giroux, 1990).

16. Aristotle, *Metaphysics,* 1032a ff.

17. Aristotle, *Metaphysics,* 1072b ff.

18. For a representative statement see, Bruce A. Ackerman, *Reconstructing American Law* (Cambridge, Mass.: Harvard University Press, 1984).

19. See, e.g., Mark R. Levy, "Polling and the Presidential Election," *Annals of the American Academy of Political and Social Science* 472 (March 1984): 85–96; John J. Dohonue III and Peter Siegelman, "Allocating Resources Among Prisons and Social Programs in the Battle Against Crime," *Journal of Legal Studies* 27 (January 1998): 1–43; David J. Spiegelhalter et al., "Probabilistic Expert Systems and Graphical Modelling: A Case Study in Drug Safety," *Philosophical Transactions: Physical Sciences and Engineering* 337 (December 15, 1991): 387–405; W. Michael Hanemann and Ivar E. Strand, "Natural Resource Damage

Assessment: Economic Implications for Fisheries Management," *The American Journal of Agricultural Economics* 75 (December 1993): 1188–1193; Dana B. Kamerud, "Benefits and Costs of the 55 m.p.h. Speed Limit: New Estimates and Their Implications," *Journal of Policy Analysis and Management* 7 (Winter 1988): 341–352; James J. Anton and Dennis A. Yao, "The Sale of Ideas: Strategic Disclosure, Property Rights, and Contracting," *The Review of Economic Studies* 69 (July 2002): 513–551.

20. See Richard A. Posner, *Economic Analysis of Law*, 3rd ed. (Boston: Little, Brown, 1986).

21. Theodore M. Porter, *The Rise of Statistical Thinking, 1820–1900* (Princeton: Princeton University Press, 1986); Robin M. Williams, Jr., "Sociology in America: The Experience of Two Centuries," in *Social Science in America*, ed. Charles M. Bonjean et al. (Austin: University of Texas Press, 1976), 77–111; Harry Elmer Barnes and Howard Becker, *Social Thought from Lore to Science*, 3rd rev. ed., 2 vols. (New York: Dover Publications, 1961).

22. Aristotle, *Politics*, trans. T. A. Sinclair (New York: Penguin Books, 1981), 1253a–1274a; Alfred Marshall, *Principles of Economics* (New York: Macmillan, 1961); Jean-Jacques Rousseau, *The Social Contract and Discourses*, trans. G. D. H. Cole (New York: Dutton, 1950), 102–109; John Zaller and Stanley Feldman, "A Simple Theory of the Survey Response: Answering Questions Versus Revealing Preferences,"

American Journal of Political Science 36 (August 1992): 579–616; James Madison, "Federalist #10," in Alexander Hamilton et al., *The Federalist Papers* (New York: New American Library, 1961), 77–84; Carol Mershon, *The Costs of Coalition* (Palo Alto: Stanford University Press, 2002).

23. Bernard Williams, "The Makropulos Case: Reflections on the Tedium of Immortality," in *Problems of the Self: Philosophical Papers 1956–1972* (Cambridge: Cambridge University Press, 1973). I have been influenced in my thinking about this subject by Heidegger's *Being and Time*, Sections 46–53.

24. See Billy Graham, *Living in God's Love: The New York Crusade* (New York: G. P. Putnam's Sons, 2005), 82 ("Come to Jesus tonight and let Him control your life and take away your sins."); Valerie J. Hoffman, "Muslim Fundamentalists: Psychosocial Profiles," in Martin R. Marty and R. Scott Appleby, eds., *Fundamentalisms Comprehended* (Chicago: University of Chicago Press, 1995), 199–230, 219 (describing among young fundamentalist Muslims a "craving for security . . . satisfied by legalistic rigidity and obedience to what is perceived as the absolute authority of the Divine"); Joseph Cardinal Ratzinger, *Turning Point for Europe*, trans. Brian McNeil (San Francisco: Ignatius Press, 1994).

25. Sophocles, *Antigone*, trans. Elizabeth Wyckoff (Chicago: University of Chicago Press, 1954), 170–171 ("Many the wonders but nothing

walks stranger than man. . . . He can always help himself. He faces no future helpless. There's only death that he cannot find an escape from.").

26. See Jonathan Lear, *Aristotle: The Desire to Understand* (Cambridge: Cambridge University Press, 1988).

27. See *Kitzmiller v. Dover*, 400 F. Supp. 2d 707 (M.D. Pa. 2005); Kristi L. Bowman, "Seeing Government Purpose Through the Objective Observer's Eyes: The Evolution-Intelligent Design Debates," *Harvard Journal of Law and Public Policy* 29 (Spring 2006): 419–490; William A. Dembski and Michael Ruse, *Debating Design: From Darwin to DNA* (Cambridge: Cambridge University, 2004); Eugenie C. Scott, *Evolution vs. Creationism: An Introduction* (Westport, Conn.: Greenwood Press, 2004); Matt Young and Taner Edis, eds., *Why Intelligent Design Fails: A Scientific Critique of the New Creationism* (New Brunswick, N.J.: Rutgers University Press, 2004).

28. See Ronald Dworkin, *Life's Dominion* (New York: Knopf, 1993).

specialization's rise, 80–83, 134–36 (*see also* specialization); university system's emergence, 75–78, 113, 136–37, 346(n29) (*see also* research ideal). *See also* history of formal study of life's meaning

Columbia University, 53, 95, 320

communism, 212

compensatory justice, 203–09. *See also* diversity

constructivism, 230–49; definition and origins, 175–76, 230; external and internal criticisms, 219–27; multiculturalism supported, 230–33, 234, 242, 372–73(n30); vs. secular humanism, 242–48

conversation of great works, 109, 156, 158–59, 213–18, 247, 249. *See also* Yale University: Directed Studies Program

Cornell University, 78

culture: custodianship of tradition/culture, 149, 360(n36); humanities and, 289–90; understanding uniqueness of a culture/period, 127–32. *See also* multiculturalism

curricula: 17th century (Harvard), 61, 63–64; antebellum curriculum, 67–69, 72–73, 80–82, 85, 91–92, 108; great books curriculum, 52 (*see also* conversation of great works; Yale University: Directed Studies Program); prescribed vs. elective courses, 81; specialization, 80–83. *See also* liberal arts programs; *and specific institutions and fields of study*

Printed in the United States
145610LV00004B/25/A